RUNNING
IN BORROWED SHOES

RUNNING
IN BORROWED SHOES
Thane Baker and the 1952 Summer Games

CATHERINE
BAKER
NICHOLSON

FORT WORTH, TEXAS

Copyright © 2024 by Catherine Baker Nicholson

Library of Congress Cataloging-in-Publication Data

Names: Nicholson, Catherine Baker, 1959– author. | Baker, Thane, 1931– writer of foreword.
Title: Running in Borrowed Shoes : Thane Baker and the 1952 Summer Games / Catherine Baker Nicholson.
Description: Fort Worth : TCU Press, [2024] | Includes bibliographical references and index. | Summary: "Running in Borrowed Shoes journeys with the United States Track and Field Team from the tryouts in Los Angeles to the 1952 Olympics and afterwards, as the Olympians traveled and competed in local competitions throughout a Europe still recovering from World War II. Running in Borrowed Shoes focuses on pivotal days in the life of Thane Baker, who won silver in 1952 and gold in the 1956 games. Running in Borrowed Shoes relates his first triumph, when the young Kansan overcame physical, educational, and financial obstacles to compete in the 1952 Olympics in Helsinki. When an accident at work left the fourteen-year-old with a piece of metal lodged under a kneecap, Thane's doctors told him he would never run again. But when a legendary coach at Kansas University admitted Thane to the team, Thane understood that his tenacity and hard work in the intervening years had paid off. Thane Baker's daughter Catherine Nicholson worked with her father to record his story. Seen through twenty-year-old Thane Baker's eyes, Running in Borrowed Shoes plunges the reader into the world of the young American athletes who competed in the first Olympics to reach a wide US audience through television. Primitive by today's standards, Helsinki's 1952 Olympic Village is brought into sharp focus, as are the characters who represented a USA fearful of Communism and still under the grip of Jim Crow. The Olympic competitions themselves, and Thane's sometimes risky travels throughout war-torn Europe, are rendered in acute detail by a young athlete relating his most unforgettable experience"—Provided by publisher.
Identifiers: LCCN 2024005188 (print) | LCCN 2024005189 (ebook) | ISBN 9780875658698 (trade paperback) | ISBN 9780875658773 (ebook)
Subjects: LCSH: Baker, Thane, 1931– | Olympic Games (15th : 1952 : Helsinki, Finland)—Biography. | Sprinters--United States--Biography. | LCGFT: Biographies.
Classification: LCC GV1061.15.B355 N53 2024 (print) | LCC GV1061.15.B355 (ebook) | DDC 796.42/2092 [B]—dc23/eng/20240206
LC record available at https://lccn.loc.gov/2024005188
LC ebook record available at https://lccn.loc.gov/2024005189

Front cover painting: Watercolor of Thane Baker, 2020. By Dan Degrassi. Used with permission.

TCU Box 298300
Fort Worth, Texas 76129
817.257.7822

Design by Preston Thomas, Cadence Design Studio

THE OLYMPIC CREED

"The important thing in life is
not the triumph, but the fight;
the essential thing is not to have won,
but to have fought well."[1]

DEDICATION

For Thane Baker, my father,
who taught me to dream while grounding me.

For Sally Baker, my mother,
who taught me resilience.

For Chuck Nicholson, my husband,
who encouraged me to pursue my dreams.

For Will, McKenna, Sarah, Ben, David, Anastasia, Charlie,
Jamie, Julia, and Madeleine, may you always follow your dreams.

For John Patrick, our son, who died in our arms after a
seven-year battle with brain cancer, thank you for sharing your
amazing life with us.

EXCERPT FROM "THE DREAMS OF YOUTH"

The dreams of youth are fairest,
The dreams of youth are rarest;
The dreams of youth are brighter
Than the dreams we'll know again.
Hope is the fairy weaver
For youth, a firm believer,
And great the things we'll master
In the days when we are men.

There's neither pain nor sorrow
In the great and grand tomorrow
For the boy who lies a-dreaming
Underneath the apple tree.
There's neither hate nor malice
In the shining, golden chalice
The painter of the future holds
For every boy to see.

For his eyes are turned to gladness
And he sees no tear of sadness
In the visions of the future
That his soul is drinking in.
In the days to come he'll journey
With a brave heart to life's tourney,
And he dreams about the prizes
That in the future years he'll win.

EDGAR ALBERT GUEST[2]

CONTENTS

FOREWORD BY THANE BAKER xi
PREFACE xiii
INTRODUCTION 1

PART ONE	Growing up in Kansas	5
CHAPTER 1	The Dream Discovered	7
CHAPTER 2	The Dream Destroyed	18
CHAPTER 3	Daring to Dream Again	31
PART TWO	Games of the XV Olympiad	41
CHAPTER 4	Departure	43
CHAPTER 5	New York City	67
CHAPTER 6	Welcome to Helsinki	85
CHAPTER 7	New Coaches and Old Friends	104
CHAPTER 8	Opening Ceremony	116
CHAPTER 9	Let the Games Begin	136
CHAPTER 10	The Dream Comes True	157
CHAPTER 11	Exploring Helsinki	188

PART THREE	European AAU Exhibition Meets	211
CHAPTER 12	Nightmare	213
CHAPTER 13	A European Tour	217
CHAPTER 14	Vienna	231
CHAPTER 15	Night Terrors	250
CHAPTER 16	All Dreams Must End	255
PART FOUR	Return to Kansas	271
CHAPTER 17	Return to Reality	273
CHAPTER 18	Sharing the Dream at Thane Baker Day	283
APPENDIX 1	Thane Baker's Autographs of the 1952 United States Track and Field Olympians	294
APPENDIX 2	Fiftieth Reunion of the 1952 United States Olympic Teams	311
APPENDIX 3	Thane Baker's Lifetime Accomplishments	319

ACKNOWLEDGMENTS 329
FOREIGN LANGUAGE GLOSSARY 334
ABBREVIATIONS 340
NOTES 341
BIBLIOGRAPHY 372
INDEX 387

FOREWORD BY THANE BAKER

When I traveled to Helsinki, Finland, as a wide-eyed twenty-year-old to compete in the 1952 Olympics, I never could have imagined that amazing experience of a lifetime. Because I never wanted to forget a moment of my adventure, I saved everything. I even collected a complete set of autographs from all my track and field teammates to remember them better. Someday, I hoped to write a book about my memories, but I just never got around to it. Fortunately, my daughter, Catherine, this author, found the boxes with my stored items, and this book is the result.

My daughter involved me with the book every step of the way. Besides my stories and our editing discussions, we contacted all the other living 1952 Olympic Track and Field team members. It has been so rewarding to talk to them and recall those events that we shared seventy years ago!

My fellow Olympians and I relived our earlier journey together over the telephone with laughter and joy. We did not laugh when recalling our airplane motor that caught fire; we thought the plane might crash and kill the entire team. Our reminiscences made light of endless times we spent waiting, seeking luggage, traveling instead of sleeping, and not understanding other languages. Soggy dirt tracks didn't bother us in hindsight, either. (We did not have artificial track surfaces back then.) Even my experience of being lost and hiding from the police after curfew in Vienna sounded amusing in conversation, but it wasn't.

I wouldn't have reconnected with old friends if not for this book.

I hope readers of this book can imagine the dreams we all shared of making the Olympic team. I felt numb and in disbelief when I qualified to make the USA Team. I cannot describe the thrill that we experienced as we marched in the Opening Ceremonies. I cannot express in words what it felt like to stand on the victory stand with the Star-Spangled Banner playing and our country's flag rising up the mast.

If an Olympic hopeful is reading this, I want to say this to you. Every time your coach says, "One more time, better than the last one," do it! Work out when you know you need to, regardless of the weather. After hard work, your muscles may hurt for a few days, but they will be better for it. You will look back on your sacrifices, and you would do them again. Even if you miss making the Olympic team, you will never regret the rewards of your efforts. Never give up your dream.

Only a person with Catherine's knowledge and experience in track could have written this book with the detail, feeling, and understanding of running that she gave it. Thank you, Catherine, for giving me the 1952 Olympic experience again.

I want to thank Kansas State University (KSU), and especially the late Coach Ward Haylett, for the opportunity and coaching that made it all possible, and for lending me the running shoes.

THANE BAKER
October 2020

PREFACE

For many girls, their father is their first love. When I was young, my father played tag with my brother and me, along with the neighborhood kids. He would let us almost touch him before he pulled back and dodged away. The game never got old. This was my first taste of running with my father, and I was in love. Today, my father, Thane Baker, is the oldest living United States track athlete to win an Olympic medal. This book captures days critical to his first Olympic Games.

My brother and I grew up around tracks. My father often woke us early on Saturday mornings. Once dressed, my father fed us each a tablespoon of honey from the same spoon to get our blood sugar going, before driving us over to the track. We climbed over the six-foot, chain-link gate at the one place without barbed wire. The fence and barbed wire kept people from harming the track, my father explained. We could run on it because we planned to use the track properly, and I discovered much later the coach had given my father permission to use it.

Thane Baker paid forward his competitive days by working as a starter in some of the largest track meets in the Southwest. He shot the gun for nationally ranked athletes while my brother and I played around the stadiums. I would watch those world-class men finish their races with the sweat pouring off their bodies and think, "I'll never do that."

Men formed my early role models in track. In the 1960s and early 1970s, women did not participate in athletics in the numbers they do today, for cultural reasons and from a lack of funding.[3] In 1972, the United States Congress enacted Title IX, a statute which required that women receive the same funding for athletic training that men received.[4] As I began competing in 1973, my running career ran parallel to the developing impact of Title IX on women in sport.

My father's return to running coincided with my track beginnings. In 1971, when my father turned forty, he laced up his track shoes again. In 1972, he traveled to Europe for a month and encouraged others around the world to join the Masters program, an organization in which men and women over age forty competed.

Whenever I visited home from college, my father and I still snuck onto the local track and trained together. Unlike when he let me beat him once when I was eight years old, I could not defeat my father in the 100 meters. He held world records for his age group in the 100 and 200 meters, and I was not a sprinter.

In 1981, I became a national champion in the 800 meters for the Association for Intercollegiate Athletics for Women Division II and earned All-American status at the Division I National Championship. At that time, only men competed in the National Collegiate Athletic Association (NCAA). I also ran in the Texas Relays, where my father ran and officiated.

After college and law school, I homeschooled my children for twenty-two years and cared for my son, John Patrick, who suffered from brain cancer for seven years before he died in the arms of my husband and me in September 2018. He was only twenty-two but had already lived a full life defined by his faith, humor, and intellect. My father and mother helped us through our difficult marathon of caregiving. We mourned.

Over the next few years, my father and I spent several hours a day together caring for my mother, who eventually lived under hospice care in their home. He shared his 1952 Olympic experiences, and we reminisced over our mutual love for running track. We enjoyed calling his friends from the early 1950s and hearing their stories. I organized the contents of boxes full of fragile newspaper clippings, programs, letters, and autographs. This book gave us focus for our days. In early 2021, Sally Baker passed from this world at home while holding her husband's hand. My brother and I stood beside them both. Her family surrounded her with love.

Running in Borrowed Shoes captures memories of the 1952 Olympics and shares with the world my father's and my love of family, friends, and running track.

CATHERINE BAKER NICHOLSON
June 2023

To learn more about the United States Track and Field Athletes in the 1952 Helsinki Olympics, please see http://catherinebakernicholson.com.

INTRODUCTION

Born in the Dust Bowl, Thane Baker limped through two years of high school with steel stuck under his kneecap because of an accident, yet dreamed of running in the Olympics. After two surgeries failed to remove the metal, a doctor told Thane to abandon athletics forever.

Thane refused to accept his doctor-ordered limitations and ran competitively as a junior and senior in high school. As a walk-on at Kansas State College, Thane unexpectedly earned a berth on the United States 1952 Olympic Track and Field Team. Aware of this unique opportunity, Thane collected items from his Olympic experience, including autographs of his teammates, in the hope of writing a book.

Almost seventy years later, Thane and his daughter, Catherine Nicholson, unpacked his boxes of Olympic mementos. Together, they called the still-living Olympians, and old friends reminisced. Using these many resources, Nicholson shares Thane Baker's unique perspective of those long-ago Olympics held near the Arctic Circle.

Helsinki, Finland, the host of the 1952 Olympic Games, suffered during World War II. Between 1939 and 1945, Finland evacuated many of her children to other countries, fought two wars with the Soviet Union ending in lost territory, maintained an uneasy alliance with the Nazis, and later declared war against Germany. Many Finnish men died, while others suffered permanent disabilities. Over half a million Finnish refugees crowded into the country's remaining cities. Finland also owed substantial war reparations to the Soviet Union.[5] Trauma from the displacement of children continued to the next generation.[6] Despite these obstacles, Finland efficiently and effectively mobilized to host the 1952 Olympic Games.

Back in the United States, the Olympics caught and held the attention of the nation for the first time because of television, radio, newspapers, and a presidential proclamation. The United States Olympic Committee partnered with the Armed Services, Amateur Athletic Union (AAU), NCAA, and garnered grass-roots support. Volunteers everywhere from Hollywood to New York City supported the Olympians on their journey to Finland. Even children collected nickels and dimes for them.[7] Despite nationwide patriotism and sports enthusiasm, American male athletes still faced the hurdles of financial insecurity, racism, and inadequate diets on their way to Helsinki.

Both class and racial discrimination affected the amateur track and field athletes in America. In 1896, the original amateur of the Modern Olympic Games belonged to the aristocracy. Rules banned participation by anyone who had performed manual labor for money.[8] By 1952, the evolved Code of Amateurism prohibited would-be Olympic competitors from taking money for their athletic efforts, a more subtle form of class exclusion. Most athletes improved their talents through sports programs in college, which not all could afford to attend.[9] Postcollegiate Olympic hopefuls struggled to train and compete while supporting themselves and sometimes a family. Because the United States military allowed their members to prepare while on active duty, twenty-eight percent of the male American challengers in Helsinki served in the Armed Forces.[10] Conversely, Soviet and Eastern Bloc countries supported their contestants.[11]

In 1952 America, segregation in sections of the country forced people of color to remain apart. "Whites only" signs labeled hotels, restaurants, bathrooms, and drinking fountains.[12] "Sundown" towns forbade people of color from remaining inside the city limits after dark.[13] A "separate but equal" educational system existed.[14] *Running in Borrowed Shoes* demonstrates how the integrated 1952 Olympians stretched racial boundaries but could not entirely escape them.

Running in Borrowed Shoes reflects the summer of 1952. The Soviet Union and Eastern Bloc nations entered the Olympic arena during the Cold War in Europe, the "hot" war on the Korean Peninsula, and McCarthy's drive to rid America of Communists. The American athletes had concerns about their first meeting with athletes from a regime demonized in the West. Although forgotten today, the Helsinki XV Olympiad played a significant role in shaping the succeeding Olympic Games as continuing East-West tensions would dominate the Olympics for a generation.[15]

In addition to these issues, *Running in Borrowed Shoes* delves into the dietary and exercise regimes of various athletes and coaches at the time of Thane's training for and competing in the 1952 Olympics. Some of these practices followed the conventional wisdom of the time, while others were individual strategies. Given the modern understanding of dietetics and kinesiology, it is now clear that many of these practices were unhelpful or even potentially harmful.[16]

One occurrence that summer altered the Olympic course for the next twenty years. The International Olympic Committee (IOC) elected American Avery Brundage, a 1912 Olympian, as the new president. Frank Litsky of the New York Times (NYT) called Brundage "the most powerful figure in the history of organized sports. He was also one of the most controversial and misunderstood." Litsky labeled Brundage as more effective than the United Nations in international relations. He influenced the IOC responses to Communist-versus-capitalist battles, women entering the Olympics in greater numbers, colonies seeking freedom from their conquerors, the rising use of performance-enhancing drugs, racial unrest (which peaked with the 1968 protests in Mexico City), and the conflict in the Mideast which, among other tragedies, resulted in the 1972 attack in Munich that ended with the death of seventeen people, including eleven Israeli Olympians seized from the Olympic Village. Detractors today accuse Brundage of antisemitism, racism, misogyny, and despotism.[17] For good or ill, the IOC's 1952 choice of Avery Brundage for president changed the course of Olympic history.

Running in Borrowed Shoes journeys with the United States Track and Field Team from the tryouts in Los Angeles to the 1952 Helsinki Olympics and afterwards, as the Olympians traveled and competed throughout a Europe still recovering from World War II. Supportive relationships within families, among athletes, and between athletes and their coaches shine. *Running in Borrowed Shoes* focuses on the pivotal days in the life of Thane Baker, who overcame physical, educational, and financial obstacles to compete in those far-off Olympics. *Running in Borrowed Shoes* begins where Thane Baker's dream began, the day he first watched an Olympic athlete run.

PART
ONE

Growing up in Kansas

CHAPTER 1

The Dream Discovered

SATURDAY, SEPTEMBER 2, 1939, ELKHART, KANSAS

Seven-year-old Thane Baker bounced next to his family before the Doric Theater on Main Street in Elkhart, Kansas. He wore his new overalls rolled up at the bottom to keep from dragging. His mother had patched his shirt, and his father had glued rubber soles to the bottom of his shoes because he had worn holes in them. His friends and neighbors waited nearby. The store owners had decorated their windows and swept the dust off the sidewalks for the big day.

Thane could not wait for the parade to start. Father held his hand.

"Why is there a parade today?" Thane asked. "So many people!"

"Today is Glenn Cunningham Day for our hometown hero," Father said. "He grew up near Elkhart, and he ran a mile faster than anyone else in the entire world ever did. At about your age, a fire burned Glenn's legs real bad. The doctor almost cut them off." Thane cringed. His father kept talking. "Glenn learned to walk again by holding onto the tail of a cow. He's been to the Olympics two times. He won second place there three years ago."

"What's the Olympics?" Thane asked.

"A bunch of contests held every four years to find out who's the best. People come from around the world."

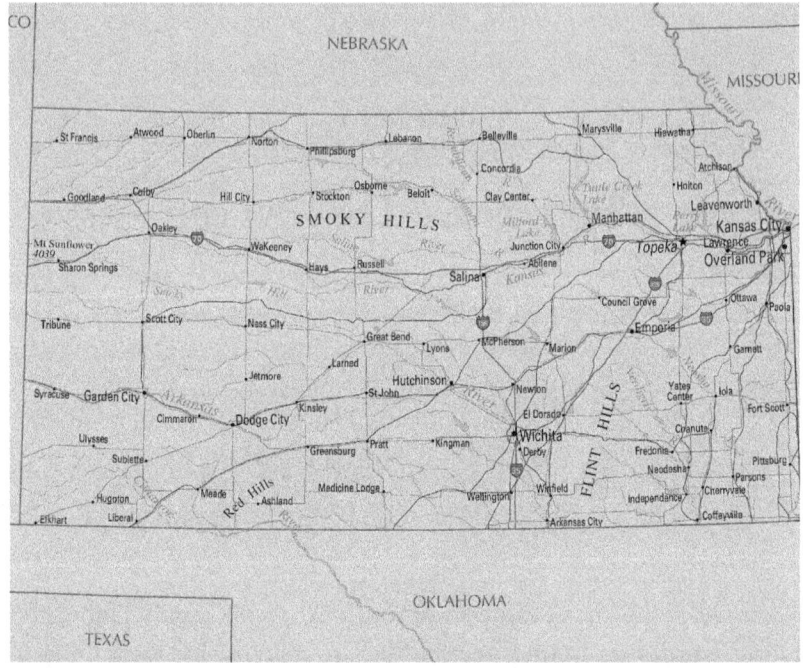

Elkhart, Kansas, sits in the southwest corner of Kansas, 2004. *Courtesy of National Atlas of the United States.*

"Where are the Olympics?"

"Back in '32, Los Angeles, California. In 1936, Berlin, Germany. Adolf Hitler was there."

Seven-year-old Thane did not know anything about Adolf Hitler. "Did Glenn Cunningham get a prize for winning second?"[1]

"Yes, he got a medal."

Thane's eyes sparkled with excitement. "Superman is the fastest man in the universe. I saw him in a comic book one of my friends showed me."[2]

Father smiled. "Glenn Cunningham is the fastest man we have around here. That's why it's Glenn Cunningham Day."

Smoke from burning trash in folks' yards stung Thane's nose as he leaned back on his heels and swung back and forth, pulling

Father's hand. His head fell back, and he stared up at the pale-blue sky tinged with dust, half listening to the grownups talking around him.

"This town ain't what it was. So many people left for California during this Depression. Some who stayed died of dust pneumonia."[3]

"Town's not what it was."

Most of Thane's playmates took off for California.[4] He missed them. His sister Ruthene got cranky with him, like when he broke the legs off her paper dolls when he helped them "walk." Ruthene didn't like to go fishing or hunt for arrowheads either. At least he had a few friends left. The instruments started to squawk and hum as the musicians tuned them.

"We haven't had a 'black roller' in a while.[5] That's got to be a good sign. Nothing like that terrible dust storm we had in '37."

Thane knew about rollers. If he saw one, he had to run inside when it made it to the end of the block. His family trooped down the narrow wooden steps to the cement basement. Mother made Thane wear a cloth mask over his face dipped in egg white. Sometimes the electricity failed for days. Dust came into the house during the storm even though Mother sealed the windows with strips of cloth dipped in starch around all the frames, and Father stopped up the fireplace. The houses in town slowed the dust a little, but Thane knew a house in the country where the dirt had piled up outside to a second-story window on the north side of the house.

"It's hot as blazes today. Yesterday, my mercury said it was 104 degrees."

"Think we'll get any rain? How long can we keep going without rain?" [6]

"Did ya hear Hitler is bombing cities in Poland?"[7]

"Darn shame."

Thane kept swinging his father's arm. How long did he have to wait for the parade? He wiggled his feet in his shoes. The rough patch where his mother had darned his sock scratched his big toe.

Would the parade ever start?

Dust storm in downtown Elkhart, Kansas, when Thane Baker was five years old, May 21, 1937. *Photographer from the United States Farm Security Administration. Courtesy of Morton County Historical Society, Elkhart, Kansas.*

The announcer called over the loudspeaker, "Elkhart, Kansas, welcomes back one of its own. Olympic Silver Medalist and world-record holder, Glenn Cunningham!" Thane gazed up the street. Glenn rode on Gus Johnson's pinto. Everyone cheered. Thane jumped up and down and waved his arms. He did not feel the heat now.[8]

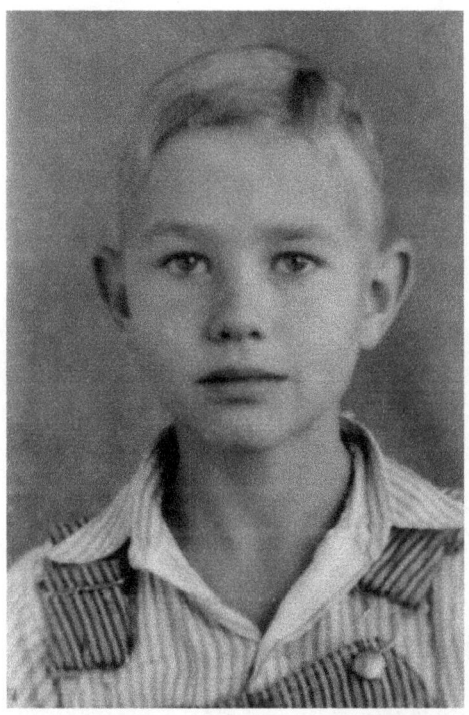

Thane Baker's school photo at age seven, 1939. *Courtesy of the Thane Baker Collection.*

The Elkhart band marched down the red brick street. A band from Rolla, a nearby town, followed. Music played louder than when the Methodist church congregation sang "Church in the Wildwood." Thane felt the drums inside his chest. He clapped as the bands passed.

After the parade, Thane stayed with Father. Ruthene and Mother went their own way. The men by the pool hall pretended to have a badger under a keg, and women drove nails into wood in a hammer contest. They walked back toward the Rives Drug Store.

"Look, Father, those boys tied their legs together."

"It's three-legged race time."

"Better if they're even."

"What's that, son?"

"That fella's big. The other's little."

"You are right. A matched pair might work better."

Glenn Cunningham, 1932 or 1936. *Courtesy of the Crawford Family U.S. Olympic & Paralympic Committee Digital Archives.*

A man called out. "On your mark! Get set! Go!" Everyone started yelling. Three teams fell. Most got back up and went on. Thane hopped from one foot to the other, imitating the racers.

Afterwards, the older boys lined up. Thane pointed to Glenn Cunningham. "He's got a gun!"

"Cover your ears, Thane. He's going to shoot the gun to start the quarter-mile race. They'll run around the streets and finish here." The gun went off. Again, everyone yelled. After the race, some boys leaned over panting, while others walked on shaky legs. A few lay on the ground. One boy puked.

"That's not fun. Why'd they do that?"

"They like the challenge." Father pulled Thane's hand. "The greased pole contest is next." They stepped off the curb to cross the street. No cars drove on it today.

"Why's grease on a pole?"

"It's harder to climb that way."

"Who wants to climb a pole? It would hurt if you fell."

"It's just the ground."

"I'd want something soft under me."

Mother and Ruthene joined them again. They watched the boys struggle up the pole. Then they walked over to the girls' chocolate pie-eating contest.

"That's more fun than climbing a greasy pole," Thane said. The girls sat on their hands and smashed their faces into the pies, producing pie mustaches and beards.

The train whistled. Everyone moved two blocks toward the track for one of their favorite activities, watching the train clear dirt blown across the tracks. The engine's snowplow thrust earth to either side of the tracks until a buildup slowed the train to a stop. Then the engine backed up, got up to speed, and hit the drift again, sending plumes of dust flying. Everyone cheered. The train repeated the action four or five more times until it found a clean track. Then it gathered speed toward the next dirt drift. Mounds ran along each side of the track left over from previous track clearings.

"Show's over, Thane," Father said. "Let's get back."

Back downtown, the loudspeaker squawked. "Everyone, line up on the sidewalks. Glenn Cunningham agreed to show us his world-famous legs. Let's give him a big round of applause."

The crowd obliged

"Think we'll see the scars on his legs from the fire?" Father asked.

Everyone got quiet. Thane peered around the crowd to see Glenn Cunningham standing by the Church of God. He leaned over and stood motionless. Then Glenn Cunningham ran. Never, ever had Thane seen someone move like that. Like a hero from a fairytale. Glenn came closer and closer. Powerful Glenn Cunningham lifted his knees while his arms pumped. His feet hardly touched the ground as he floated past Thane.

What had Thane just seen? Was it real? He wanted to hold on to that memory.

The announcer called out, "Come on, youngsters. It's time for the greased-pig contest." Thane chased the porker until the exhausted pig fell next to someone's back porch. An older boy flopped on it and flung his arms around it, winning the pig.[9]

Thane rejoined his family.

"It's time to go home for dinner." Mother said, "Let's go to the car."

Glenn Cunningham runs in his University of Kansas uniform, early 1930s. *Courtesy of the University Archives, Kenneth Spencer Research Library, University of Kansas.*

Thane's childhood home, Elkhart, Kansas, 1930s. *Courtesy of the Thane Baker Collection.*

"Watch me! Watch me! See how fast I can run!" Thane took off for the car. Ruthene joined him. She touched their car first.

"I won!"

"Nuh-uh. I was near the car first."

"I touched it first."

"Quiet, children," Father said. The hot and sweaty Baker family loaded back into their old Ford, rolled the windows down to let in a breeze, and headed the eight blocks for home on gravel roads.

When they arrived home, Mother said, "Wasn't it nice that we could celebrate in Elkhart? It didn't cost one red cent."

Mother went to the icebox with its ten-pound block of ice and pulled out leftovers from lunch for their dinner. Thane and Ruthene washed their hands. They shoved each other, tussling to stick their hands under the faucet first. In the kitchen, Thane slid across the bench to make room for his sister. His parents sat across from them.

"I sure hope we get rain soon." Mother said to Father. "It's been years since we've had a healthy growing season here."[10]

"We just have to hold on," Father acknowledged. "We've made it this far."

Thane asked for the butter he had helped make. He spread it on his roll.

Taking a deep breath, Thane announced, "I decided something."

"What did you decide?" Mother asked as she forked her chicken.

"I want to be in the Olympics, like my hero, Glenn Cunningham."

"You're silly," Ruthene said.

Thane grew solemn. "No. I want to."

Thane's father turned serious as well. "If that's what you really want, you will have to work harder than you ever thought you could. You will give up things you want to keep moving toward your goal. Maybe you'll make it. Maybe not. But worthwhile dreams are useful to follow. They make you a better man."

Mother served her strawberry-rhubarb pie for dessert, Thane's favorite. "Tell you what," his mother spoke up. "During the week, you stand on the edge of the school grounds when it's time to come home for lunch, and I'll get my alarm clock. When Father sounds the noon whistle, I'll check the time. You run home as quick as you can, I'll go outside and wait for you on the front porch. We'll see how fast you can run those seven blocks. I wish that old clock had a second hand, but I should be able to figure out if you get faster."

"Fast!" Thane yelled.

"Thane!" Father said.

Thane ducked his head. "Sorry."

Ruthene leaned forward. "I want to race, too. I beat you to the car today."

Father sat back on the bench. "Running sounds like a good idea. Do your best."

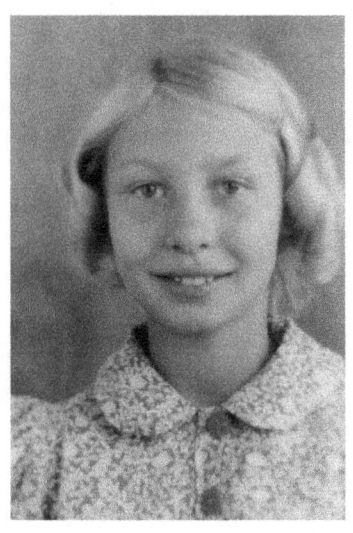

(*left*) Ruthene Baker's school photo age nine, 1939. *Courtesy of the Thane Baker Collection.*

(*below*) Thane's parents, Walter and Susie Baker, at Susie's parent's farm north of Elkhart, 1920s. *Courtesy of the Thane Baker Collection.*

CHAPTER 2

The Dream Destroyed

WEDNESDAY, OCTOBER 17, 1945, HAYS, KANSAS

Thane opened his eyes. Two women in white dresses stood over him. Something covered their hair. His eyes shut.

He opened his eyes. A woman held his wrist and gazed at her watch. He remembered Father called her a sister.[1] His eyelids drooped.

"Thane, Thane, can you hear me? Open your eyes, Thane. Can you squeeze my hand?"

It took time to make his hand work. He closed his fingers and drifted off.

"Thane, we're going to move you now."

He opened his eyes. Four women wearing white lifted him on his sheet and slid him onto another bed. The darkness claimed him again.

Thane's eyelids fluttered. He saw Mother and Father by his bed.

"How do you feel, Thane?" Mother asked.

"Tired," Thane mumbled.

"Rest," she said, taking his hand.

The next time Thane opened his eyes, he was more awake. Mother said, "I think that hypo they gave you before your operation today wasn't near as bad as that ether the Elkhart doctor used two days ago. Ether can kill a body."²

"Mmm," Thane replied.

"How's your knee?"

He tried to shift his leg propped up with pillows and groaned, "Water."

After he drank Father eased him back onto his pillow. Thane drifted off.

When he opened his eyes, another sister held his wrist and stared at her watch. He remembered he was in a hospital. Then the sister pulled out a thermometer and shook it.

"Put this under your tongue. Good, close your mouth."

Thane thought it tasted awful.

"Thane! Wake up! You need to keep your mouth closed. Don't sleep."

He opened his eyes wide. Mother held his other hand and squeezed it to help him stay awake.

"Just a little fever. Nothing to worry about," the sister said before she left.

Thane let his mind drift.

Six years ago, Father had come home from work and told eight-year-old Thane, "I've got good news. My boss said you can work at Muncy every Saturday morning." Muncy and Sons was the Ford garage in town where Thane's father worked. "He'll pay you thirty-five cents a day. You're lucky to get this job. Work real hard. You hear me?"

"Yes, Father. That's a lot of money!"

Every Saturday morning at the Ford garage, Thane swept the car storage area. The work took up the better part of the morning. The garage held sixteen cars, including the old 1912 Model T up on blocks. In the summer, dirt and oil covered the floor. Thane spread sawdust on the oil spots, then swept it away. During the winter, snow, slush, and mud made Thane's job more difficult. He scraped everything up and dumped it in a 55-gallon drum beside the garage.

While he swept, Thane dodged around a motor running on the floor with an open belt connected to an axle hanging from the ceiling. It had three more belts hanging down. Those belts ran the drill press, the stone-grinding wheel, and a wire brush. Thane didn't want to get caught in one.

"I finished the floors, boss, and I took out the office trash. What now?" Thane asked.

"Dust the showroom and clean the front windows."

"Yes, sir."

Later, Thane asked, "What should I do now?"

"Clean out any oil pans in the shop."

"Yes, sir." During tough times, most folks did not change their oil too often. A layer of sludge often covered the bottom of the oil pans. Thane used a putty knife to scrape out the old gunk. To cut the last of the oil, he poured gasoline into the pans and scrubbed them with an old rag.

"The oil pans are clean. What should I do now?"

"I can't think of anything else for you to do today. Here's your thirty-five cents. Be back here next Saturday at eight."

"Yes, sir."

One evening, Father sat down with Thane at the table. "A couple of men came to my boss to ask for your job at your wages. They said it wasn't right that a boy held a job that a man needed.[3] The Depression hurts everyone. You need to keep working hard to hold on to your job."

Eyes wide, Thane nodded.

As Thane grew older, his jobs became more varied, and his work hours extended until six in the evening on Saturdays. He worked six days a week all summer. One time, he painted the entire floor of the repair shop. He would mark off a ten-by-ten-foot-square area, sweep it, and use Oil-Dri to get the liquid oil off the floor.[4] Then he scraped any dried oil and mud off with a putty knife. Thane mopped the floor with gasoline. Luckily, no one lit a cigarette.

When the floor dried, he painted the scrubbed area on his

One of Thane Baker's work uniforms from Muncy & Sons, a car repair shop in Elkhart, Kansas, 1945–1952. *Photograph by Doyle Baker.*

hands and knees with a brush, then moved to the next area. Thane also learned how to take the inner tubes out of tires and hot patch them. He'd scrape the carbon off the engine blocks and heads and do brake jobs, too. As his skills improved, so did his wages. By age fourteen, Thane earned two dollars a day.

Thane scrubbed the disgusting bathroom once a week. All the folks who worked and visited the Ford garage used it. On weekends, farm workers came to town. Their alcohol consumption added another layer of filth. Some bought "Beef, Iron, and Wine Tonic" from Bloodhart's Drug Store.[5] Kansas prohibition law said no one could buy hard liquor in Elkhart, but the manufacturers concocted their tonic with 20% alcohol, much stronger than the 3.2 beer sold at the pool hall.[6] Anything the farm workers needed to get out of their insides, going up or down, ended up in that awful bathroom.

Last Saturday, his boss said, "Break down those empty wood boxes behind the garage. Pull the nails out. We want to use the wood again."

"Yes, sir."

The three-feet long, two-feet wide and two-feet tall crates had held car engines and consisted of hard-as-iron boards from "bodark" (bois d'arc) trees.[7] Thane wedged the claw of a hammer between two boards. No matter how hard he tried, they would not come apart. He braced the wood under his knee and hit the first hammer with a second. A piece of one of the hammer heads broke off and pierced his left knee.

He limped to his father working in the shop. Thane showed him the hammer with its missing part and explained what happened.

Father peered at the blood oozing through Thane's overalls. "Let's go across the street. Let the doctor look at it."

The doctor inspected Thane's leg and manipulated his knee. "I can't feel anything in there. Before I cut, I want to be sure what's what. Take Thane to Liberal, Kansas, to get an x-ray. I'll pack powdered sulfa into the cut. It will keep it from getting infected."[8]

"That's over an hour away. I can drive him to the hospital tomorrow, but for now, I need to finish my workday," Father replied.

"Fine. Bring me the films when you have them."

Thane sat in the Ford garage until Father finished his work, and they drove home.

The next day, Thane and his parents went to Liberal, Kansas.

Thane was quiet for a while in the car. Missing church would mean he wouldn't get the perfect attendance pin he'd counted on.

"Does it hurt much?" Father finally asked, looking at Thane in the rear-view mirror.

"No, not really. It feels like a knife cut me, but not any worse."

The hospital staff took an x-ray of the top and side of Thane's knee. It confirmed the metal behind his kneecap. His parents stayed silent on the way back to Elkhart. When they got home, they walked next door to the doctor's house.

"Come to the Elkhart Hospital tomorrow morning." The doctor said, holding the x-rays up to the sunlight. "I need to cut out that metal."

Monday morning, Thane entered a room on the first floor of the Elkhart Hospital. He took off his regular clothes and tied on a hospital gown. He lay on a bed with enormous wheels. The hospital workers pushed him down the hall and inside a pulley-operated elevator. Orderlies strained on the ropes wrapped around the pulleys above to raise the elevator to the second floor. A nurse rolled Thane into the operating room. The doctor had taped his knee x-rays to the window. He stared at Thane's knee, then turned around and studied the film. After doing that a few times, the doctor made marks on Thane's knee. The nurse positioned a cone-shaped gauze over Thane's mouth and nose, then the doctor poured liquid ether on the gauze.

Thane woke up vomiting.

Later, the doctor and his parents came to speak to him.

"Thane," the doctor said, "I couldn't get the metal out of your knee. You have a cavity behind your kneecap, and that's where the metal is. I've been talking to your parents. You need to go to Saint Anthony Hospital in Hays, Kansas.[9] They've got a fluoroscope up there. That way, the doctor can see inside your knee as he operates on it."

"A fluoroscope?" Thane asked.

"You know that box where you put your foot when you're trying on new shoes? You push the button and see your bones and the outline of your foot to see if the new shoe fits. Well, that's a fluoroscope."[10]

"When do we go to Hays?"

"I see no reason to wait. I've talked to a doctor up there about your case. If you drive to Hays tomorrow, he can operate on Wednesday."

Tuesday morning, Thane's boss knocked on the front door.

"I brought over our demonstrator car from the garage," the boss said. "Thane got hurt at work. I want him to be comfortable, and I figured he would be better traveling in a larger car. This 1942 Ford has more leg room for Thane than your old '36.

"I can't imagine anyone would want to see the demonstrator car today," he continued. "The war's over, and I've had several orders for new cars. I expect the 1946 model will look different from the 1942."[11]

Father shook hands. "Thank you. We appreciate it."

Thane scooted into the four-door car. "This sure is nice."

"Settle in. The trip will take at least five hours."

When they arrived in Hays, Father drove up to an imposing red-brick building. "These people believe in Jesus, but they do things a bit differently than we do. I've heard tell this is a pretty good hospital."

As they walked up to his room on the second floor, Thane noticed the ladies in long, white dresses with large, white collars. A white cloth on their heads covered their hair. His father nodded toward them and whispered. "They are religious sisters." Thane also noticed statues of people. Maybe they were from the Bible.

When he arrived in his room, a nurse's aide rolled a cloth partition between his bed and his roommate's. "Get undressed and in bed." She turned her back, while Thane followed her orders. The aide revealed Thane's top half and washed him to his waist using a pan of warm water, soap, and a cloth. She then uncovered and washed his feet and up his legs.

"Alright. I washed down as far as *possible,* and I washed up as far as *possible.*" She gave Thane the damp, soapy rag. "I'll step outside of the room while you wash *possible.* Put this gown on and get back in bed."

St. Anthony Hospital, Hays, Kansas, where Thane had his second surgery, twentieth century. Postcard. *Courtesy of the author's collection.*

Members of the Sisters of St. Agnes, the religious order, who cared for Thane. The hospital sisters wore white habits, 1968. *Courtesy of the Congregation of the Sisters of St. Agnes Archives.*

Thane hopped out, scrubbed, fixed his gown, and climbed back into bed. The sheets were coarse, not like the soft sheets of home. That evening, two aides came to play cards with Thane, Father, and Mother so Thane did not have time to worry about his upcoming surgery. After they left, Thane lay in bed, anticipating his second surgery in three days. Despite the rough sheets, Thane slept well.

After the surgery, the Saint Anthony surgeon stepped into the room. "You awake, Thane?"

"Yes, sir."

The surgeon sat on the edge of Thane's bed. "Good. How are you feeling?"

"Sleepy."

"I'm not surprised. We wanted you asleep while we worked on your leg. That anesthetic takes a while to wear off. Does your knee hurt?"

"If I keep still, it's not too bad."

The doctor smiled and patted Thane's good leg. "You and your parents need to hear this together. I couldn't get that metal out from underneath your kneecap. I could have opened your knee, moved ligaments, cut muscles, and let all the fluid out, but I didn't. It wouldn't be normal if I had. You would never walk well again. That metal in your knee may not bother you too much. Gristle may cover it. If it becomes a problem, I could take it out then. The metal might move down your leg, and we could remove it when it's no longer in the knee area."

Father winced. "You made the right decision, doctor. Thane walked into this hospital room on his own. He can climb up and down stairs. We don't want it worse."

"The bad news is you must give up athletics. You can still do other things. Do you like music, drawing, or business? The surgery caused lots of muscle damage. You'll have scar tissue."

"You mean I have to give up running forever?" Thane stared at him.

"It would be for the best. You'll need to use crutches for a time. You have a four-inch cut on the side of your knee. Those stitches will pull and be uncomfortable. After a while, you'll use a cane. Eventually, you should walk without pain."

Thane stared at Mother. Tears ran down her cheeks. Father grimaced.

"But I play on the varsity football team for Elkhart High School this year. I know I'm a lightweight, but I'm fast. That's why they let me play. Last week I returned a kickoff and gained thirty yards."

"I'm sorry, son. Football is not part of your future either." The doctor stood up and moved toward the door. He gazed at Thane with one hand on the doorframe. "If you need anything, let me know. I'll stop by every day to see how you're doing."

"How long will Thane be here?" Father asked.

"Expect Thane to be in the hospital for about a week," the doctor said. "We'll watch him for fever and infection. Thane, stay in bed. Don't stand on that knee just yet."

Thane nodded. He watched the doctor leave.

"Well, I best be getting on the road," Father said to Mother. "I need to be at work early tomorrow."[12] He focused on Thane. "I love you, son."

He left.

Thane glared at the white walls in his room. The white cast-iron rods on his bed frame resembled bars on a jail cell. Light from the window brightened the room. Thane needed dark clouds to match his mood.

"Mother." Thane bit his lower lip.

"Yes, Thane."

"I wanted to run fast, like Glenn Cunningham."

"Listen to the doctor now."

"But I worked so hard," Thane said. He had raced home from school every day for the last seven years, except in bad weather, with his mother timing him as promised. He had practiced on a one-lane track their neighbor had made behind the Bakers' back fence.

His mother knew. "I understand, son."

"Now I can beat Earl and Ben. They used to be faster than me."

"I know."

Blinking tears away, Thane sighed. "Can I still do the broad jump and high jump?" He and his friends had even dug landing pits for practice.

"Thane, I can't say I'm sad you won't be doing the high jump anymore. I never liked you doing the scissor jump over that pole and landing on the ground."

He glanced up. "You know we spaded up the dirt to soften it."

"I don't care. It wasn't that soft."

"What am I gonna do?" Thane closed his eyes and pressed his head against his pillow.

Mother picked up her needle and the pillowcase she had been embroidering and considered his question. "Running means a great deal to you, but it's not your only hobby. You like to build things and play with Mike."

"Mike's the best dog ever." Thane said softly. "I taught him tricks."

Mother reached over to hold Thane's hand with her narrow fingers. "It seems to me like you work on projects and do things with your friends besides just running. I know you don't see it right now. You have a great deal to be thankful for. You have a home, food, clothing, and a family who loves you. With the rationing, the government only lets you get one pair of shoes a year. But you get two because your father repairs his own shoes and gives you his shoe coupon.

"Japan surrendered last month. World War II is over. The dying can stop, and the living can begin. Do what the doctor tells you. Remember what your Grandmother Baker says, 'If you don't listen, you're gonna hafta feel it.' What does that mean to you?"

Thane rolled his eyes and replied in a sing-song voice. "If I don't listen to people, then I'm going to get hurt." Thane

Thane's dog, Mike, sits on Thane's bike, 1940s. *Courtesy of the Thane Baker Collection.*

Thane Baker's School Photo, 1946.
Courtesy of the Thane Baker Collection.

bounced his head against his pillow. "But I dreamed of running in the Olympics."

"I guess you'll have to find a new dream, a new goal."

"But I love running!"

"Thane, you will find something else or someone else to love."

Thane was silent for a moment. "Think they might bring me pie for dessert?" he asked. "Pie might make me feel better."

His mother smiled. "I'll ask them."

CHAPTER 3

Daring to Dream Again

TUESDAY, DECEMBER 20, 1949,
KANSAS STATE COLLEGE, MANHATTAN, KANSAS

Eighteen-year-old Thane left his shared rented room on Fairchild Avenue. He hurried toward Nichols Gym on the Kansas State College (KSC) campus in the early evening darkness. The north wind pierced his coat. The sleet burned his face, the only exposed part of his body. It was only fifteen degrees, and the shin bones on his thin legs ached through most of his ten-minute walk.[1] In the cold and dark, it seemed to take much longer. Thane shivered not only from the cold, but also from apprehension.

An article in yesterday's campus newspaper, the *Kansas State Collegian*, lured him away from his warm room. He had been packing to go back home to Elkhart for Christmas break, but the article said that Ward Haylett, the track and field coach at Kansas State, had invited any young men interested in participating on his team to an informational meeting. He would show a movie about a recent national collegiate track and field competition. Thane wanted to run track for K-State.

After limping through two years of high school, sixteen-year-old Thane had gotten permission from the doctor to try sports again

Nichols Gymnasium at Kansas State University, prior to 1953. *Reproduced by permission from Photo Services at Kansas State University.*

in Elkhart. There was a world of difference between competing at a high school in southwestern Kansas and running for a Big Seven Conference team.

The architect designed Nichols Gym like a castle, with a frozen cannon squatted next to its door. Thane hesitated for a moment. He needed to succeed at something extra at K-State. He wanted to go to the Olympics, but feared he was not good enough to be here. But what could it hurt? Taking a deep breath, he entered and turned into the K-State Room. Twenty other young men sat at desks waiting for the coach.[2]

Thane sat down next to a young man who stuck out his hand. "How are you? Name's Dick Towers."

"Thane Baker." He replied as they shook hands.

"K-State gave me a football scholarship here, but I wanted to go out for track, too." Dick said, leaning back in his seat, "I love to run."[3]

"Me, too." Thane rubbed his hands up and down his thighs.

"I heard Ward Haylett has coached here longer than we've been alive."

Just then, a big man, rounded with age and more than a few good meals, walked to the front of the room. He wore glasses, dress pants, a rumpled white shirt, a tie, and a letter jacket. He carried a clipboard and a film can.

"Hello, and thanks for coming out on this frigid evening. Let me tell you a little about myself, then I'll meet each of you individually.

"Name's Ward Haylett. I coach all track and field events here at Kansas State. I've been doing this for a long time. Just so you know, I graduated from Doane College in Nebraska with sixteen athletic letters.[4] In my day, I competed in a lot of different track and field events. I didn't run the two miles, but that's about all.[5] I watched the 1932 Olympics.[6] In 1937, I coached the winning American team at the Pan American Games. You've probably heard by now I coached the decathlon in the '48 Olympics. The USA won gold in that event with a high-school kid named Bob Mathias, and we won bronze with Floyd Simmons. Against the best in the world.[7] This means I understand a great deal about something you might want to learn more about.

"Now, it would be my pleasure to guide you boys, some of you with little or no athletic background, to reach your potential. I'll work hard for you. I expect you to work hard for me. If you're serious about your training, then I will help you become the best you can be. If you aren't serious about it, then don't waste your time and mine."

"I'm going to show you a movie." Ward Haylett said, as he turned to pull down the projector screen attached to the front wall. "It'll give you an idea of what to expect."

He walked to the back. Thane turned around to watch as Mr. Haylett opened the side of a big projector and installed the film reel on the top of the machine. He threaded the film into the smaller

Ward Haylett, Kansas State College Track and Field Coach from 1928-1963, inside the Ahern Field House, 1952 *Courtesy of Collegian Media Group, Kansas State University.*

reel in the bottom. Thane marveled that Kansas State had reel-to-reel projectors in their classrooms.

"Someone get the lights?"

A student up front turned them off.

Mr. Haylett turned on the machine. Thane watched the silent black and white film. He studied the sprint races and waited impatiently through the rest. After the movie ended, Mr. Haylett walked back to the front and turned on the lights. "Well, that shows each event. Upper-level students compete and may earn a sports letter. First-year students race by time against other schools in 'postal meets.' The coaches mail the results to each other to see who won. Since I did not recruit you to come here, K-State will classify you as 'walk-on' athletes, but I will treat you the same as anyone else. We help each other become better for ourselves and for the entire team."

Ward checked the notes on his clipboard and walked between the desks. "Let's talk about what daily training will look like. I'll put up each event's workout for the day on the blackboard. It's up to you to get out there and get it done. I'm a one-man operation here. I'll loan you a stopwatch to time yourself or have someone else do it. Jumpers and throwers, you carry a tape measure and help each other measure heights or distances. First-year students help upper-level students. We will be on the track together. I'll go around and talk to each of you on your own. We'll discuss what you have done, what you hope to accomplish, or where you think you need improvement. Together, we'll work on a personal plan to help you get better."

Thane nodded. He could work hard. He just needed the advice of someone like Mr. Haylett.

Ward Haylett walked over to the projector screen and raised it. "For now, we won't often be on the track, jumping pits, or throwing circles. As you noticed tonight, it's cold. Winter limits what we can do outside. This time of year, we warm up in this building, then go work out under Memorial Stadium's east side. Some trackmen call it Pneumonia Downs. That sixty-yard track under the stadium has snow, mud, and potholes.

"Let me tell you a story about one of our athletes. Elmer Hackney, who put the shot, used to shove his shot put in a gunny sack. He'd soak it in a bucket of hot water before practice. That way, the steel shot would stay warm. Otherwise, that sixteen-pound shot might stick to his sweat-covered hands and tear his skin off. Must have worked. He won the NCAA's two years in a row, set an American record, and qualified for the 1940 Olympics, which didn't happen on account of the war. He didn't let a little wintry weather slow him down. Don't let it slow you down, either.[8]

"Now, let's talk about equipment. As a member of the thinclads—that's what we call ourselves—you will be issued a t-shirt, socks, shorts, towel, and a jockstrap daily. Everyone gets his own locker. On long-term loan, you'll each receive warm-ups, a pair of rubber-soled US Keds, and a pair of black leather Riddell running shoes with holes on the bottom to insert spikes.[9] We'll also provide the spikes that you'll change out as needed. Jumpers and throwers, you'll get the appropriate shoes for your sport. Previous team members may have used those same shoes. If your spikes or shoes wear out, trade them in for others. Cinder tracks tear them up fast. When you compete on different college tracks, we'll issue you the correct length of spikes for each surface. We have good equipment here that serves us well."

Clean workout clothes daily sounded great to Thane. It would save Mother work, as he mailed his dirty clothes to her every other week. She washed them and sent them back. He had never owned a pair of Keds before. He did not care if someone else had worn them first; it beat having to buy his own shoes.

"Now, I've told you about our program. I want to get to know each one of you and learn about your previous experiences. Sit with me, one at a time, and talk to me. Thank you all for coming, and I look forward to having you on the team."

Thane liked what the coach said. He waited as the other students talked to the coach. His knee bounced up and down. What did Mr. Haylett want to hear? What did the other students say?

Dick Towers came out. "You're next, Thane. Can you believe it? He had not heard I was at K-State to play football. But he's glad I want to run. See you around, Thane."

"It was nice to meet you, Dick."

Mr. Haylett nodded to Thane, who waited while Mr. Haylett finished his notes on Towers. Haylett started a new page on his clipboard. He turned to Thane, partially stood, and thrust his hand out.[10] They shook hands.

"Son, what's your name?"

"My name's Walter Thane Baker. Everyone calls me Thane. My father's Walter."

"How do you spell that?"

"T-H-A-N-E."

He wrote that down. "Where are you from?"

"Elkhart, Kansas." Mr. Haylett made a note.

"Ever gone out for a sport before?"

"I lettered in football and track my junior and senior years. I also lettered in basketball my senior year."

"That's great."

"No, not really." Thane said. "My high school class only had fourteen boys in it. Only ten of them competed. They needed me. You should also know I've got some metal under my knee."

"Is it still there? And are you able to do sports now?"[11]

"Yes," Thane answered. "And yes."

The coach continued to write on his clipboard, then looked up.

"What did you do for your high school track and field team?" Mr. Haylett asked.

"I ran the 100, 220, 440 yards, hurdles, and relays, along with the broad jump and discus," Thane replied.

"How did you do?" Mr. Haylett asked.

"I made it to the state meet finals in the 100 and 220-yard dashes but came last. Our district meet was on a half-mile horse track in loose dirt." He watched Mr. Haylett write.

"Do you know your times?"

Thane Baker's high school graduation photograph, 1949. *Photograph by Marquise Studio. Courtesy of Thane Baker Collection.*

Thane answered. "My best time in the 100 yards was 10.1 seconds. I had a 22.5 in the 220. My quarter mile time was 54.9." Mr. Haylett recorded his times.[12]

"Have you been working out?"

Thane nodded. "I'm in your physical education class." He hesitated, then blurted out, "I'm serious about my running. Strawberry-rhubarb pie is my favorite food in the world. When I'm in training, I don't eat any kind of pie."

"No pie, huh? You must be serious." The coach smiled. "All right, Thane. Tell me about your time in high school." Thane talked about his awards, job, perfect attendance, and how he liked to dance. Thane believed his dancing might have improved his knee.

Mr. Haylett nodded. "How are you situated here at school?"

"Well, I share a room in a widow's home. I have money saved from work. My older sister attends the University of Kansas. With me here, my folks didn't have enough money to make ends meet. They had to ask my uncle for a loan."

"It sounds like your parents support your being here," Mr. Haylett said. "Do you think they would approve of you running track?"

"Sure, they would. Ever since I was seven years old and saw Glenn Cunningham run in my hometown, I wanted to go to the Olympics—just like he did. Above our high school trophy case was a photo of Glenn Cunningham running and a newspaper article of him breaking a world record. That motivated me every day.[13] My parents always supported my education and my dream of running. They made sure I understood I had to work for it."

"You and Glenn came from the same town. Tell you what. Why don't you come out for the team? I think I could make a good quarter miler out of you. It seems like I've spent my entire coaching career looking for a good fourth man for our relay teams. You could be that man."

Thane left Nichols Gym and slipped and slid as he ran back to the room he shared. The sleet had turned to snow and soaked his shoes. But inside, Thane felt warm. He dared to dream again.

PART TWO

Games of the XV Olympiad

CHAPTER 4

Departure

MONDAY, JUNE 30, 1952, LOS ANGELES TO NEW YORK

At ten in the morning, two days after the finish of the 1952 Olympic Tryouts in Los Angeles, twenty-year-old Thane Baker stood with his Olympic teammates for a photograph next to their airplane at the Inglewood, California, airport. Afterward, he excitedly climbed the stairs to board Trans World Airlines Flight #18. He and the rest of the United States Olympic Men's Track and Field Team would fly to New York City.[1] From there, the team would depart for Helsinki, Finland, and the XV Olympiad.[2] Thane would represent his country in the 200-meter dash.

A smiling flight attendant soon approached him and offered him a drink before takeoff. Thane ordered an orange soda. When she returned to serve him she sat for a moment, and they discussed the Bob Hope telethon that raised money for the Olympians' travel expenses.[3] Thane told her this was his first time on a big aircraft. She told him this airplane had something new, a pressurized cabin, which allowed them to fly at 20,000 feet. Their Constellation class plane, nicknamed "Connie," had four propeller engines and three tails.[4]

The flight attendant popped up to serve more arriving passengers.

This Lockheed L-1649 Starliner represents the Trans World Airlines flight that carried the 1952 United States Olympic Track & Field Team from Los Angeles to New York City on June 30, 1952, 1950s. *Photograph from the Ames Imaging Library System and NASA.*

"Excuse me, please," she said with a smile.

Thane smiled back. He watched the other athletes board the plane. The throwers in the field events were massive, while the distance runners appeared much smaller and leaner. Some he knew from competitions in the Midwest. Others he had seen in the last few weeks at big national meets.

Ever gregarious, Dean Smith leaned over the chair in front of Thane. "Hey, Thane! How ya doin'?"[5]

"Doing great, Dean."[6]

"Surely was cold at those tryouts. Hard on us athletes. I like to froze to death."[7] Dean pretended to shiver.

"Wasn't too cold for a Kansas boy like me." Thane replied.

"Thane," Dean began, moving to sit next to Thane, "did ya ever think that two ol' country boys like me from Texas and you from Kansas would go to the Olympics?"

"I'm still in shock.[8] From the time we marched in the closing ceremonies at the tryouts, to finding out we could stay at the Alexandria Hotel for free, and then getting on this huge plane, it's a dream come true.[10] I mean, I thought about the Olympics a little last year. Maybe more this year. I didn't plan too heavy on it. It's almost hard to believe it's really happening."

"Me neither." Dean agreed, "Before the NCAAs, the newspaper listed both of us as some of the top sprinters in the country.[11] But it still doesn't seem real.

"How many times have we seen each other, Thane? Ya just finished your junior year at K-State, right?"[12]

They had been together at both the Texas and Kansas Relays, at the NCAA meet at UC Berkeley in the middle of June, and at the AAU National Track and Field Championships at Long Beach, California, the following week.[13]

"We've seen each other quite a bit. You won the 100 at Long Beach," Thane said. "I had to run the qualifying heats of the 100 meters Friday night at 8:20 and 9:05, followed by the finals. Saturday, I had 200-meter heats at 2:15 and 3:00 p.m. with the finals fifty minutes later."[14]

Los Angeles Memorial Coliseum postcard, mid-twentieth century.
Photograph by David Mills. Distributed by the Souvenir Color Card Co. Converted to black and white.

1952 U.S. Olympic Souvenir Book, Track and Field Tryouts for Men, June 27–28, 1952. *Courtesy of the Thane Baker Collection and reprinted by permission from the United States Olympic & Paralympic Committee.*

"They like to keep us on our toes." Dean joked. "Get it? Sprinters run on their toes."

"Dean, maybe you're a ballerina, but I run on the balls of my feet."

"Speaking of the NCAAs," Thane said. "I got telegrams at the hotel wishing me good luck. Most of them came from my hometown."

"Cool," Dean said. "Folks back in Texas are pulling for me, too."[15]

Thane watched the last Olympians and coaches board the plane. Thane and Dean watched out both windows as one, two, three, and four engines started, one for each propeller. The low grinding noise of the engines came through the walls. Thane had been on buses, trains, and a small airplane, but this was something else. As the plane moved toward the runway, the roar from all four engines increased. The acceleration pushed the passengers back into their seats as they left the ground. Thane, Dean, and the rest of the passengers watched the world underneath them get smaller and smaller.

"Wasn't that something?"

"I'm going to write home about this." Astonished comments surrounded Thane. He was not the only person in a large aircraft for the first time.

After a time, Dean turned to Thane. "I beat you at Texas, but I don't remember seeing' ya at the Drake Relays."[16]

"Kansas State always goes to the Colorado Relays instead of Drake," Thane said. "K-State can win in Colorado. Drake's a little tougher. We run indoor and outdoor meets at the University of Colorado."

"See any pretty girls in Colorado, Thane?" Dean teased.

"I did. They had a Colorado Relay Queen who gave out the awards," Thane replied.

"You do alright in Colorado?" Dean asked.

"It didn't really bother me to run up in the mountains, but some of the distance runners had more trouble. I did okay." Thane had tied the indoor world record in the 60-yard dash prelims back in March. When Mr. Haylett told him how fast he had run, Thane had cried. He did not tell Dean about it. He didn't want to brag.[17]

The Colorado Relay Queen, Gwen Van Derbur, presents a running trophy to Thane Baker, 1951. *Courtesy of the University of Colorado Athletic Department and the Thane Baker Collection.*

"Thane, you and me, we're friends," Dean said. "But we're tenacious. Anytime I can, I'll whip ya. And you'd do the same to me."

"I wouldn't have it any other way. I might have won the 100 yards at the Texas Relays last year, but I made a rookie mistake. I got confused about where the finish line was and quit too soon. I was used to the 60-yard dash indoors, and that was my first major outdoor college meet."

"And ya almost beat me in the 100 at Texas this year. My start is faster than yours. Our coach at Texas practices starts with us three times a week using a gun."

"My coach only practices starts once a week."

"That's why I'm a better starter. I get a good start, get out in front, hold my breath, and try to stay out front. But you, Thane, you're one of the best come-from-behind runners I've ever seen."

"Thanks, Dean. But anything can happen."

"We measure most running distances here in yards." Dean made a wry face. "It'll be different in Finland. Everything there is in meters."

"I read that 200 meters is just inches less than 220 yards, which I usually run," Thane replied. "The 100 meters is over nine yards farther than the 100 yards. You'll have to work longer."

Thane thought about the finals in the 100 meters at the Olympic tryouts.[18] Jimmy Gathers and Dean Smith tied for third. The officials took a long time to determine who qualified for the Olympic Team. Thane wondered if Dean's coach from the University of Texas argued for Dean to make the Olympic team. Gathers was Black, and Dean was white. Thane wanted to believe that the picture must have shown Dean placed before Gathers, who would be competing in the 200 meters with Thane.[19]

After a moment, Dean frowned, "Thane, I'm sorry you didn't make the Olympics in the 100," Dean said. "It doesn't seem right."

Only four men qualified for the Olympic tryouts in both the 100 and 200 like Thane did. He won the 100 at the Kansas Relays two years in a row.

"Well, you beat me fair and square," Thane said. He had run the 100 meters in 10.7 in the tryout finals the previous weekend, but Dean had run it in 10.6.

"Thank goodness ya qualified in the 200," Dean replied.[20] "What was your time?"

Dean Smith practices the start of his race at Memorial Stadium at the University of Texas, 1955. *Courtesy of the Dean Smith Collection and reprinted by permission from the University of Texas.*

"I got second, 20.9 seconds. I was nervous, but that was my fastest time ever. So many spectators!"

"Ya weren't slow," Dean said. "Say, it takes over six hours to fly from Los Angeles to New York. Let's get better acquainted. Tell me about yourself."

"Dean, I don't like to talk about myself."

"Okay, I'll start. I get a scholarship plus $10 a month for expenses.[21] Did your coach recruit ya to run for K-State?"

"No, I'm just a walk on."

"So, how are you getting on for money?"

"I get on all right, Dean," Thane said.

Thane Baker works on his start at Kansas State's Memorial Stadium, 1951–1953. *Photograph by Laurence Blaker. Courtesy of the Kansas State University Athletic Department and the Thane Baker Collection.*

It had not been easy, though. At the beginning of his sophomore year, Thane told Mr. Haylett he needed financial help. Mr. Haylett put Thane on scholarship for $67.50 a semester for tuition and found him a job mopping out a laundromat seven days a week.

Haylett located Thane a job in the athletic department and another herding pigs. Thane eventually decided the pigs were smarter than he was.[22] Thane also sold programs at athletic events and received a small stipend for being in the Advanced Air Force ROTC. His rent for his share of a low-ceilinged basement apartment was only $15 per month, but Mr. Haylett worried Thane was not eating enough. Food cost money. Mr. Haylett sent him to the doctor for vitamins. When the Delta Tau Delta fraternity invited Thane to pledge with them, he agreed to join them only if he could work in their kitchen for two meals a day. He no longer went hungry.[23]

"Here comes the flight attendant with our grub," Dean said. With everyone standing and walking around, the flight attendants found it difficult to move. The athletes ducked into seats, ready to eat.

"I work in the kitchen at the Delt house back at K-State." Thane said as they tucked into their meal. "One day after a football game, we rang the dinner chimes, and the fraternity brothers and their dates started towards the dining room. This worker had a cast-iron roaster full of cooked hamburger patties. He tripped and dropped it. Those patties rolled all over the kitchen floor like hockey pucks. We just stood there and stared at each other for a second. Then we scrambled to chase them. We shoved the patties back in the roaster as nice as you please, then served them up."

"I can't believe y'all would do that!" Dean exclaimed.

"What else could we do? We didn't want the dates to go hungry. Besides, we always kept that floor clean enough to eat off."

"Think the flight attendant dropped our food?"

"We'll never know."

They grinned at each other. Thane always appreciated free food, but he did not want too much of it. He believed that if he gained weight, he would run slower.

"Ya gonna eat that pie, Thane?"

"No, you can have it."

"Don't ya like pie?"

"I like it, just not when I'm in training."[24]

After he finished Thane's pie, Dean looked over at Thane. "Let me get this straight. Ya don't drink alcohol, right?"

"I never did. At our fraternity house parties, I'd staff the three-two beer keg and serve other people. I could be part of the party but wouldn't drink myself."[25]

"And ya don't smoke, and ya don't eat pie." Dean was incredulous.

"No pie while I'm in training," Thane repeated.

"Dang! And I thought I was loco!"

After the flight attendants cleaned up the meal, athletes walked around and chatted. Others took turns sitting in the cockpit with the pilot.

Dean suggested they walk while they continued to talk, so that they wouldn't get stiff.

They both got up and stood near the cockpit. Thane held the back of a seat with one hand, bent his knee and pulled back on the top of his foot with his other. Dean spread his legs and twisted his torso back and forth.

"Thane, if ya walked on, how did ya get so fast?"

"I need to thank Ward Haylett and Dick Towers for that." Thane changed hands and stretched the other thigh. Dean stuck his hands on his waist and leaned over left and right.

"Dick Towers? Isn't he an 880 man? How did a middle-distance fellow make ya fast enough to go to the Olympics?"

"And a 440-yard hurdler. He ran that at the Olympic Tryouts, but he didn't make the team. He was my rabbit."

"Huh?"

"He was a rabbit because I tried to catch him. We ran repeat 100s. He'd start five yards ahead of me. We'd begin at three-quarter speed to get smooth. We picked it up to seven-eighths speed. We ran all out for the last fifty yards. I had to pass him. We would walk the curve and do it again. We practiced together every day."

"What did Towers get out of that?"

"He improved his top speed. Improved his competition time."

Left to right: Thane and Dick Towers, taken in a Photomatic booth in Salt Lake City, Utah, June 1952. *Courtesy of the Thane Baker Collection.*

Both Thane and Dean leaned over to touch the carpeted aisle to stretch the backs of their legs.

"Say," Dean continued, "did ya read what Wes Santee said in the LA Times?[26] 'I'll be under 14:30 in the 5000 meters in Helsinki, and that's going to put me into the finals. You wait and see.' He's awful sure of himself."[27]

"Oh, he's always boasting. That's just who he is. He goes to the University of Kansas, and I go to Kansas State. We had meets together frequently. He has a prancing style of running. Once, during a track meet, Santee came over and asked me to transfer from K-State to KU. He promised me a full scholarship. Don't know where Wes got the authority to offer money. Maybe his coach put him up to it. I said no, thanks. One time, my parents heard a sports radio announcer from Colorado compare Santee and me." Thane hesitated, shy. "He said, unlike Santee, I was humble. My mother told me that my father cried when he heard that."

Thane grabbed a seat back and situated one foot straight

David Wesley "Wes" Santee, 5,000 m, July 1952. *Courtesy of the Crawford Family U.S. Olympic & Paralympic Committee Digital Archives.*

behind him. He focused on pushing his rear foot flat on the floor to lengthen his calf muscle. Dean followed his example.

"That's nice. My mother died before I was two. Tuberculosis.[28] But God gave me these legs. I showed people I could use them."

"It's good your coach is going with us. I wish Ward Haylett were here. This summer, he drove five of us out to California for the qualifying meets and the Tryouts. If there was a sight to see or tasty food to eat, he stopped. He's better than any tour guide regarding his US history. Salt flats, mining towns, shepherds with their sheep. We had places to train on the way. He made sure of that."

With six men in the coach's car, the summer drive had been sweltering, even with the windows down. They went through Denver, Boulder, Provo, Salt Lake, Reno, Stockton, and Sacramento and slept near the Rocky Mountain National Park and on the Utah-Nevada border. Mr. Haylett took them to Yosemite National Park twice to see both the north and west sides.[29]

"Mr. Haylett was with me every step of the way." Thane said

Ward Haylett standing by his car on the trip to California, June 1952.
Photograph by Thane Baker. Courtesy of the Thane Baker Collection.

as he straightened. "I wouldn't be here without him. It's strange he isn't here now."

As they headed back to their seats, Thane continued. "Haylett told me back in Kansas to get my passport photos taken before the tryouts. I sure am glad I did! The Olympic Committee said the State Department will push the forms through, and we'll get our passports in New York." In addition to passports, the athletes needed smallpox vaccination certificates and permission from the draft board to travel outside the country.[30]

"Doesn't it seem to ya, Thane, that if they wanted us to have

Thane Baker riding in his coach's car on the way to California, June 1952. *Courtesy of the Thane Baker Collection.*

passports, they should have paid for them? Ten dollars for a passport was hard on my thin wallet!"[31]

"Same here," Thane responded. "And I don't get why all our luggage is on a different plane. I sure hope it ends up where we do,"

"Better be on your best behavior," Dean grinned towards a man approaching. "Here comes the Vaulting Vicar, the Pole-Vaulting Parson."

Bob Richards, older, with more confidence than Dean and Thane, plunked his knees on the seat ahead of Thane and peered over the chair back at them. He had won Olympic bronze in '48 and received the Sullivan Award and Helms World Trophy Award the previous year.

"What are you plotting back here?" Richards spoke in the dramatic, clipped manner of a professional speaker. "I saw you two putting your heads together and knew you were up to no good."

"Parson, we got halos." Dean chortled. "Trouble is, I left mine in my luggage!"

Thane stuck his hand out. "Name's Thane Baker. I'll run 200 meters. This guy is Dean Smith, 100 meters."

"Bob Richards, pole vault and decathlon, but I'll just be doing the pole vault in Helsinki. I figure you folks need the counsel of a minister to figure out where the finish line is."

"We ain't ed-u-mu-ca-ted like you, Bob." Dean retorted, exaggerating his Texas accent. "When ya ain't flying off the end of a pole, you're a theology professor, right?"

"Yes, the church ordained me in 1946. Why do I pray so hard? You try flying up to heaven with nothing but a stick."

Dean grinned. "At least it's not a broomstick."

Richards rolled his eyes. "I just hope Helsinki is better than London. In '48, it rained for nine straight hours during the pole vault competition. It's hard to hang on to a slippery pole."[32]

Thane shuddered at the thought and changed the subject. "I saw you lifting weights on the cover of *Strength and Health* magazine."[33]

"That's right. I'm also in this issue of *Guideposts*. It's a religious magazine."

"My coach won't let me lift weights or even go swimming," Thane said with a shake of his head. "He doesn't want me to be musclebound. It would slow me down. I do pushups, squats, and sit-ups on my own, though."[34]

"To each his own. But my arms need to propel me fifteen feet in the air. I need some muscle."

"I see your point."

"You folks are new here." Bob continued, "The older athletes have seen each other often in competitions. Let me make some

Reverend Robert Eugene "Bob" Richards, pole vault, July 1952. *Courtesy of the Crawford Family U.S. Olympic & Paralympic Committee Digital Archives.*

introductions! There's my old roommate, Harrison Dillard. We competed in Europe together back in '47." Richards called toward the back of the airplane, "Bones, get over here! I've got new folks for you to meet." Bob turned back to Thane and Dean. "His nickname is Bones because he was a skinny kid."

Dillard, a thin Black man of medium height, approached from the rear.

"Hello, Bob." Dillard said.

"Bones, these boys are so new they don't know come here from sic 'em. I want to introduce you. This is Dean Smith, 100 meters, and Thane Baker, 200 meters. You may have seen them at the tryouts. Thane, Dean, this is Harrison Dillard, Jesse Owens's protégé. Tell 'em how you know Owens, Bones."

William Harrison "Bones" Dillard, 110-m hurdles, July 1952. *Courtesy of the Crawford Family U.S. Olympic & Paralympic Committee Digital Archives.*

"We're both from Cleveland." Dillard answered in his modest way, "and went to the same high school. He's been my hero for so long. He gave me running tips. When I was competing in old shoes, he brought me a fresh pair."

"I told these youngsters that we roomed together on that exhibition tour the summer before the last Olympics."

"We did," Dillard nodded. "We had a ball."

Richards explained that Harrison Dillard had won the 110-meter hurdles over eighty times in a row going into the 1948 Olympic Tryouts. He tripped over a hurdle and ended his Olympic quest in that event. Fortunately, he had already qualified for the 100 meters. Dillard won Olympic gold in the 100 meters and the four-by-one-hundred (4x100)-meter relay.

"A couple days ago," Bob Richards said. "Bones qualified in his best event, the 110-meter hurdles and may run on a relay."

"Harrison, or may I call you Bones?" Thane asked. "Bob says he lifts weights. Do you?"

"Bones is fine. No, my coaches don't want me to get bulky muscles or lose flexibility. I include pushups and sit-ups, though."

Thane nodded, glad to see that his training conformed to that of a reigning gold medalist. "That's what I do. Thanks for sharing."

"Nice to meet you both. If you'll excuse me, I'm going back to rest."[35]

Bob Richards introduced Dean and Thane to other Olympic veterans in the surrounding seats. Mal Whitfield had run the 400, 800, and four-by-four-hundred(4x400)-meter relay. Fortune Gordien and Jim Fuchs had thrown the discus. While not a previous Olympian, officials ranked Bud Held the best in the world the previous year in the javelin.

With a mischievous grin, Bud told a story about rooming with Bob Richards in Europe. "Bob's always doing pushups while doing a handstand. Once, we were in a hotel room with a metal bar for a footboard."

"Now, Bud, do you need to tell them everything you know?" Bob Richards interrupted.

"Bob, these rookies think you are perfect, being a preacher and all. I just need to set the record straight."

Bob shook his head, crossed his arms, and looked amused.

"Like I was saying," Bud Held said, "Bob got it in his head to grab hold of the iron bar at the end of the bed and do his handstand pushups there. Then, if he got tired, he just fell back on the bed."

Thane couldn't imagine doing handstand pushups, let alone doing them while holding onto a round metal bar. He guessed that was good practice for a pole vaulter.

"B-u-u-u-d," Bob Richards intoned.

"B-ah-ah-ah-b," Bud Held echoed. "So, things were going well, until that one time, when Bob kicked the chandelier. He ripped it off the ceiling. Glass shards! Everywhere!" Bud spread his arms for effect.

"What did ya do then?" Dean asked.

"What could we do?" Bob asked. "We cleaned all that glass up just as clean as a whistle."

"Every bit," Bud Held said. Then he looked around before he delivered the punchline. "And we put all that glass in the closet, said nothing, and checked out the next day."

"Not my best moment," Bob Richards grimaced.[36]

The good-natured teasing continued. Thane kept quiet around the more experienced athletes. It was hard to feel like he belonged among them.

"Let's try to be serious now." Bob said, changing the subject. "This is the first time we'll compete against the Soviets in the Olympics.[37] Back in the '48 Olympics in London, Soviet coaches asked us questions about what we did. They wanted to learn techniques to take back to their compatriots. With the Korean War piling up casualties every day, I'm planning to make up a delegation to greet the Communist athletes. Jesus asks us to love everyone. Anyone want to join me?"

Franklin Wesley "Bud" Held, javelin, July 1952. *Courtesy of the Crawford Family U.S. Olympic & Paralympic Committee Digital Archives.*

Before anyone had a chance to respond, a panicked shout rose out of the crowd.

"FIRE!"

"Where's fire?" Thane jumped to his feet, straining to see, "Think it's just the cigarette smoke filling the cabin from the smoking coaches and athletes?"

"The wing!" Bob Richards exclaimed, pointing out the window.

Thane spotted the flames streaming behind an engine. Black and grey smoke poured out behind the flames. Thane felt dizzy and frozen in place.

They were so high up! He gasped repeatedly, trying to draw air into his lungs, but it didn't seem to work.

"There are mountains down there!" Dean, eyes wide, yelled over the terrified athletes. "Where we gonna land?"

"This is the captain," came a calm voice over the speakers. "We have a fire in one of our prop engines. We're flying over 20,000 feet. I'm going to dive to about two thousand feet to extinguish the fire. Everyone, please take a seat and brace yourself."

They scrambled into their seats with seconds to spare.

The pilot cut the engines.

The plane dropped.

Thane felt himself rising in his seat. With muscles rigid, he gripped the armrests and stuck his feet under the seat in front of him, straining to resist the powerful forces trying to toss him across the cabin like a rag doll. They were all going to die. Screams filled the cabins.

Everything not tied down flew inside the cabin. Bags, hats, food, glasses, coats, and shoes crashed into anyone or anything in their way. A flight attendant floated above him. Thane let go of his armrests and tried to hold onto her, but dynamic forces ripped her from his grasp. Four other athletes caught and held the poor woman.

The horrifying plummet seemed to last forever, but the aircraft finally leveled out. The wing outside the window was no longer on fire. The plains stretched out below the blackened engine.[38]

"The fire's out." The pilot announced, "I'm looking for a place to set down."

Thane could finally breathe again, but he felt like he was going to vomit. Judging by the sounds, he wasn't the only one who felt that way. More than one of his travel companions had tears in his eyes.

When he finally found his voice, Thane asked "Do you realize, Dean, we could have just lost the entire US Olympic track and field team?"

"Except for the marathon runners, who would've looked mighty silly running the 100 meters," Dean said with a shaky smirk. The marathon runners would meet them in New York.[39]

"You can joke?" Thane couldn't believe it.

"Beats crying. I gotta tell you, that scared the fool out of me."

"Me, too. I thought I was going to die."

"What were you thinking when it happened, Bob?"

His hands together, Bob Richard's fingers touched his lips. His palms pressed together so tightly that they trembled. He cleared his throat and focused his eyes on Thane. "Our Father, who art in Heaven."

"Amen," Thane whispered.

The Olympic Committee had hired a nurse to join their company. She tended the banged-up flight attendant and the other injured.

The flight attendants resumed their duties slowly in their rumpled uniforms. Returning property to the rightful owners took time. Everyone chipped in to straighten the chaos.

The airplane landed for an inspection at an airport, and everyone deplaned. Some searched for food inside the terminal.[40]

Thane stood alone in the aircraft's shadow. The sun drained energy. During track meets, he often wore a wet towel draped over his head if he couldn't be in the shade.

The pilot and copilot, along with workers from the airport, inspected the wing and the rest of the plane. After a lengthy discussion, they decided.

"Okay, everyone, back on the plane."

Many athletes expressed their concerns, but most entered the aircraft. Despite the terror he had just experienced, Thane still wanted to be on the Olympic team and joined those returning to the plane. Out his window, Thane watched the more reluctant passengers standing obstinately at the bottom of the steps. Finally, the coaches, pilots, and last reluctant fliers boarded.

The ebullient mood of the new members on the Olympic team ended. As the adrenaline from their free-fall waned, exhaustion crept throughout the cabin.

The plane refueled in St. Louis, and by the time the team landed in New York City, Thane felt as if he had completed a marathon.

CHAPTER 5

New York City

MONDAY, JUNE 30–MONDAY, JULY 7, 1952, NEW YORK CITY

Thane gathered his belongings and descended from the airplane. Late afternoon heat pressed down on him. The track and field team boarded several chartered buses and traveled toward downtown. Thane pushed his window down to catch a breeze. He turned to Dean. "Say, you ever look at such tall buildings in your life?"

"Only in the movies."

"I'm looking forward to checking out New York," Thane said.

"Think you'll have time?" Dean asked. "The coaches packed our schedule for the next few days. I heard something about marching in a parade, too. They'll keep us busy."

They both stared out the window at the buildings and crowds. People walked in and out of the subway entrance. Thane had never been on one of those underground trains.

The bus pulled into Times Square. The setting sun hid behind the buildings. Neon advertisements flashed everywhere. Chevrolet, Kensey Blended Whiskey, Canadian Club, and Admiral Television lit up one end. Not to be outdone, Coca-Cola, Pepsi-Cola, Camel Cigarettes, and Arrow shirts also advertised, along with beers Thane did not recognize. Marquees listed names of movies and plays. How did anyone sleep with all those lights flashing?

The team arrived at the Hotel Paramount about a block and a half from Times Square. The bus driver told them the hotel had been here for over twenty years. Thane stared at a tall building with a dozen arches supported by columns across its front. Ribbons and flowers of stone decorated the floor above. A little roof covered every window on the next floor up. It looked like a wedding cake on the top of the hotel.[1] How different the hotel looked from his home in Elkhart or even Kansas State College.

Thane followed the other athletes under an awning into the lobby. The hotel had stored their luggage on carts in a room off the lobby. The team rolled them out one by one, and the luggage-sorting melee began. Athletes threw suitcases to their owners. Thane stood back until his bag appeared. He took it out of the way and sat on it. With the entire Olympic track and field team to settle, he resigned himself to waiting for his room assignment and key. He looked up at the high ceiling above him and at everyone crowded into the lobby. The inside of this grand hotel had seen better days.

After getting to his room, Thane took a long shower. He had started the day in Los Angeles, flown in a burning aircraft, survived a dive without engines, and ended up in a hotel near Times Square. His bed beckoned. He needed to conserve his strength while he could. If today set the pattern, the days ahead might be as tiring as the Olympic Games themselves.

Thane's time on the East Coast passed quickly. Tuesday, the team took a train to Princeton, New Jersey, where they lived in the dorms and practiced at Palmer Stadium. When not practicing on the track, Thane played pool with Bud Held.

On July 1, a newspaper photographer snapped a picture of Thane running in lane one on the smooth Princeton track. Dean Smith ran in lane two. Four other Olympians ran in the outside lanes. Lots of newspapers printed that picture, maybe because only Dean Smith wore a T-shirt. Thane felt a little uncomfortable that folks from his hometown might see him wearing only thin cotton shorts.

Another photographer snapped an image of Walt "Buddy" Davis using the "Western Roll" over the high jump bar. Thane and several of the athletes ceased their workout to watch. Clyde Littlefield, Dean Smith's coach from the University of Texas, held one end of the bar. Walt ran toward the bar with one leg fast and the other slow. He threw his head in the direction he came from and swung his legs up so when he went over the bar, his entire body lined up parallel with the bar and faced toward the raked sand pit below. Buddy cleared it.[2]

The team had planned to stay in Princeton a while longer, but some of the team members encountered problems with their passports. With federal offices closed on Friday, July 4, and departure set for the following Monday, the team returned to New York on the third, hoping to resolve the issues.

That evening, Thane and other Olympians caught a Brooklyn Dodgers game at Ebbets Field with almost seventeen thousand other spectators. Thane had never attended a professional baseball game but had listened to plenty over the radio. The red brick facade, the green grass, the colors of the uniforms, and the spectators etched into his mind. Radio broadcasts would never be the same. Jackie Robinson, second baseman, batted third for the Dodgers.[3]

Thane got to know Meredith "Flash" Gourdine, who sat beside him at the game. Flash, an engineering student, spoke in his slow, thoughtful way about his journey from New York City gangs to Columbia University. He gave credit to a math teacher who refused to accept anything less than his best. After three hours of play, the New York Giants won 4-3.[4]

On the way back to the hotel, Thane talked with Lee Yoder, a 400-meter hurdler. "I'd never actually seen a professional baseball game before. Had you?"

"Sure. I'm from Philadelphia and a Phillies fan." Lee had a strong Philly accent.

Front cover of the program for the baseball game between the Brooklyn Dodgers and the New York Yankees, July 3, 1952. *Courtesy of the Thane Baker collection. Major League Baseball trademarks and copyrights are used with permission of Major League Baseball. Visit MLB.com.*

Ticket to the baseball game between the Brooklyn Dodgers and the New York Yankees, July 3, 1952. *Courtesy of the Thane Baker Collection. Major League Baseball trademarks and copyrights are used with permission of Major League Baseball. Visit MLB.com.*

Meredith "Flash" Gourdine, July 1952. *Courtesy of the Crawford Family U.S. Olympic & Paralympic Committee Digital Archives.*

Thane explained he played fastpitch softball back in Kansas with indifferent pitchers who gave up multiple hits, and batters who scored many runs. Thane had expected a higher scoring game. Yoder said the better pitchers in the major leagues obviously led to lower scores, but Thane thought the game was slow. They continued their conversation on the way back to the hotel and shared their experiences of seeing California for the first time the past June.[5]

On the fourth, Thane would have lit fireworks back home, but in New York he walked around to see more of the city. An

Dewey "Lee" Yoder, July 1952. *Courtesy of the Crawford Family U.S. Olympic & Paralympic Committee Digital Archives.*

afternoon thunderstorm cut his wanderings short.[6] That night, the Olympians watched a magic show at the hotel. By the end of the evening, with all the thunder and lightning, Thane figured they had enjoyed quite enough fireworks for one day.[7]

On Saturday, July 5, at nine thirty in the morning, Thane stood in line with the other track and field athletes in the Bowman Room at the Hotel Biltmore. The Olympic Committee needed to process each person before they departed for Helsinki.

While waiting, Thane picked up a blue booklet that listed all the Summer Olympic competitors and their sports, along with their coaches and managers. Surprise and hope filled Thane when he read his name listed as an alternate for both the 400-meter and the 1600-meter relays. The United States listed eight runners for each relay. Thane's name topped each list, but only because the team alphabetized the names. He did not expect to run a relay, but he guessed the US Olympic Committee sent their registration to Finland before the coaches picked their final roster.

Thane moved down the line and signed paperwork, promising that he had read the rules and would abide by them. He executed a release promising that he and his heirs would not sue the Olympic Committee and signed the Olympic Oath of Amateurism stating Thane had not competed as a professional athlete. He also agreed to take part in post-Olympic competitions sponsored by the Amateur Athletic Union of the United States.

When he finished his processing, Thane hustled back to the Paramount Hotel to pick up his Olympic uniforms. He wished to avoid another lengthy line. This time, he did not wait long. He took his outfits back to his room and hoped they fit.

After checking out his uniforms, Thane lined up downstairs to have his picture taken. After having competed in the NCAAs, AAUs, Olympic Tryouts, and spending a week together, Thane put names, faces, and events together for each of the other athletes lined up with him.

The Olympic Team often held meetings in the hotel. At one meeting, Thane learned Finnish stores did not sell chewing gum, and most Finns had not encountered it before. If the American athletes wanted to buy a low-cost gift to share with their hosts, they might want to stock up on chewing gum. Thane and his fellow Olympians added packages of Wrigley's Spearmint and Juicy Fruit, along with Adam's Clove and licorice flavored Black Jack to their luggage.

Thane Baker, July 1952. *Courtesy of the Crawford Family U.S. Olympic & Paralympic Committee Digital Archives.*

The Olympic Committee supplied meal money.[8] On Saturday night, he and Dean Smith spent $4 each for dinner at Mama Leone's on West 48th Street. The delicious food justified their splurge.

"Meals didn't come in courses back in Texas," Dean remarked.

Thane started with a shrimp cocktail. Smoked Nova Scotia salmon, vegetables, and a green salad followed.

"I'll tell ya, Thane, this is the best spaghetti I've ever eaten. Why d'ya pick fish?"

"I like fish, Dean."

Dessert followed. Thane picked half a grapefruit with sugar on it. Grapefruit was a special treat back home in Kansas. Dean chose a cheesecake.[9]

In the hotel on Sunday morning, the Reverend Bob Richards preached. With his tent-revival style, he told of successful athletes whose relationship with God motivated them. He concluded, "Analyze yourself, work on your weaknesses, welcome competition, put out more, be a good sport, be enthusiastic, and take God into your life. With Him, you can reach life's great heights."[10]

Afterwards, Thane shook hands with Bob. "How do you speak in front of a crowd like that? Anytime I speak, I work on my speech for days. I lose sleep from worry. You must have a gift."

Bob rested a hand on Thane's shoulder. "It just takes practice."

That afternoon, while a million other New Yorkers visited the beach for the Independence Day weekend, the United States Olympic Committee hosted the Olympic Carnival at Triborough Stadium on Randall's Island on a cloudless eighty-degree day with five thousand spectators.[11] It began at two thirty with a parade of athletes. This fundraiser demonstrated many unusual distances for track runners, plus field events, fencing, cycling, weightlifting, race walking, and gymnastics. The women contributed three fencers, eight gymnasts, and a few for the 100-yard dash. After the other events, the Olympic men's soccer team scrimmaged. The New York City Fire and Sanitation Department Bands supplied the music. The radio station WMYC broadcast the event live. Proceeds from the gate for the day's competitions provided additional funds for the Olympic team.[12]

At two fifty that afternoon, Thane won the 150-yard dash. A little guy from New York, Lindy Remigino, came in second, with Dean Smith from Texas finishing third.[13] Ten minutes later, Thane watched an intense-looking Charlie Moore, a 400-meter hurdler, win and set a record in the 352-yard dash.[14] Other running events were the three-fourths of a mile and two-mile runs. Thane enjoyed a beautiful afternoon and evening watching sports he usually did not have a chance to see.[15]

Monday morning Thane packed his suitcase and dressed in his wool Olympic suit.[16] His suitcase would not come anywhere near the 66-pound weight limit, as he carried his toiletries with his metal bottle of Old Spice After Shave on board.[17] When Thane left Kansas in early June to compete on the West Coast, he had only packed the essentials. He never dreamed that he would carry that same suitcase to Finland.

The New York Mayor's Reception Committee provided a bus to Battery Place, the starting point of the Olympic Parade. New York City Police Academy Military Training School members helped form the Olympians into ranks by size.

At five after noon, Thane and the rest of the United States Olympic Team began their march in a ticker-tape parade on Broadway to City Hall, escorted by former Olympians. Their honor escort included the Army, Marine, Navy, Air Corps, and Coast Guard, as well as New York's Finest, both mounted and walking. The Fire and Sanitation Departments and other bands played music.[18] Police guarded wooden barricades that blocked off layers of New Yorkers out to watch the parade. Just like they hailed Army General Douglas MacArthur, New York City toasted the 1952 Olympic Team as heroes.[19]

Relieved to get off his feet after breaking in his new white buckskin shoes on the uneven streets of New York, Thane sat in a folding chair at City Hall Plaza. Red, white, and blue bunting hung from a railing in front of a grandstand built in front of City Hall. At the podium in the center, an Olympic flag hung in front of the speakers. Behind the podium, a gigantic Olympic flag and more bunting hung from the second story. For the parading of the colors, Thane stood, took his hat off, and placed it over his heart with the other athletes. Men in uniform saluted. Speeches by Mayor Impellitteri and three other speakers followed as the sun braised the wool-suited Olympians.[20]

Bob Richards responded on behalf of the Olympians. "Thank

you all for letting me speak on behalf of the Olympic athletes. We are going over to Helsinki to do our best to make America proud. Our Olympic Oath says it all. 'We swear that we will take part in the Olympic Games in loyal competition, respecting the regulations which govern them and with the desire of participating in them in the true spirit of sportsmanship for the honor of our country and for the glory of the sport.' Thank you for all the encouragement you have given us today."[21]

Thane appreciated the brevity of Bob's talk.

After the recessional, buses took Thane and the rest of the Olympians to the Waldorf Astoria for lunch. Dean complained to Thane the fancy new shoes raised a blister on his foot. He and his fellow athletes took an elevator to the Starlight Room on the eighteenth floor. Two Olympic flags hung behind the head table. A stained-glass roof set in the vaulted ceiling, supported by great pillars, made the room seem like a church. The floor-to-ceiling windows produced a beautiful view of New York City.[22]

The titles on the menu sounded fancy. "Supreme of Fruit Lucullus" and "Breast of Chicken Virginia" were regular fruit and chicken like they served in Kansas.[23]

At eight thirty that evening, Thane waited with the rest of the track and field athletes, who joked and called out over one another. The Pan American Airways buses picked them up and delivered them to Idlewild Airport for their nighttime departure to Helsinki. Everyone carried a shoulder bag donated by the airline, marked PAA and Pan American World Airlines (Pan Am) on one side, the other side bearing the United States Olympic team logo and "United States Olympic Team 1952."

In the airport, photographers for Pan Am captured the Olympians as they waited for their flight. One photographer asked for Thane, Bob Richards, Dean Smith's coach, and several of the field athletes to pose together. Thane's big smile nearly eclipsed his face. At six feet tall, Thane stood about half a head shorter than the throwing giants on either side of him.[25]

Waldorf Astoria Hotel postcard, mid-twentieth century. *Courtesy of the author.*

UNITED STATES OLYMPIC TEAM

NAME *Walter Thane Baker*
PAA FLIGHT No. _____ DATE _____
FROM _____ TIME _____
BOOKED TO _____ VIA _____
Address at Destination
_____
_____
TEAM: *Track + Field*

Pan American World Airlines provided stickers to attach to the luggage of the athletes, July 1952. *Courtesy of the author.*

Once on the runway, the seventy-one track and field men, seven trainers, and two others posed for a photograph in their uniform suits next to their shiny Pan Am Super 6 Clipper. An athlete held a sign that read "Track and Field Team." With several flights of US Olympians departing for Europe, perhaps both the photographers and the United States Olympic Committee wished to identify the departing groups.

Thane noticed on the right of the cabin door someone had taped a sign, "*PAA WELCOMES the 1952 OLYMPIC TEAMS . . . GOOD LUCK . . .*"[26] After Thane settled into his seat, the plane taxied to the end of the runway.[27] Then it returned to the gate.

Dean turned to Thane. "Think we're jinxed? More mechanical problems."[28]

Inside the terminal, Thane found a seat away from the others. He slouched down and slipped his uniform hat over his face. Fatigue closed his eyes.

Voices grumbled. "This is the second time on two flights that we've had engine trouble."

Left to right: Waiting at the airport prior to departing for Finland, Assistant Coach Clyde Littlefield; Bob Richards, pole vault; Don Laz, pole vault; Cy Young, javelin; Thane Baker, 200 m (arrow); Bob Backus, hammer throw; and Franklin "Bud" Held, javelin, July 7, 1952. *Photograph produced by Pan American World Airways. Courtesy of the Thane Baker Collection.*

"Why can't we just use a ship to cross the Atlantic like normal people?"

"The basketball team gets to cross in a ship."

The 1948 track and field team members reminded them they did not exercise for two weeks while they sailed on the ship. After a time, the other athletes quieted. Three and a half hours later, the Olympians boarded again.[29]

The coaches assigned seats to require the competitors for each event to sit next to each other. That way, they could become better acquainted during the airplane ride. This plan integrated the team by race, as well. For the smaller athletes, the plan worked well.

James "Jim" or "Jimmy" Gathers, 200 m, July 1952. *Courtesy of the Crawford Family U.S. Olympic & Paralympic Committee Digital Archives.*

However, the bigger field event men squeezed into their seats, surrounded by equally large men.[30]

Thane joined Jim Gathers and Andy Stanfield, the other 200-meter competitors. He learned Jim had attended Tillotson College in Austin, Texas, and now served in the Air Force. Since Thane had competed at the Texas Relays in Austin, and was in Air Force ROTC, Austin and the military gave them starting points for their conversation.[31] However, the Texas Relays banned Jim because of his skin color.

Andrew "Andy" William Stanfield, 200 m, July 1952. *Courtesy of the Crawford Family U.S. Olympic & Paralympic Committee Digital Archives.*

While Jim Gathers was about Thane's age, size, and weight, Andy Stanfield, another Black man, looked older and larger. Thane had met both at the AAU Track and Field National Championships in Long Beach in mid-June, where Andy won the 200 meters. He also won the Olympic Tryouts. Andy graduated from Seton Hall and came from New York City, but he grew up in Jersey City, New Jersey.[32] Thane did not mind Andy's size, but he hated inhaling all the smoke from Andy's cigarettes. Thane also worried his Olympic suit would smell like smoke before the flight ended.

At one thirty in the morning, the plane began its journey. Thane watched the city lights below fade as they climbed. Exhausted athletes rested. No one spoke much. The farther they traveled, the thicker the smoke grew in the cabin. The PAA flight refueled in Newfoundland, made an unplanned but necessary fuel stop in Shannon, Ireland, and an expected pause in London, England.[33] At every stop, the Olympians disembarked and moved around to stretch their legs. The track and field athletes arrived in Helsinki, Finland, on Wednesday, July 9, at five in the morning local time, twenty-plus hours after leaving Idlewild Airport in New York.

CHAPTER 6

Welcome to Helsinki

WEDNESDAY MORNING, JULY 9, 1952, HELSINKI, FINLAND

A brilliant turquoise sky welcomed the Olympic team to *Suomi*, the Finnish name for Finland. As the aircraft descended, Thane saw hundreds of lakes and far more trees than at home on the Kansas prairie, even though the United States government and the farmers had planted millions of trees in shelterbelts to stop the Depression-era dust storms.[1]

Thane stepped off the plane at the newly opened Seutula Airfield.[2] His gritty eyes squinted against the bright sunlight. A nearby church tower bell tolled five times, too early to be out of bed. He reset his watch. He and the rest of the track and field team had not seen a bed in over forty hours.[3] Thane had tried to sleep on the plane, but he kept waking up.

Photographers snapped pictures of the arriving Americans in their wilted suits.

The baggage handlers laid all the luggage on the tarmac.[4] Thane grabbed his suitcase and stood in line with his passport with the rest of his team.[5] They cast long shadows in the early morning sun. Over the door to the terminal was an enormous banner, which said, "USA Olympic Team, Welcome to the XV Olympiad Helsinki."

The United States Olympic Track and Field Team arrive in Finland on their Pan American airplane, July 9, 1952. *Photograph #613, possibly by Olympia-Kuva OY. Courtesy of the Thane Baker Collection.*

Despite being tired, Thane felt alert as he boarded the bus to Helsinki.[6] Their driver took the team on an early morning tour of the city. The Olympic rings were everywhere. Perfectly tended flowers grew in the shape and colors of the Olympic symbol on a grassy area in front of an imposing, multi-columned building, which their driver identified as the Parliament House. Rings hung suspended between tall downtown buildings. The train station, department store windows, and a theater also bore the Olympic logo. The Finns even decorated grills on the front of their cars in honor of the Olympics.[7] With light poles sporting the Olympic rings, Thane knew he was not in Kansas anymore.[8]

The bus crawled along the brick streets near Helsinki Senate Square. Thane tried to keep his eyes open to take in the Helsinki Cathedral gleaming white against the sky, its four smaller green domes surrounding the great green center dome. His forehead burned with a headache, but he was determined to enjoy his first

First-place winners at the Kansas Relays received a watch in the early 1950s. Thane earned four. This is his watch from 1952. *Photograph by author. Courtesy of the Thane Baker Collection.*

view of the University of Helsinki and the Government Palace that also shared the square.[9] The white buildings reminded Thane of pictures in books about Ancient Greece.[10] Unlike New Yorkers, the Finns kept the Helsinki streets clean.

Police officers directed traffic in formal attire with oversized white gloves. Green and yellow trolley cars mixed with other traffic, which yielded the right-of-way as their bus traveled through Helsinki's brick-covered streets.[11] Their driver gestured to

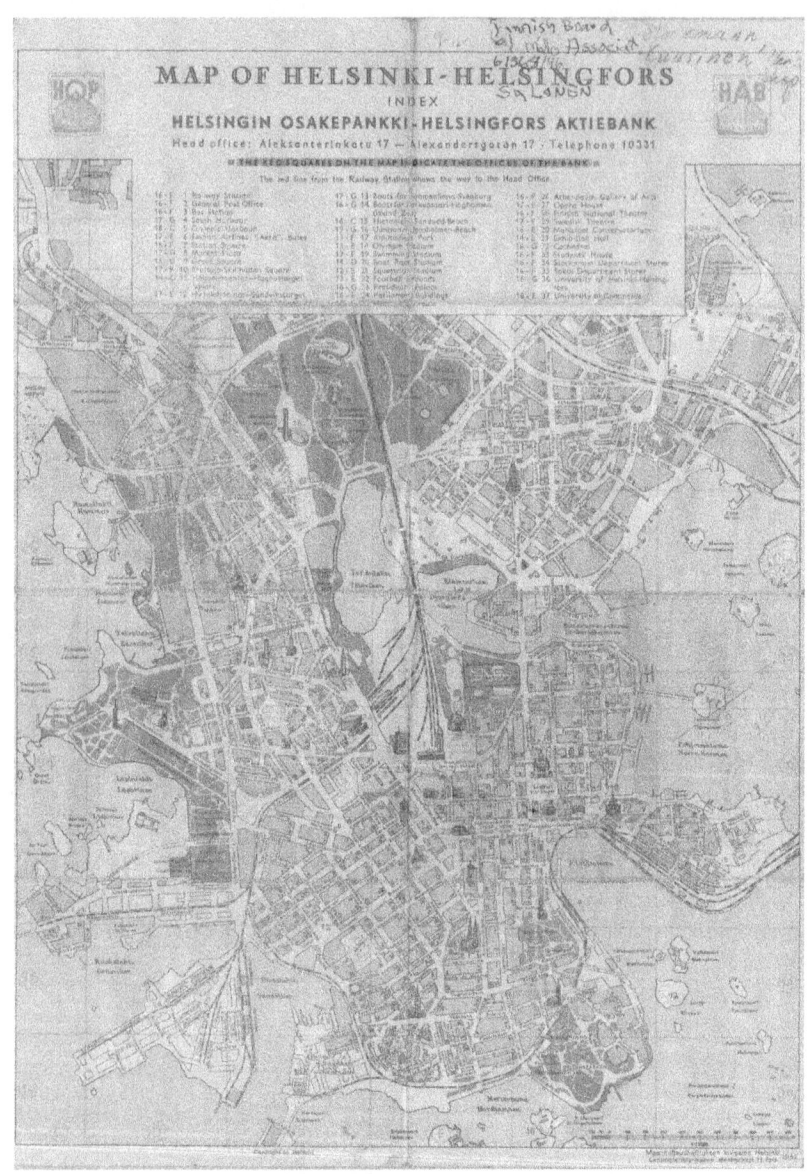

Helsinki. 1952. *Distributed by Helsingin Osakepankki-Helsingfors Aktiebank, © National Land Survey of Finland and courtesy of the Thane Baker Collection.*

Kauppatori, an open-air market near the waterfront. People set up their canvas-covered stands, overflowing with fruit, flowers, and traditional Finish foods, including local soups and breads. Near the harbor, vendors displayed fish just off the boats next to a covered meat market.[12]

"We've gotta come back here." Dean Smith said with a gleam in his eye.

Thane nodded.

Töölönlahti Bay led out to deeper ocean waters. Until a month ago, Thane had seen little salt water. A Kansas boy, he never traveled farther than a car could carry him. Last month, he ran where the Pacific touched San Francisco and Long Beach. Last week, New York City reached out to the Atlantic. Salt water united them all.

Their driver stopped in front of the Olympic stadium. Wide awake now, Thane sat up. A thrill coursed through him. Flags from all the competing countries fluttered against the sky from tall poles in front of the stadium. He had dreamed of this for years.

Thane nudged his seatmate, Dean Smith.[13] "Wake up! The Olympic Stadium!"

Dean lowered his knees from the seat in front of him, shoved the hat off his face, and sat up. "Whoo-ee! Will you look at that! That's why we're here."

"I probably won't win, but I'm sure glad to be here. Anything can happen," Thane said.

"Right you are!" Dean answered.

"The Olympic Tower is seventy-two meters high," the driver said, pointing to the huge spiral tower next to the stadium. "Soon, the Olympic flame, carried all the way from Greece, will burn on top of it. That tower has been waiting since we opened the stadium in June 1938. We planned to host the 1940 Games.[14] Then World War II happened.[15] Now, we have improved the stadium and welcome the world to the Fifteenth Olympiad. Finland has declared an Olympic peace, just like the Ancient Greeks. We call this the 'Friendly Games.'"

The Helsinki Olympic Stadium, 1952. *Photograph by U. A. Saarinen. Courtesy of the Finnish Heritage Society. License by CC by 4.0.*

The thin Olympic Tower on the side of the stadium must have been about twenty stories.

In front of the Olympic stadium, a statue of a naked runner stood on a stone block with the words Paavo Nurmi etched into it. "Paavo Nurmi, the Flying Finn, is a great hero in Finland," the bus driver explained. "He earned nine gold medals and three silver medals between 1920 and 1928."[16]

The buses stopped again at a rectangular arch that marked the entrance to Käpylä Olympic Village. The flags with Olympic rings floated above the gateway. On the right side of the building were the words *Citius, Altius, Fortius*. Their bus driver explained that it was the Olympic motto written in Latin, meaning "Faster, Higher, Stronger."[17] Guards protected the gate. A tall barrier made of chicken wire, supported by two-by-fours, surrounded the village.[18]

Entrance to the Olympic Village from outside the gate, July 1952. *Photograph by Thane Baker. Courtesy of the Thane Baker Collection.*

One of the US Track and Field coaches stepped on the bus.

"I have a badge for each of you to pin on your clothing," the coach explained, "The orange ribbon below the medal identifies you as an athlete. Coaches and officials have their own colored ribbons. You're also getting a blue card with your picture on it. This ticket gets you into wherever you need to go, including the Olympic Village here. It'll also admit you into the athletes' section to watch events and the dressing room or holding area for your own sport.[19] It's your ticket to ride the athletes' buses that run to the stadium area and back and will even get you onto streetcars. Hold on to these."

The coach walked down the bus aisle, handing out cards and pins. Thane pinned the badge on his uniform jacket and slipped the card into his wallet.[20]

"Required track and field meeting at five o'clock this evening out at the practice track," the coach said when he returned to the

Thane Baker's participation pin from the 1952 Olympics. *Photograph by author.*

front of the bus. "Grab some sleep while you can. Come dressed for an easy workout."[21]

The house steward greeted the athletes and gathered everyone together.

"Welcome to Käpylä Olympic Village. We built Käpylä for public housing. The Olympians are the first residents here. We expect 4,800 male competitors to stay in the village during the Games.[22] The other two thousand live in different accommodations, even private homes." Only ten American women would compete in track and field; they stayed at a nursing school. The Finns had painted the buildings in the village Olympic colors of red, blue, green, black, and yellow.

"Those flags extending from the right of the gate as you came in represent the athletes who live here." The steward continued. "Your American flag is already up because the Puerto Rican delegation is here. However, you will take part in your country's official flag-raising ceremony soon.[23] Once we raise a country's flag, the banner flies until the morning after the last athlete from that country departs."

"Where's the Soviet flag?" Dean asked Thane in a whisper.

"Perhaps they haven't arrived yet, or they aren't staying here."

"Follow me." The steward continued the tour, showing them

View in the Olympic Village from the restaurant tent toward the main gate. The flags on the left represent the countries of the inhabitants of the Olympic Village. Straight ahead is the main gate. On the right is the restaurant tent, July 1952. *Photograph by Olympia-Kuva Oy and courtesy of the Helsinki City Museum. License by CC by 4.0.*

the Käpylä Sports Park. A fence like the one around the Olympic Village surrounded the workout area.[24]

The steward escorted everyone back to the main gate, pointing out the enormous restaurant tent along the way. They turned right along Koskelantie, the road leading to the gate. The group stopped at a three-story cement building near a small, guarded gate in the fence.

"This is Building 11B, where you will stay. The apartments are unfinished but will provide a nice place for you."[25]

Buildings in Käpylä Olympic Village where the athletes lived, July 1952. *Photograph by Thane Baker. Courtesy of the Thane Baker Collection.*

A cheerful young Finnish cadet functioned as caretaker for their building and showed them to their apartment. Thane's two-bedroom upstairs apartment contained seven beds, some chairs, cement floors, a cold-water bathroom, and a small balcony. Even incomplete, this apartment would do.

Each bedframe had a card attached. The English-speaking Finnish private assigned to their room encouraged everyone to sign his name to it for the next occupant of the bed, who will either be in a nursing home or a hospital.

A sign on the wall said, "We wish you a hearty welcome to your village!"[26]

The private pointed out that no one assigned to their apartment would compete against anyone else in their suite. He gave the seven men three keys to share. After he left, Thane and his roommates left their door unlocked. That way, athletes with different schedules would not need to unlock the room for others.

Images from Thane Baker's room in the Olympic Village. Left to right: the view out the front, a flagpole behind, the side towards the flags in front of the Olympic Village, and the courtyard behind Thane's room, July 1952. *Photograph by Thane Baker. Courtesy of the Thane Baker Collection.*

Parry O'Brien, a favorite in the shot put with a new, creative way of throwing it, took the bed in the kitchen. When Parry figured out that their apartment lacked closets, he grabbed some nails and pounded them into the walls with his fists to hang his clothes.[27]

Thane left his suitcase in one of the shared bedrooms but brought his Brownie camera with him, slipping his fingers under the little leather handle attached to the cube-shaped camera. He took pictures of various views from his apartment, like the large boulders the size of cars bulging up from the ground all around.

After heading downstairs and outside, Thane went for breakfast. Now that his adrenaline had faded, a headache ground against his eyes again. If only he slept, he might feel better. He even felt a little nauseous. He joined Bob Richards and Dean Smith on the way to the tent.

RESTAURANT, spelled out in red letters, stood high in the air supported by unfinished wooden boards. Surrounded by flowers and plants, the white tent had vertical blue stripes on the sides and a wooden floor inside. His stomach growled at the smell of frying bacon and brewing coffee.

The servers wore blue and white checked dresses with white collars and cuffs. One sweet-smiling woman greeted Thane and his friends.

"Hello! Welcome! This is your restaurant tent. It is five thousand and five hundred square meters. We serve almost five thousand men at each meal. We have five separate kitchens and serving lines. You may go through any you wish. One line has Latin-American food. British and American food is over here. Our Scandinavian food is over there. We also have Central European and Asian lines. Some countries, such as Israel, Italy, and France, have their own private kitchens."

"Here, take a tray. Servers speak the language associated with the food they serve. You'll also see labels on the tables to tell you what everything is."[28]

"Thank you for explaining everything to us." Bob Richards raised his tray in a salute.

After seeing Thane and his friends line up, she turned to greet the next arrivals. "Hello! Welcome! This is your restaurant tent . . ."

"So much food!" Thane exclaimed. "It all smells great!"

"I'm starving." Bob rubbed his stomach.

Dean grimaced. "Nothin' here appeals to me. I saw some SPAM and crackers. I'm goin' to check that out."[29]

"SPAM?" Thane said, confused.

Bob raised his eyebrows.

Thane collected waffles with butter, syrup, and bacon on the side, served on a porcelain plate. He added a biscuit with butter and honey on a smaller one. Thane always tried to eat honey at every meal, since it gave him an extra burst of energy.[30] He carried his plates to a trestle table covered with a white tablecloth, returned for orange juice, and returned once more for hot chocolate. Bob and Dean joined him at the table, which accommodated four per side. Even though the coaches had integrated the team on the airplane, the Black athletes sat separately here.

"SPAM, huh?" Bob asked Dean.

"That fish gave me the willies. Who eats fish for breakfast?"

"People who live near the sea," Bob replied.

"In Texas, I might have some fried catfish and hush puppies

Jesse William "J. W." Mashburn, 1952. *Courtesy of the Crawford Family U.S. Olympic & Paralympic Committee Digital Archives.*

for supper, but this fish looked too fresh to me." Dean shuddered. "They still had their eyeballs!"

"I've gone fishing with my parents. Let me tell you, when we went out before dawn, caught fish, and cooked them over an open fire," Thane remembered with relish, "mm, that fish tasted great in the early morning."

Dean just shrugged as another man approached their table.

"Mind if I join you? J. W. Mashburn from Oklahoma."

Dean kicked out a chair across from him. "Sure. I'm Dean Smith, University of Texas. This here's Thane Baker from Kansas State, and Bob Richards from . . . Where're ya from, Bob?"

"California."

"Right. Do you attend college, Mashburn?" Dean wanted to know.

"I just finished high school. I plan to attend college in Oklahoma in the fall. Did you ever see so much food in your life?

I just couldn't decide, so I took some of everything."

"Aren't you worried your eyes are bigger than your stomach?" Thane asked. "My coach always says not to get heavy, or I might get slow."

"Nope, I'm pretty sure I can eat all this," J. W. replied with a grin. "I'm a growing boy."

"What are you here for?" Bob asked.

"I'm the fourth man on the 4x400-meter relay team. The Americans won that relay in '48, and we're going to win it again this year."[31]

"Good for you, J. W. Have you folks noticed that folks from other countries want to trade pins and stuff with us?" Bob asked.

Thane and Dean both nodded.

"We just don't have a thing to hand out," Dean contributed. "The other countries came prepared."

Thane added, "I didn't realize we were supposed to trade."[32]

Dean picked up a cracker. "Notice our mattresses? Stuffed with straw, I'd bet."

"My bed was hard." Thane took a sip of his juice. "But I figured hard beds must be good for runners."

"Well, our Lord slept on a bed of hay." Bob contributed, leaning in.

Dean sat back in his chair. "Well, I hate ta break it to ya, Parson, but we're livin' in the twentieth century, not the first."

After breakfast, Thane felt a little better. He wandered around the shops in the Olympic village with his friends. He saw a magazine and newspaper stand that sold nothing written in English. A tailor, barber, and shoemaker readied their workplaces. A photography studio developed film for athletes. Stores sold tobacco, sweets, soft drinks, souvenirs, and basic sports equipment. Thane did not need to buy razor blades, because Schick had given an electric razor and a voltage converter to every member of the team.

There was even a taxi stand, which seemed unnecessary. He could take the bus for free and looked forward to his first ride in

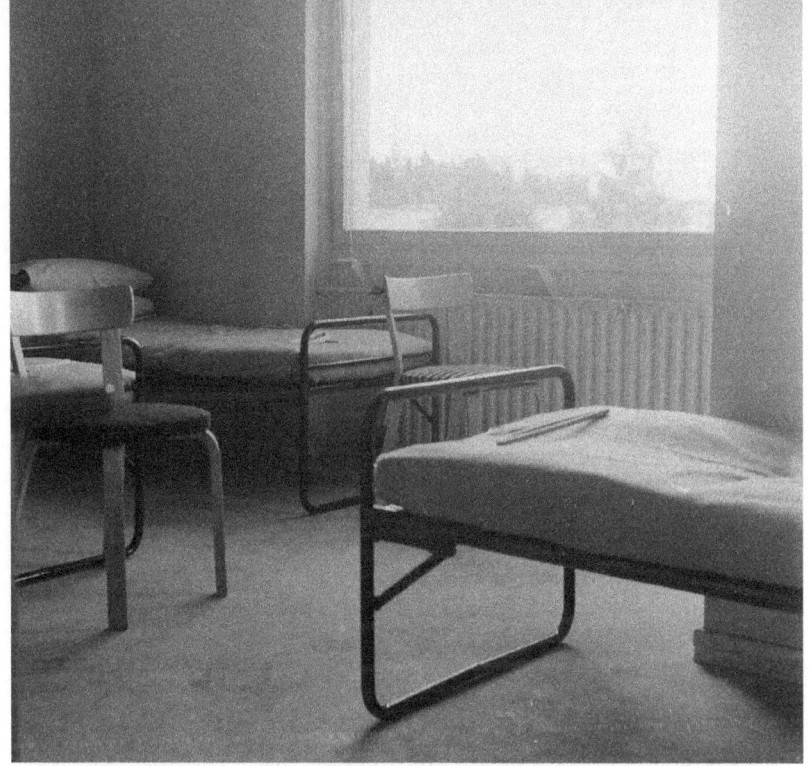

"Sleeping accommodation of Olympic participants," July 1952. *Photograph by Harry Pot. Courtesy of the Anefo Collection in the National Archives of the Netherlands. License by CC by 4.0.*

a streetcar. He lived in a village. The planners provided everything he needed.

"I thought we would not get any expense money, so I wrote a check for fifty dollars in New York. I won't need it now. We're rich," Thane commented. "What with the two dollars a day that the US Olympic Committee pays us for expenses."

"Good thing it doesn't count against our amateur status," Bob Richards commented.

"Only problem is, I'd like to convert some money into *markkas*," Thane said. "Back in town, I saw some places. I hear the stores will give us a better exchange rate if we buy something from them with dollars."

"*Pankki* means bank." Bob looked around. "Anyone find that word?"

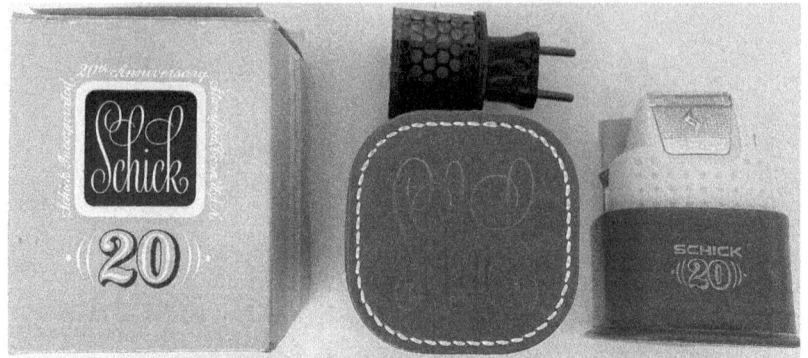

A Schick electric razor, leather container, and European transformer provided to each 1952 United States Olympian by Schick. Photograph by author. *Courtesy of the Thane Baker Collection.*

"There it is." Thane pointed.

They walked over to the bank. A man stood outside, sweeping the step. He opened the door for them to enter. Inside, a counter with a glass partition divided the customers from the cashiers. Thane exchanged United States dollars with a nice young woman who wore a white shirt with a small round collar, buttoned to the top. She spoke English, which helped. They left with paper and coins jingling in their pockets.[33]

"I want to buy a blank book to collect autographs from the Olympic track and field team, and I'll need some stationery and stamps to write home to my folks," Thane said.

"Souvenirs for my family," Dean declared. "That's what I need to find. I need to do well in the Olympics, for my wife and boy. Her family thinks I ain't worth spit."[34]

"I want what both of you want. I need to write to my wife and boys back home, plus find gifts to bring them that'll fit in my suitcase."

"Bob, how 'bout you fetch 'em an Olympic medal?" Dean suggested.

"From your mouth to God's ear. To be truthful, I hurt my leg in the tryouts. I'll work out in the swimming pool and pray for the best."³⁵ Bob lifted his head and shifted his shoulders back. He shook his head and smiled. "Thy will be done. Hey, we're at the Olympics. Let's do our best."

"This is the greatest adventure of my life." Thane said, "My eyes are as wide open as they can be. I'm trying to take everything in. I'll never have a chance like this again."

The somber mood lifted. They walked on.

They wandered over to a bus that served as a temporary post office. Thane checked out the postage prices.

"Fifteen *markkas* for a postcard and more for a letter. Let's see." Thane pulled a pencil and a scrap of paper from his pocket and calculated. "Two hundred thirty-one Finnish *markkas* to the dollar. Hmm. They charge about six and a half cents to mail a postcard. The rate for that thin airmail paper that folds into an envelope is eleven cents. A regular letter costs up to thirty cents. That's outrageous! I can mail a postcard in Kansas for three cents."³⁶

Thane filled out a postcard anyway and mailed it to his mother and father to tell them he'd arrived.

When he had called his parents collect from Los Angeles to tell them he had made the Olympic team, Mother sounded worried when she accepted the call. She must have expected sad news. When Thane told her he qualified for the Olympic team, she started crying. He heard her tell Father.

"Do your best! Do your best! Do your best!" Father chanted before they had to end the expensive call.

Thane glanced over at the fence that separated the competitors from the townspeople. Little girls with bobbed haircuts competed with Brylcreemed boys for a position at the divider, pushing slips of paper through holes in the chicken wire barricade for Olympians to sign.³⁷ Adults formed a second layer as they lined the fence to stare inside. Thane, Dean, and Bob moved to the fence.

"Sign, pliss," the autograph seekers said. "Your name, pliss." Thane, Bob, and Dean signed papers shoved through the fence

Fans surround the Helsinki Olympic Village, summer 1952. *Photograph by U. A. Saarinen. Courtesy of the Finnish Heritage Agency..*

for some time, but people kept coming. Flash Gourdine, broad jumper, and Andy Stanfield, winner of the tryout 200 meters, also stood nearby and signed. Some people seemed fascinated with them because they were Black. Thane was popular, because when he passed his signature back through the fence, he included a stick of chewing gum.

"Uh-oh." Bob looked at his wristwatch. "We need to rest our heads on our pillows before practicing this afternoon. Here comes Don Laz, another one of our pole vaulters. He's hunting for a new hollow steel pole. His broke during the tryouts."

"What kind of pole do you need, Don?" Thane asked.

"I have a tremendous swing and high grip that will break a pole quicker than anything. It's got to be seven millimeters thick, and they should have one in Sweden. But so far, no luck."

Bob interrupted, "Laz, you want to race back to our building?"

Laz set his body ready to run.

"No fair using your legs." Bob planted his hands on the ground and thrust his feet up in the air. Don Laz got on his hands, too. Did they plan to race on their hands? They did! A handstand against a wall proved challenging for Thane.

"Go," shouted Dean.

A crowd gathered around, encouraging them. The competitors' arm muscles bulged, and neck muscles strained as they arched their backs and bent their knees to keep their balance as they raced.

"Come on, Richards!"

"Show him, Laz!"

The Finnish spectators cheered from behind the fence.

When they reached the porch, Bob Richards and Don Laz climbed up the stairs using their hands! When they touched Building 11B, they both stopped and landed back on their feet.

Thane clapped Bob on the back and laughed. "You and Don are amazing. I've never seen anything like that."

His face red, Bob shook his head. "We kid around like that all the time. Let's get some sleep."[38]

"I'll beat y'all upstairs," Dean challenged. Thane hustled into the building. Bob, with an almost imperceptible limp, moved more slowly.

CHAPTER 7

New Coaches and Old Friends

WEDNESDAY EVENING, JULY 9, 1952, HELSINKI, FINLAND

That evening, after a much-needed nap on sheets made of rough canvas, Thane sat next to other athletes from Kansas, Oklahoma, Texas, and California, stretching his muscles on a grass field in the center of the track.[1] Tall evergreen trees and their pine-needle carpets guarded the 400-meter oval where Thane had already coasted through a warmup quarter mile. The weather was perfect.[2]

Waiting for everyone to arrive, Thane took photographs of his fellow athletes. Everyone wore their newly issued T-Shirts that said "USA" in red and "Helsinki-1952" in blue, except Wes Santee. He wore his University of Kansas track suit.

The head coach, Brutus Hamilton, a soft-spoken man from California, introduced the other coaches. Hamilton was a good friend of Thane's coach Ward Haylett back in Kansas. Here, Clyde Littlefield, Dean's coach from the University of Texas, assumed responsibility for sprinters like Thane.[3] Hamilton told Thane's group if they encountered a situation, they should ask Littlefield for help.

Dean Smith leaned close to Thane and whispered. "Mr. Littlefield's more like a father to me than my own, who's just a drunk.[4] Mr. Littlefield drives up to Dallas from Austin about three

Wes Santee, 5000 m, on the right, July 1952. *Photograph by Thane Baker. Courtesy of the Thane Baker Collection.*

Thane Baker's 1952 Olympic workout T-shirt. *Photograph by author. Courtesy of the Thane Baker Collection.*

times a year to buy me a new pair of these special kangaroo-hide running shoes."

Thane whispered back, "My shoes aren't new, but I like to put those leather pushers inside them. I hope Mr. Littlefield treats all of us as well as he does you."

Thane wore socks and Keds loaned from K-State. His black competition shoes with spikes, also borrowed from K-State, sat on the grass beside him.

Mr. Hamilton said the coaches did not plan to teach the athletes much. They were already Olympians. He would make facilities available for the athletes to do their own individual workouts. Thane had hoped the coaches would take a more active role in their training. Similar thoughts reflected on the faces of some of his fellow athletes.[5]

Coach Hamilton explained that everyone needed to wear their clean dress uniforms at the Opening Ceremony. Because various administrators complained that the Americans looked sloppy coming into the stadium during previous Olympic Ceremonies, all members of the team would have marching practice before the Games. Olympians who served in the Armed Forces were invited to assist with drilling.[6] Every athlete would have an assigned position in the column, as they walked around the entire track for the spectators to observe them. Sprinters would line up first. Dean looked over his shoulder at Bob Richards. "Sprinters will beat ya ever' time."

Hamilton paused and leveled a stare at Dean to quiet him.

The coach continued, "We are in reasonably good shape, but it will take a few days to loosen up."[7] Stiffness plagued Thane's muscles. Bob Richards attempt to pole vault earlier but quit because of his injury.[8] "I believe the track here will make for slower times in the sprints and hurdles and better marks in the longer races. It is softer than the usual American cinder paths. The reason is that the Finns go in for more distance stuff."[9]

If the track slowed Thane down, it would hurt everyone else, too. Placing well mattered more than fast times in the Olympics.

Thane stuck both legs straight out in front and barely reached an inch past his toes. He had never been limber.

"These Games will be different." Mr. Hamilton continued, "They will be dramatic. You may be sure there will be some tenseness, but we will be able to meet any situation that arises. Be a perfect guest to a perfect host nation. I know all of you will be trying to do a little better than your best at Helsinki."[10]

Mr. Hamilton explained the new rule says anytime an athlete breaks a record, whether in preliminaries or finals, it will be a new Olympic record. In the past, only records beaten in the finals set a record. "Now an athlete might break an Olympic record and still not win a gold medal."

"We'll just be ourselves." Coach Hamilton said, finally addressing the issue on everybody's mind: their Cold War adversary, the Soviet Union, would compete in the Olympics for the first time. "We'll congratulate them and shake their hands and gab with them, too, if they'll let us. There won't be any trouble. We'll have to be wary and set a good example. I don't anticipate any rhubarbs."[11]

The Coach warned the athletes not to involve themselves with anyone trying to escape from another country. That seemed odd. Didn't the Americans want to give the defectors freedom? The Soviet border loomed a little over a hundred miles away by land. Soviet-occupied Estonia was even closer across the water. Maybe they did not want to create an international incident. Russian planes could be here in short order. The Korean War flamed higher every day. The world did not need another crisis.[12] Thane spread his straight legs in a "V." He leaned over, pulling his torso toward the ground.

"We don't have a Jesse Owens.[13] We have a good strong team. On the basis of our records, this is the best team we have ever sent to the Olympic Games. Of course, we realize the rest of the world has improved, too. So, it's doubtful that we will win as many gold medals as in 1948. But we will certainly make a good showing."[14]

Coach Hamilton explained that by allowing West Germany and Japan to compete in 1952, unlike in 1948, and adding the Soviet Union, the medal count for the United States would lower.

"All in all, we should maintain our place at the top of the track and field world," the coach continued.[15] "We're strong in every place. Just compare our times. The Russians have some good boys. They have a fine chance in the steeplechase, some of the distance runs, and the hop, step, and jump. But who's going to stop Whitfield, Dillard, Mathias?"[16]

Thane looked over at the three mentioned by Mr. Hamilton. All of them earned gold medals in the 1948 Games. It must be intimidating to be the best in the world, then come back four years later to try to defend that title.

Thane struggled to stretch, trying to improve his own flexibility. He appreciated those older men with more experience and success.[17] But the "victory follows the experienced" philosophy did not apply to Bob Mathias.

Only four months before the 1948 Olympics, Bob Mathias's high school coach had suggested he try the decathlon, the two-day test of ten track and field skills. Three months later, Bob qualified for the Olympics. Ward Haylett, Thane's Kansas State coach, mentored Mathias through the London Games. On a field lit by car headlights and flashlights, Mathias earned his first Olympic gold medal at only seventeen years of age. Now Mathias, a year older than Thane, held the world record in the decathlon.[18] Thane would only compete in one event. Mathias came prepared for ten.

Thane was grateful to belong on a team with such talented athletes. He still struggled to believe that he was at the Olympic Games, an ocean away from home. A second Olympiad might be impossible for Thane. In four years, he would be out of college and would need to work. Stretching, he reached for his right foot with his left hand.

Coach Hamilton warned the runners the commands for the race starts would be in Finnish. *Paikoillenne* meant "on your mark" and *valmiit* stood for "set."[19] Thane tried to repeat the words to himself. The coach told the runners not to worry. Runners would drill in the new language during the eleven days before the Olympics began.

Surprisingly, Coach Hamilton counseled everyone to get enough sleep. Because they stayed so close to the Arctic Circle, the summer sun shone eighteen hours a day. It rose about three in the morning and set at nine thirty. Dusk lingered until after eleven at night, and dawn began a little before two in the morning. Tonight, a full moon would illuminate the brief night.[20] The team manager would distribute sleeping masks.

Coach Hamilton's advice not to overeat in the dining tent was not a surprise. Ward Haylett had often reminded Thane that extra weight led to a slower time.

In the past, the Olympics included art contests. This year, the Olympic Committee eliminated them, but artists would show their work at the Art Exhibition Hall.[21] They invited the athletes to view their work, but Thane doubted he would have time to attend.

The track and field athletes received a reminder to review the letter from Avery Brundage, President of the American Olympic Association. The highlights included instructions that they came to Helsinki "to do more than win Olympic prizes; we must create a lasting, favorable impression of Americans. . . . We can do this by becoming genuinely interested in Finland before leaving and by showing true sportsmanship on and off the athletic field." Athletes were to avoid public smoking so as not to startle foreigners. Of note, "Anti-American demonstrations of various kinds may even be staged." The athletes should "be aware that hostile eyes and ears from countries which are antagonistic to the United States" placed the Americans "under continuous surveillance . . . Every American attending the Games, in whatever capacity, should be careful of his words and actions and ever watchful to protect American prestige."[22]

Coach Hamilton gave instructions to work their kinks out on the track today, but not push too hard. He advised them to stay

American Olympians take a break during their workout, July 1952.
Photograph by Thane Baker. Courtesy of the Thane Baker Collection.

awake until after dinner to help them overcome their jet lag. He ended his speech. "What fun is it? Why all that hard, exhausting work? Where does it get you? Where's the good of it? It is one of the strange ironies of this strange life that those who work the hardest, who subject themselves to the strictest discipline, who give up certain pleasurable things in order to achieve a goal, are the happiest."[23]

Thane did a light workout. During his breaks, he took another photograph of his fellow athletes.

On his way back to his apartment, someone stopped him and asked him to pose with a set of blocks. Thane was happy to comply.[24]

A reporter originally from Hays, Kansas, asked Thane a few questions. Before long, they stopped talking about the Olympics and discussed the more critical issue of the current Kansas wheat crop.[25]

Thane went back to his dorm room after his workout. He cleaned up in the chilly water and changed into his street clothes.

Thane Baker sets his blocks in front of a Coca-Cola stand, July 1952.
© 1952 The Coca-Cola Company. All Rights Reserved. Photograph by Lee Dolan. Courtesy of the Thane Baker Collection.

Thane sat outside Building 3 in the Olympic Village on a four by eight-foot rectangular rock and watched the world go by, trying to stay awake. He straightened. A small man in an Olympic competition uniform passed.

"I know you!" Thane called out.

The man denied it.

"I know you! Bobby Bickle! You lived in my hometown when I was a kid!" Thane and Bobby shook hands. Thane reminded Bobby of a time he fought in front of the high school against a much larger opponent.

"Your fists were lightning fast," Thane said.

Bobby told Thane that he had qualified to come to the Olympics in the "featherweight" division but would compete in the "lightweight" division.[26]

Back in Elkhart, Thane had heard rumors that Bobby used to go down to Guymon, Oklahoma, on Saturday nights to fight for $25 a night. If true, that would disqualify him from the Olympics. Thane did not mention it.

"Will you take our photograph on my camera?" Thane asked a teammate before handing over his Brownie. After the photo, Thane thanked his temporary photographer, and Bobby went on. Thane shook his head. What a coincidence!

Three of his teammates joined him on the rock. They held two newspapers. The reporters had not written in English.

"What are you doing with those?" Thane doubted they read other languages.

"We have a puzzle to tussle. Here's a German newspaper and a Norwegian paper. We're looking for the same Associated Press articles in each paper. We'll compare them and discover if we can figure out the gist. You wanna help?"

"Sure. Sounds like fun. Why didn't you buy a Finnish newspaper?"

"Because no one understands Finnish."

Thane and his compatriots studied the newspapers and

Thane Baker and Robert Leroy "Bobby" Bickle, July 1952. *Courtesy of the Thane Baker Collection.*

understood a few articles. Three of Thane's grandparents came from Germany. Maybe that helped.

After a while, the newspaper words blurred. Thane's head sank into his chest. The surrounding voices mingled with his dreams.

"Thane Baker?" The call of a messenger jolted Thane awake.

"That's me." Thane straightened.

"Someone's at the gate for you." The announcement surprised him. Who would want to see him? His fellow rock-sitters looked interested as well.

At the front gate, Everett Wareham, one of the Wareham brothers from the Wareham Hotel in Manhattan, Kansas, greeted

Thane. Mr. Wareham was a friend of Ward Haylett and a huge fan of K-State athletics. Mr. Wareham came to practices and track meets back home. But for him to come all the way to Finland!

Flabbergasted, Thane shook his hand. "Mr. Wareham, what a surprise! Come on in. I'll show you around."

The Wareham family owned a substantial hotel near Kansas State. During that terrible flood last summer, seven feet of river water covered the main floor of their building.[27] After the Kansas River receded, workers cleaned out a great deal of mud. Thane had seen the high-water mark on the hotel's limestone walls when he visited the Wareham Hotel.[28]

Thane led the way past the gate with its silent sentinels. He showed Mr. Wareham his upstairs apartment. If Mr. Wareham thought it odd that one bed was squeezed lengthwise in the kitchen, he did not comment on it.

Afterward, they took another exit from the apartment building and walked over to the athletic fields.

"Mr. Wareham, this is where we practice."

"You've got to see where we eat," Thane said when they finished studying the practice fields. "It's that enormous tent over there. Come join me for dinner."

After dinner, Thane readied for bed. Since he last enjoyed a good night's sleep, he marched in a parade in New York City, lunched at the Waldorf-Astoria Hotel, traveled by airplane to Newfoundland, Ireland, London, and Helsinki. He visited the Olympic Stadium and settled in the Olympic Village. He napped and worked out. People from the only two places he had ever lived greeted him.[29] Too tired for dreams, Thane slept.

The Wareham Hotel in the Manhattan, Kansas, flood, 1951. *Reproduced by permission from the Kansas Historical Society.*

CHAPTER 8

Opening Ceremony

SATURDAY, JULY 19, 1952, HELSINKI, FINLAND

Saturday morning, July 19, 1952, seven men in Thane's apartment shared one bathroom as they prepared for the Opening Ceremony. Searching for missing ties or socks consumed too much time. Blanket-blocked windows kept out the sun that rose too early and set too late. Smelling of his Old Spice After Shave, Thane dressed in his Olympic uniform with the Olympic shield on the blue wool flannel jacket along with "Helsinki 1952." Grey flannel pants and a white shirt completed his suit. The silver buttons on his jacket displayed the same US Olympic shield that sat on his hat and competition singlet. He added his red, white, and blue woven belt. Thane tied his Olympic tie as he jockeyed for mirror space. Thane then pulled on the argyle socks the team provided. He pushed his feet into his buffed white shoes with their red soles, then attached his participant pin with its ribbon onto the lapel of his jacket. He never needed the blue card the coach handed out on their first day here. Everyone honored his pin as proof of Thane's participation in the Games. He grabbed his poplin hat and dashed out the door to join the other Americans waiting outside.[1] Thane took a picture of his teammates in front of his building. American Buddy Davis towered over everyone.

United States Olympians in their dress uniforms in front of their temporary home, July 1952. *Photograph by Thane Baker. Courtesy of the Thane Baker Collection.*

The last time Thane had seen all his fellow American in their formal uniforms was last Saturday, the day of the village flag raising ceremony for the United States. Beginning about eleven thirty in the morning, the entire Olympic team, men and women, plus coaches, trainers, and managers, about 350 people, marched four across from the housing area to the flag area across from the Restaurant tent. An older gentleman led the procession. The ceremony began at noon, with a Finnish band playing introductory music, followed by welcoming speeches. Avery Brundage, the United States Olympic Committee president, replied on behalf of

Walter "Buddy" Davis, high jump, July 1952. *Photograph by U. A. Saarinen. Courtesy of the National Board of Antiquities. License by CC by 4.0.*

the Americans. Finnish cadets raised the American flag while the band played the Star-Spangled Banner. Crowds of spectators stood behind the fence that ran parallel to the flag poles to watch the spectacle. At the end, the band played a closing march. It only lasted a few minutes, but it was impressive.[2]

Every day had been perfect for their Olympic preparation. Because of early athletic adventurers, Mr. Hamilton decreed no one could work out before eleven in the morning. Less than twenty-four hours after their arrival in Helsinki and only a few

Avery Brundage, head of the United States Olympic Committee, approaches the podium at the United States flag-raising ceremony, July 1952. *Photograph #1036 by Olympia-Kuva OY. Courtesy of the Thane Baker Collection.*

hours of sleep, Bob Richards had shaken Bud Held awake and dragged him to the workout track before sunrise. Bob explained it was only five in the evening in California! Dr. Adolf Weinacker, a fifty-kilometer walker, and some distance runners had also enjoyed a beautiful run through the forest before dawn.[3] Today, cool, cloudy weather replaced the beautiful sunshine as the athletes gathered by country.[4]

"Pay attention!" A United States team manager yelled into a bullhorn, "It's the birthday of your head coach, Brutus Hamilton. Now, you don't need to worry about buying him a fancy present. He said, 'The best birthday gift the American athletes can give me is gold medals for themselves.' So, this week, let's win lots of gold medals for yourselves, your coach, and your country."[5]

Thane joined his teammates in enthusiastic applause. With the excitement and hope coursing through the crowd, anything felt possible.

"First thing we're going to do is take some team photographs. For the track and field photograph, we decided on the flags of the competitors in the village for the background. Let's walk over now," the manager instructed.

"Remove your hats for the pictures, please. While they're setting up, let's have the men's track and field team get ready in front of the flags. We want two rows standing and one row squatting down. Back row, we want your heads between the shoulders of the two men in front of you. Again, take off your hats, please."

Thane moved into the back row, twelfth person in from his right side. J. W. Mashburn of Oklahoma stood to his right. Thane looked over Wes Santee's shoulder. The coaches and trainers joined the group. Thane combed his hair back from his face. When the photographer, who wore a US Army uniform, decided he captured everyone in his camera lens, Thane smiled.

"The photographer finished," the manager said.[6] "Thank you for your patience. Let's take a quick break and meet up again at the main gate in fifteen minutes. You won't have time to yourself until the ceremony is over at three o'clock."

Thane and many others stopped in their rooms for a moment. He left his Brownie camera. No sense in carrying that around all day.

Back at the front gate, the manager spoke again, "Everyone, listen up. We've practiced marching several times. Remember, demonstrate professionalism once we enter the stadium. Special thanks to the eighty US Olympians who also serve in the Armed Forces. They were a tremendous help in teaching us to march, particularly with turns.[7] Let's give them a round of applause."

Thane clapped with everyone else. Because of his ROTC experience, he knew how to march. The number of active-duty men surprised Thane, since he had not noticed many service members on the track and field team.

"May I have your attention again?" Several whistles helped calm the crowd. "Yesterday, representing the Americans, a sign-holding Finnish cadet, one of our team managers, and our flag bearer had a

United States Track and Field team in their dress uniforms. David Wesley "Wes" Santee, center, and Jesse William "J.W." Mashburn, right, face the camera. July 1952. *Photograph by Thane Baker. Courtesy of the Thane Baker Collection.*

Some of the United States Track and Field men in front of the flags. Left to right: Jack Davis, 110 m hurdles; James Gathers, 200 m; Roland Blackmon, 400 m hurdles; Walter Ashbaugh, triple jump; Bill Miller, javelin; Kenneth Wiesner, high jump; Arthur Bernard, 110 m hurdles; Meredith Gourdine, long jump; John Demi, 50 km walk; and Samuel Felton, hammer throw, July 1952. *Photograph by Thane Baker. Courtesy of the Thane Baker Collection.*

Official photograph of the United States Track and Field Team found in Bushnell's Olympic Book on pages 72–73. Back row, left to right: Theodore Corbitt, Meredith Gourdine, George Brown, James Gathers, Asst. Manager Pincus Sober, George Shaw, Jerome Biffle, Reginald Pearman, Arnold Betton, J. W. Mashburn, Wes Santee, Thane Baker, Arthur Barnard, Jack Davis, Lindy Remigino, Ollie Matson, James Gerhardt, Arthur Bragg, Darrow Hooper, Browning Ross, Kenneth Wiesner, George Mattos, James Dillon, John Barnes, Walter Davis, Cy Young, Franklin Held, Floyd Simmons, Warren Druetzler, Donald Laz, James Fuchs, William Ashenfelter, Gene Cole, Robert Backus, Javier Montez, Walter Ashbaugh, Price King, Samuel Felton, Charles Moore, Asst. Coach Lawrence Snyder, Robert McMillen, Asst. Coach Clyde Littlefield, and Asst. Coach Charles Werner. Front row kneeling, left to right: Fortune Gordien, Manager Robert Kane, Roland Blackman, Andrew Stanfield, Henry Laskau, Lee Yoder, Thomas Jones, Victor Dyrgall, Horace Ashenfelter, Harrison Dillard, Leo Sjogren, John Deni, Curtis Stone, Charles Capozzoli, Dean Smith, Trainer Hill, Trainer Wojecki, Kenneth Howard, Asst. Manager Lawrence Houston and Asst. Manager Harold Berliner, July 1952. *Photograph by the United States Army. Courtesy of the Crawford Family United States Olympic & Paralympic Committee Digital Archives.*

rehearsal with every country who planned to march in the Opening Ceremonies. Plus, little cardboard signs will show us where we line up both at the practice field and in the stadium. What with coaches and trainers, we have over 340 Americans marching today.[8] I know you will do everything you can to stay organized."

The United States Olympic Committee provided each Olympian with a small flag to use in the Olympic Opening Ceremonies, July 1952. *Photograph by author. Courtesy of the Thane Baker Collection.*

The manager continued, "Norman Armitage, fencer, will carry the United States flag into the Olympic Stadium. Norman, raise your flag so everyone can find you."[9] The manager then held up a sign that said, *YHDYSVALLAT.* "This word means the United States in Finnish.[10] You want to be behind a sign with this word on it. If not, you're in the wrong place." The team manager asked for volunteers to hand out American flags for the athletes to wave in the stadium.

"The transportation will carry us to *Eläintarha,* the women's workout field.[11] We will wait there until our turn to enter the stadium. Our team will be the second to last group to enter. Our hosts, the Finns, follow us. The planners of this event expect 5,500 athletes to march into their assigned position in one hour."

Surprised mutterings scattered through the crowd.

"Don't forget men, hats off and over our hearts when we pass the grandstand. When we exit, we will march in columns out of the two eastern gates. This should go faster than our entrance."

Thane hoped so. He expected to be on his feet all day.

"The United States will be the last team to board the buses for the Opening Ceremonies. We've already had word from the Finns this morning about other countries who lagged in their loading. Eleven buses depart from Käpylä every seven minutes. We don't want to hold up the show. When it's our turn, look sharp.

"Right now, move into your assigned place for the parade. Remember, we're walking seven across. We want to load the bus in the same order we will unload and march. When we get there, coaches march into the stadium first, followed by the women. Men in military uniforms process in next. Then you men will be last. Everyone, do your best. They expect 70,000 spectators in the stands, plus reporters and cameras will broadcast this ceremony all over the world."[12]

Thane had heard that the US Olympic Committee required the women to alter their uniform skirts to make the end of the fabric on each skirt to be the same distance from the ground because someone had decided it looked better. That sounded like too much work for the women, who had to train as much as the men!

Thane stood at the front of the men's columns with the other sprinters. He searched, but did not find his fellow sprinters, Dean Smith or Andy Stanfield. The scent of rain hinted at worsening weather, and the clouds looked darker and heavier than when they first came outside. Soon it poured, drenching his new Olympic uniform that had neither a raincoat nor an umbrella.

"The buses are here. Load up."

Glad to get out of the rain, Thane looked out the window. As the bus crept toward the stadium, thousands of people wearing raincoats, slickers, trench coats, and carrying umbrellas walked toward the same destination.[13] They moved out of the way of the athletes' buses.

Two hours later, Thane still stood on the women's training field in the driving rain. The smell of wet wool was overwhelming. His soaked suit weighed him down. Even his white buck shoes filled with water, and his hat sagged over his ears. His once spotless uniform was now a mess, and the wind bit through his soaked clothes. Shivering, Thane planted his shoes on tufts of grass, hoping to stop them from sinking into the mud.[14]

Despite the downpour, the band inside the stadium played marches in the distance as the crowd sounds rose and fell.[15] By one o'clock, athletes from other countries drained out of the practice field.

"United States, it's our turn now," a team manager called through the bullhorn. "Prepare your lines military-style."

The American line moved along a road. Members of the police and military lined the roads.[16] Crowds of spectators on a grassy hillside watched them march past. Some coaches wore raincoats until they reached the stadium.[17] The band sounded much louder now. Cheers erupted as new delegations entered the stands.

The United States followed the small Vietnamese delegation through the Marathon Gate and into the stadium. A young Finnish man wearing gray trousers and a white open-necked shirt held the *YHDYSVALLAT* sign for the Americans to follow. Noise from the crowds exploded around Thane on all sides. The Americans held their heads high and marched in step through the torrential rain. As they came into the stadium on the east side, Thane executed a sharp right turn onto the outside lanes of the track. The inside lanes remained empty. The athletes on the right side took small steps, while those on the left took larger steps. This maneuver kept their lines in formation.

As they rounded the curve on the north side, small potted evergreen trees in front of tarps prevented the marchers from following an alternate track toward the water jump. Behind that, a dozen drummers drummed next to the stadium seating. Above them, the band played. Higher, a large electronic sign displayed,

Citius, Altius, Fortius.[18] Unlike his first day in Finland, Thane now understood the Olympic motto meant "Swifter, Higher, Stronger." He hoped he would be swifter than he had ever been before when he ran his heats of the 200 meters.

The Americans moved before the grandstand.[19] Unlike flag bearers from other countries, Norman Armitage did not dip the flag in submission, following precedent set by previous Americans.[20] When he passed dignitaries, Thane took his hat off and placed it over his heart. Afterwards, he plopped it back on. The hat did not keep his head dry, but at least it kept the heavy rain out of his eyes. Some Olympians from other countries lined up next to the track on the infield to watch the marchers.

When the Finnish team entered behind the Americans, the multitude roared. Only a fourth of the crowd received protection from the elements, yet the deluge did not dampen the enthusiasm.

People in wheelchairs or with crutches sat at track level against the low wall of the seating area. The groundskeepers covered all the pits for the broad jump, high jump, and pole vault to keep out the rain. Even during the ceremony, they checked under the tarps to monitor them.

Thane focused on the track beneath his feet. He would run here in three days. The red-brick dust track held standing water and was a churned-up mess below his feet. The thousands of athletes who preceded him had roughened up its surface. Thane hoped the track caretakers smoothed out the track before the races started tomorrow. The brick dust stained his white shoes pink.

When the American team finished their lap, they walked to their position on the crowded infield that held thousands. The previous marchers compressed paths into the grass where they passed.[21] The mud further discolored Thane's no-longer-white shoes. After the Finnish competitors joined them on the field, the ceremony began. Thane glanced at his wristwatch. The scheduled hour-long parade took fifty-six minutes–these Finns valued punctuality. Even though the parade ceased, the rain continued.

Postcard showing the United States Olympic Team marching before the viewing stand. The American flag remains unbowed. Avery Brundage leads, followed by the coaches. Thane Baker is on the front row of the athletes' section. The circle near the top is from the postage cancellation stamp on the other side, July 19, 1952. *Postcard produced by the United States Olympic Committee. Courtesy of the author's collection.*

A man approached a rostrum set on a low platform facing the grandstand. He spoke in several languages. When he spoke in accented English, the speaker thanked various Olympic Committees and neighboring countries.

"We welcome this occasion for Finland to form the neutral site where West and East can meet in noble combat, where happy winners will be singled out without bitterness and the desire for revenge on the part of the losers. If the Olympic spirit and international understanding will have grown among the world's youth, then the organizers will have been granted the gold medal they have earnestly aspired to earn."

A photograph of the Olympic Opening Ceremony from low in the north side of the stadium. The rain makes the far side of the stadium difficult to see, July 19, 1952. *Photograph by Janne Rentola. Courtesy of the Society of Swedish Literature in Finland. License by CC by 4.0.*

"I declare the XV Olympic Games open," the Finnish president announced.[22]

The band played the Olympic Fanfare.[23] Led by another soldier, six men in uniform marched around the track with the large white satin Olympic flag held shoulder height between them. The flag and its bearers arrived at the flagpole. Working together, they attached the flag to its mast. The Olympic flag rose.

Thane counted twenty-one big guns that fired outside the stadium. From the north end of the stadium, thousands of doves danced into the air.[24] They circled inside the stadium for a few laps like the runners would do this week, then dispersed. Thane forgot about the cold or his drenched clothes. This moment's excitement triumphed over his discomfort.

The crowds screamed. Thane looked to the scoreboard, which read, "The Olympic Torch is being brought into the Stadium by Paavo Nurmi." Nurmi, the man depicted by the nude statue in front of the stadium, entered the stadium wearing shorts and a singlet. The five thousand Olympians standing on the infield broke rank and rushed to the eastern edge to witness Nurmi carry the Olympic flame. They pressed in several rows thick. Competitors in the back jumped high in the air to glimpse the famed Nurmi. Some stepped on the track to get a better view. Nurmi dodged around and ran through them.[25] It reminded Thane of Glenn Cunningham's run thirteen years ago in Elkhart. But in Elkhart, folks stayed out of Glenn's way. Nurmi carried a wooden-handled torch with a narrow silver cone on top. As soon as Nurmi passed, the Olympians turned like a murmuration of starlings and ran to the other side of the field to follow him.

On the southern end of the infield next to the flagpole, the conic-shaped cauldron rested on four rooted poles in a square formation, with an additional one in the center. Soldiers guarded it. The balding Nurmi stood tall with his arm extended and lit the flame with his torch.[26] Fire flew up six to eight feet above the cauldron. Wind caught it, and the flame flashed out to the side. Nurmi continued running to the base of the tower. The Olympic choir sang a hymn, and younger athletes ran a torch relay up the spiral steps to the top.[27] Thane could see the flame circling the tower as it went higher. The scoreboard announced that four-time Olympic gold medalist Hannes Kolehmainen lit the flame at the tower's summit.[28]

A woman wearing a long, flowing white gown and sensible black shoes ran 200 meters around the track and gained the podium. Thane thought she was part of the ceremony.[29]

Paavo Nurmi runs by the Olympic athletes, July 19, 1952. *Courtesy of the Society of Swedish Literature in Finland. License by CC by 4.0.*

"Paavo Nurmi lights the Olympic fire in Helsinki," July 19, 1952. *Photograph by Räshid Nasretdin. Courtesy of the National Board of Antiquities. License by CC by 4.0.*

Flag bearers from each country form a semicircle in front of the viewing stand, July 19, 1952. *Photograph #2775 by Olympia-Kuva OY (marked with RP/224, KK, 5, and 108). Courtesy of the Thane Baker Collection.*

"Ladies and gentlemen," she began before Finnish officials wrestled her away from the microphone as she clung to the rostrum. They escorted her briskly off the field. The program continued without interruption.

In his robes, the archbishop said a prayer in a foreign language.[30]

The Finnish flag bearer brought his flag next to the rostrum. On the infield, Norman and all the other flag bearers formed a crescent shape by standing on light marks on the grass.[31] They must have learned where to stand at their rehearsal yesterday.

An athlete from Finland held the bottom of the Finnish flag and spoke. Then the band accompanied the enthusiastic crowd as they sang. Along with words in other languages, the scoreboard revealed the Olympic Creed: "Great is to Triumph Greater Far Noble Combat."

The flag bearers returned to stand with their own countries. Thane and the rest of the athletes formed up behind their respective flags. The athletes exited the stadium from two gates. According to Thane's watch, the ceremony ended on time to the minute.

Thane stood in the rain until he boarded an athletes' bus to return to the Olympic Village. While he waited, thousands of spectators flooded past him. Friendly children handed autograph books to any athlete who would sign. The height of the American basketball players and high jumpers and the width of the throwers awed the children. Despite feeling cold and wet, Thane signed until his bus arrived, hunched over to block the rain and keep the children's autograph paper dry.

After pulling on dry clothes in the Olympic Village, Thane hung up his wet suit. He hoped his clothes would dry without shrinking. Adrenaline spent, he wanted to crawl under the covers and warm up. Cold and wet for hours, his strength ebbed, and his muscles stiffened. He needed to eat, though. Out the window, the rain dominated the landscape and doused anyone who dared to trespass. He tucked his new autograph book inside his jacket to keep it dry, clomped down the stairs, held an old newspaper over his head, and dashed for the restaurant tent.

Thane got into the food line. Hot soup, bread with butter and honey, and hot chocolate were heaven sent after the soggy, chilly day.

Thane took his meal to where Dean Smith sat and pulled out a chair.

"Why are you still eating SPAM and crackers?" Thane asked. "Or is that boiled ham?"

"Ya know I don't like anythin' they serve here."[32]

"Hey, the food here tastes great." Thane said with a smile. "Listen to that rain hitting the top of the tent like sticks banging on a drum. I can't hear myself think. Why didn't you march in the parade today?"

"Clyde Littlefield, my coach at Texas, got me a seat under the overhang. I stayed dry as could be."

Athletes go through the serving line in the restaurant tent, July 1952. *Photograph by U.A. Saarinen. Courtesy of the Finnish Heritage Society. License by CC by 4.0.*

"I'm glad your coach helped you. Some of the other sprinters, hurdlers, and I had complications with Coach Littlefield. Twice, we made appointments with him to come out to the track and give us practice starts. Twice, he didn't show. We got a middle-distance coach to do our starts for us. It all worked out."

"Mr. Littlefield came out and worked with me on starts, but then he got sick."[33]

"Oh, I'm sorry."

Andy Stanfield, Thane's rival in the 200 meters, also had not been in the parade. Andy had not been to practice much, either.

"Wasn't it a hoot when they released those birds?" Dean laughed. "The athletes got droppings all over their uniforms."

Thane nodded and winced as he enjoyed his soup.

"Didn't that track hold water like a bowl today?" Dean continued. "It'll be muddy tomorrow, for sure."[34]

"We've all run on worse. When you Texas guys came to visit, we always wanted the Kansas Relays to be cold and damp for you."

"Let me tell ya what. The Americans got the loudest applause, 'cept for the Finns. Someone sittin' next to me said they admired us 'cause we defeated the Nazis and stood up to the Soviets."[35] Dean said, chewing on his cracker.

"I'd been outside the stadium, so I couldn't compare. I'm going to get some autographs, and I'll use my track and field roster to find everyone."

"Sounds good. I'll sign it later when I'm not eatin'. If I don't see you before you run on Tuesday, good luck, Thane."

"Thanks, Dean. I'll be in the stands during your preliminary heats of the 100-meter tomorrow. Good luck to you, too."

"Don't you want dessert? Good-looking cobblers over there."

"No, thanks. See you later."

Thane gathered signatures, then went back to his room. He slipped on his pajamas and climbed into bed, grateful for the heavy, warm, wool blanket the Finns provided. He picked up his autograph book to read his latest entries. The midnight sun provided plenty of light. Later, Thane set his autograph book aside and let fatigue win. He curled on his side and pulled his blankets over his shoulders. In three days, he would run before the world. He dreamed of the 200-meter finals.

CHAPTER 9

Let the Games Begin

TUESDAY, JULY 22, 1952, HELSINKI, FINLAND

Tuesday morning brought rain and hail.¹ After an early lunch, the weather calmed enough that Thane sat on the large rock in front of his apartment building. He would run his first Olympic race at three-thirty. Based on times posted, he should beat the athletes from Greece and Switzerland, but the Soviet runner in his heat represented an unknown. The Soviets reported fast times behind the Iron Curtain. So far, they had not repeated those times against the West.²

Sunday, Thane had watched the track and field competitions, but had stayed in the Olympic Village yesterday. Watching the events from the crowded athletes' section in the rain was not much fun and would not have helped him prepare for his own races today.

Thane had missed Monday's controversial 100-meter final. Officials studied the "blanket finish" photo for twenty minutes. The lunge at the finish tape by Lindy Remigino, an American named for Charles Lindbergh, won the race, one inch in front of second place. The first four runners all shared the same time of 10.4 seconds. Thane's friend, Dean Smith, placed fourth, only six inches behind first place. Coach Hamilton called it the "Cinderella story of the year."³ Talking about that race kept everyone occupied.⁴ No one thought a skinny, five-foot seven-inch runner, who had never performed well back in the States, could win the 100-meter dash, but he did. Maybe Thane had a chance, too.

After three days of rain, the clouds held their water for now. He hoped it would not rain during his races this afternoon.

Thane adjusted the starting blocks he collected from a 400-meter hurdler the night before. Dried red mud flaked off the bottom as he worked on them. He thought it "penny wise and pound foolish" that the entire United States Men's Olympic Team brought only three sets of starting blocks to the Olympic Games. True, they would need only three pairs during the competition. But on the practice track, eighteen sprinters, hurdlers, and decathletes needed blocks. Athletes stood around waiting for a set of blocks to become available. Since each runner moved the foot pads to suit their own foot placement, handing over the blocks from one athlete to another wasted valuable training time. Worse, on competition days, the blocks often transferred from one runner to another between races and needed resetting each time. A few runners brought their own blocks, but that did not help the rest.⁵ If he made it to the semifinals on Wednesday, Thane would have only minutes from the end of the 110-meter-high hurdle heat to change the blocks for his own race.⁶

Thane unscrewed the thumb nut holding the left triangular-shaped footrest and slid it to his own position of six and a half inches. Then he tightened it. He moved the right block to eighteen and a half. Thane screwed the thumb nuts as tight as possible so the blocks would not slip and ruin the start of his race. When he finished, Thane took a bus to the stadium.

About two o'clock that afternoon, Thane readied for his first-round race in the holding area under the stadium seats. Multi-paned windows set into the wall gazed out at track level, since the holding area was below it. Inside, a wide sidewalk ran parallel to that wall. Farther under the stands, a short warm-up track waited for runners to try their spikes on the dirt surface. Seventy other 200-meter runners also prepared on that small 40-meter practice track. Without a common language, all agreed to run a few athletes at a time in one direction to avoid collisions. Thane took his turns with the rest.

The officials divided the 200-meter competitors into eighteen heats for the first round. Each heat contained empty lanes. Thane felt relieved to run in the second heat, avoiding the long anxious wait some of the later runners would have. His time did not matter. If he placed below second, his Olympic hopes ended. Thane had memorized and practiced starting to *paikoillenne* and *valmiit*.

Officials only allowed one heat on the track. The rest remained behind. At the correct time, officials marched Thane and the rest of his heat through a tunnel under the track and came up inside the infield near the 100-meter start. During the Opening Ceremonies, a closed cover had hidden the underground passageway. They walked in the cold and damp around the curve in a single file to their 200-meter starting position almost 100 meters away.

Levan Sanadze, the Soviet runner, took off his navy sweats with white letters that said CCCP. Thane removed his dark blue suit with its red USA on the front. They wore similar warmup gear that contained a world of difference in the color and meaning in their lettering. Everyone moved into their blocks.

Thane won his heat without difficulty in 21.4 seconds. An easy victory. He and the Soviet, who came in at 22.1, advanced.[7]

The timers conferred with one another and compared stopwatch times while sitting on their narrow stand next to the stadium seating. The officials shepherded the runners, with their blocks, warmups, and alternate shoes, back under the stands to prepare for the next heat.

The windows in the warmup space presented a ground-level view of the remaining competition. Because of recent rain, little circles of water remained after each step the runners took. Thane evaluated the length of each athlete's stride before the groundskeepers

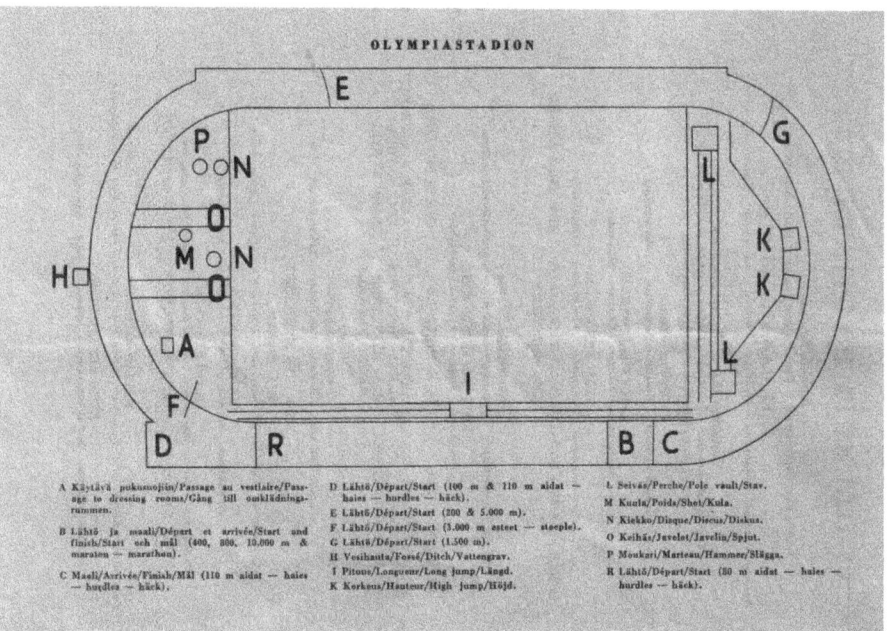

The Olympic Stadium from page 2 of the July 23, 1952, Olympic program. Block A indicates where the athletes emerged from the underground tunnel. Line E is the start of the 200-meter race and Line B is the finish. July 1952. *Printed by the Organizing Committee for the XV Olympiad. Courtesy of the Finnish Olympic Committee and the Thane Baker Collection.*

smoothed the surface between heats. Andy Stanfield, who beat Thane in the Tryouts, finished first in the seventh heat with a time of 21.8 seconds. Jim Gathers, third in the Tryouts, won the twelfth heat in 21.2. All three athletes from the United States moved to the second round.

About seven o'clock that evening, thirty-five runners in six heats tried for a spot in the semifinals. The first two finishers in each heat continued. Gathers won the first in 21.4 seconds. Thane cruised first to the tape in his second heat, repeating his earlier time of 21.4 seconds. Andy waited until the fifth heat for his victory of 20.9. Faster runners eliminated the Soviets and all but three of the Europeans. Three Americans progressed to tomorrow's semifinals.[8]

Thane Baker approaches the finish of his first heat in the 200 m, July 22, 1952.
Photograph #6865 by Olympia-Kuva OY. Courtesy of the Thane Baker collection.

Thane Baker wins his first heat in 21.4 seconds. Levan Sanadze of the USSR placed second in 22.1 seconds. Both advanced to the next round, July 22, 1952. *Photograph #9194 by Olympic World Photo Pool. Courtesy of the Thane Baker Collection.*

James "Jim" Gathers wins heat 12 in the first round of the 200 m. Notice the roller in the right foreground. The groundskeepers use it to compact and smooth the track, July 22, 1952. *Courtesy of the Crawford Family United States Olympic & Paralympic Committee Digital Archives.*

Before they left the stadium, Brutus Hamilton, the head track and field coach, came over and told the American 200-meter runners that their performances pleased him. He mentioned to Thane that he ran easily and did not appear to be putting on full steam but won his heats by five and three yards. Thane appreciated Mr. Hamilton taking the time to speak to him.

At the Olympic Village restaurant tent that evening, Dean Smith came up to Thane and clapped him on the back.

"Thane, glad you moved on to the semifinals."

Thane finished his bite of lamb chop. "Thanks, Dean."

Dean Smith autographed this photograph of the start of the 100 meters for Thane. From near to far: John Treloar (AUS), McDonald Bailey (GBR), Dean Smith (USA), Lindy Remigino (USA), Herb McKenley (JAM), and Vladimir Sukharev (USSR), July 21, 1952. Photographer unknown. *Provided by Dean Smith and courtesy of the Thane Baker Collection. Photograph by author. Courtesy of the Thane Baker Collection.*

Thane looked into Dean's eyes and realized he was still upset about his fourth-place finish in the 100 meters. "I'm so, so sorry you didn't win a medal yesterday. Dean, I'll bet you are the only person in history who tied the winning time but didn't earn a medal in the Olympics!"

"It was so frustratin'. Seemed like an hour before the officials decided who won. The four of us were so tight. It's not all bad. I picked up some photographs of the race. Let me autograph them for you. I can't believe some men were so much older than me, eight, ten, and eleven years older. Well, there's always the 4 x 100-meter relay on Sunday. Maybe I'll get a medal there. Too bad about Art Bragg, our best sprinter, though. We needed him for the relay come Sunday."

The 100 m finish autographed to Thane by Dean Smith. Results: 1st, Lindy Remigino (USA) 10.4 seconds; 2nd, Herb McKenley (Jamaica) 10.4 seconds; 3rd, McDonald Bailey (Great Britain) 10.4 seconds; 4th, Dean Smith (USA) 10.4 seconds; 5th, Vladimir Sukharev (USSR) 10.5 seconds; 6th John Treloar (Australia) 10.5 seconds, July 21, 1952. *Courtesy of the Thane Baker Collection.*

Dean told Thane how after he got second in the semifinals, he looked back for Bragg. A Soviet came in third. Bragg was limping. Dean put his arm around his Black teammate and helped him to the warmup area.

"That's terrible. Who do you think will run in the 4 x 100-meter relay now?"[9] Thane asked. He knew he was a candidate.

"Don't know. We'll see what the coaches decide," Dean said. "I bet I'll feel better by Sunday. I'm so far from home. My lower back's been hurting something fierce. That straw mattress doesn't help. This damp cold seeps into my sore back. The beds are small for us Americans."

Dean turned his grimace into a smile. He directed the conversation to Thane. "How did your races go today?"

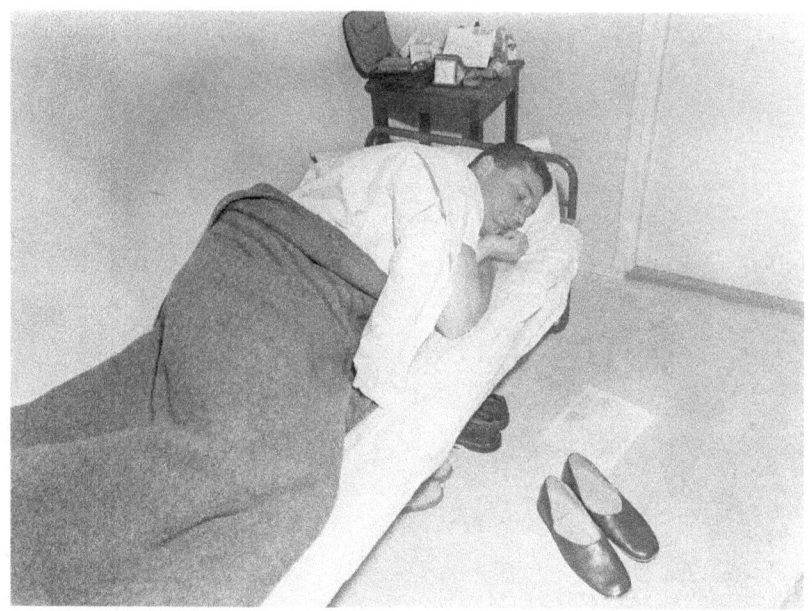

Some athletes were too large for the beds in the Olympic Village. The author suspects this is Parry O'Brien, gold medalist in the shot put, July 1952. *Photograph by U. A. Saarinen. Courtesy of the Finnish Heritage Agency. License by CC by 4.0.*

"Pretty well. I placed first in both of my heats, so I'll go to the semifinals tomorrow. That's where I'll meet better runners."

Dean worried his lower lip. "Thane, remember how Adidas gave everyone a pair of running shoes?"

"What about them, Dean?" The leather Adidas shoes had three stripes across the saddle and only four spikes that an athlete could not switch out instead of the normal six places for interchangeable spikes.

"Well, I ran in them last week and jammed my toe," Dean said. "I got a bad blood blister and ended up doctorin' it myself with my pocketknife."

"Dean! Why would you try to break in those new shoes? You keep telling me about those great kangaroo-hide shoes your coach bought you in Dallas."

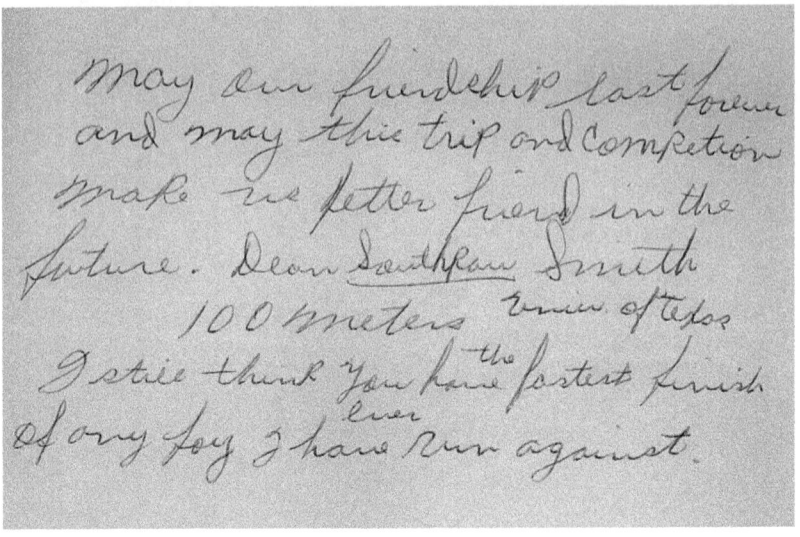

Dean Smith autograph, July 1952. *Courtesy of the Thane Baker Collection.*

"Just wanted to check 'em out. Maybe they would've made me faster."[10]

"I'm wearing the old spikes and Keds that Kansas State loaned me. I hope you get better soon, Dean."

Dean and Thane discussed how Wes Santee did not make the finals in the 5,000 meters like he promised but finished second to last. Afterwards, Santee claimed the Europeans were so much better at distances that it wasn't even funny.[11] Thane told Dean that Hamilton, the head coach, said Santee went out too fast.

"Dean, while I've got you here, will you sign my autograph book?" Thane asked.

When Dean had finished signing the book, Thane smiled at the message. "You know why I have a fast finish? No matter what distance I ran in workout, I always ran the last twenty yards faster." Thane shook hands with Dean. "Thanks. Well, best of luck in the relay on Sunday. I bet the US of A wins gold."

"I hope so. Gotta show my wife's family that I'm gonna amount to somethin'."

"You do, Dean. You're charismatic. When you walk into a room, everyone takes notice. Gold medal or not, you matter. I need to congratulate Bob Richards."

"Thanks, Thane. Appreciate your words. I talked to Richards earlier. When the best in the world run tomorrow, you'll be with them."

"Thanks, Dean. Get well for Sunday's relay."

Thane joined Bob Richards where he sat at a table with a bowl of ice cream.[12] They shook hands.

"Great job! Gold medal in the pole vault today!"[13] Thane sat next to him.

"Thank you, Thane. This afternoon, every single time I ran toward the pit, I feared my hamstring would go." Bob shivered. "You were in the warmup area except for two brief intervals. We are at Alaska's latitude here. I was *outside* for five hours with Don Laz and George Mattos. I suspect they set the qualifying standard too low. Nineteen men qualified for the finals, a long afternoon. Laz and I just kept challenging each other. Pushing each other to the top of our poles."[14] Thane had seen Bob Richards lying on a bench wrapped up in a blanket.

"After Laz and I had cleared 14 feet 9.17 inches," Bob said, "the officials moved the bar up. Don didn't make the next height. He had finished his attempts. I still had a couple more. I said, 'Oh God, please, please, help me do my best.' He answered my prayer. On my next jump, as I planted my pole, I heard 'PUSH,' and I pushed as hard as I could. Then, the voice said, 'PULL,' and I pulled with everything in me. Then, I soared and cleared fourteen feet 11.14 inches and set a new Olympic record. Afterwards, I jumped in the air, my sore muscle forgotten."

"I heard about your bounding out there."[15]

"I could not help but sing praises to the Lord, for his strength, for his greatness. My body is His instrument. He came to my assistance. Praise the Lord!"[16]

"You were enthusiastic!"

"Thane, I'm a preacher and a theology professor. The word enthusiasm comes from the Greek *entheos*. I translate that as 'in-Godded.'[17] With God in my life, I reached new heights. 'They that wait upon the Lord shall renew their strength; they shall mount up with wings as eagles.'[18]

"I watched you race in your first heat, Thane. You tore up the track. The dirt flew out behind your feet at every step. You looked extremely fast. That second-placed Soviet must have been about fifteen feet back."

"Thanks, Bob. We'll see how I do tomorrow."

"You are so humble, Thane. You seem uncomfortable with praise. Not like Wes Santee. You both come from Kansas, but you couldn't be more opposite. Santee's been talking about himself since I met him."

"Some people avoid him because he's always building himself up." Thane said. "I always make a point of speaking with him. We are the only two athletes from the Big Seven in the Olympics. It's too bad he failed to qualify in the prelims today."

"Now, you listen to me, Thane. You are modest, but you are as good at sport as you are a man. You encourage everyone around you to do their best. You lift them up. But you are a fierce competitor."

This embarrassed Thane.

"Now don't worry. You're going to be great tomorrow."

"I want to tell you something else," Bob said. "I reached out to the Soviet vaulters. We became friendly. They seemed surprised that American athletes only focused on one or two specialties. They said they trained in every track and field event. The Soviets asked me if I prayed. I said I did. They told me they prayed, too. They asked me what I prayed for. I told them what I told you. I prayed to do my best. God helps me. If you believe deep down in your heart, He'll help you, too."

"They pray in a Communist country?"

"They do," Bob said. "Very supportive, too. During competition if I did well on a vault, the Soviets said, 'Boo-tee-ful.' If one of

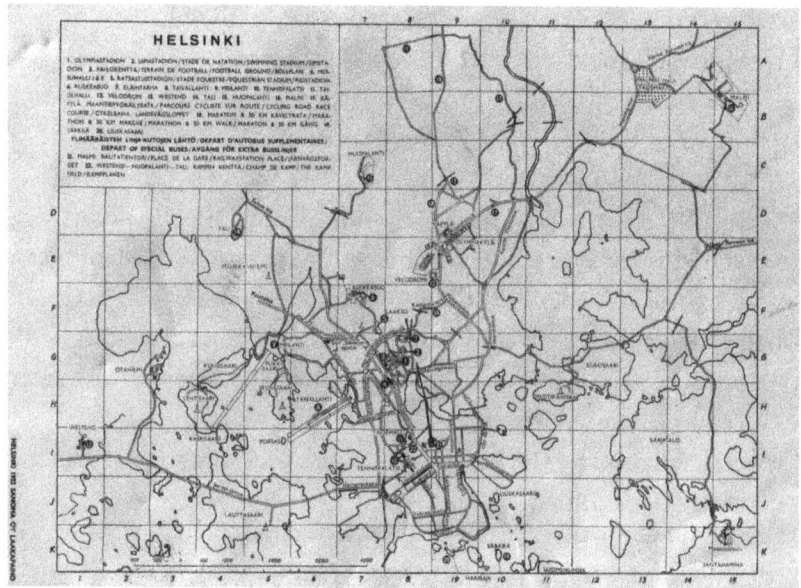

Helsinki Olympic venues from the back cover of the July 23, 1952, Olympic program. Käpylä Olympic Village 9D, Otaniemi Olympic Village 2G, where the Soviet Union and Eastern Bloc countries stayed, Olympic Stadium 8G. July 1952. *Printed by the Organizing Committee of the XV Olympiad, courtesy of the Finnish Olympic Committee and the Thane Baker Collection.*

them did a good job, I said, '*Khorosho,*' which means 'good job' in Russian. They are wonderful people. They were just grand. I can't understand why people can't get along as competitors. After my last vault, one of the Soviet vaulters lifted me into the air. Another kissed me. Believe it or not, I kissed him back."[19]

"Good for you, Bob." Thane realized the field event people had an easier time of making friends with the Soviets than the track runners. Whenever the Soviets were on the practice track at the same time as the Americans, each of their athletes always had two escorts. They wore long coats over their suits and looked official. One accompanied the runner to the starting line. The other met the athlete at the finish line. Thane had heard a rumor that the men from Russia lived on board a ship in the harbor and only came on land to train and compete, but that was false. They had their own Olympic Village on the west side of Helsinki called *Otaniemi*.[20]

"All the best for you tomorrow, Thane. I'll be praying for you."

"Thanks, Bob. I'll need it. See you later."

"You, too, Thane."

Bob Mathias, 1948 Olympic Gold medalist in the decathlon, relaxed in his chair nearby. After the outgoing personalities of Dean Smith and Bob Richards, Thane appreciated the reserve of Mathias. Thane had spoken with him before and found him conversational, one-on-one. Thane thought Mathias was tired of being the center of attention. Everyone kept asking him the same questions about his 1948 Olympic gold medal in the Decathlon at age seventeen after only four months of training.[21]

Mathias said that he noticed Thane talking to Bob Richards earlier. Mathias said Richards was a "stand-up guy." Mathias explained that even though Richards competed today for the gold medal, yesterday he had spent time with Mathias out on the practice field to help with his pole-vaulting skills. Since coming to Helsinki, he had helped the decathletes from America and pole vaulters from other countries.

"Bob, my big day is tomorrow," Thane said. "Nerves are getting to me a little. You look calm. Competition for you starts in about three days. How come you aren't tense?"

Mathias admitted he was a little tight in the stomach. "It's like waiting for a funeral." Mathias said it got better once he started competing. He reminded Thane, "They don't give you points for worrying. I had a little trouble sleeping the first night because the sun never seems to set in this country."[22]

They said their farewells, and Matthias ambled over to his fellow American decathletes, Milt Campbell and Floyd Simmons. It pleased Thane to know that mild-mannered Bob Mathias, one of the most famous athletes in the world, was still just as nice as he could be.

Thane saw Lindy Remigino and asked for his autograph. "What was your strategy for winning the 100, Lindy?"

"There's only one plan in the 100 meters, and that's get in front and stay there. You're not gonna take anyone like McKenley from behind, so I wanted to get a good, good start, an excellent start. I was way out in front about fifty, sixty meters. And I did something tactfully wrong. I see the tape coming up. I'm going to win this thing. I'm going to win it. So, I started leaning into it. And lo and behold, you don't realize how far you are away from that tape. I started slowing up because my stride is getting shorter. The whole field is closing in on me, and lo and behold, I thought I'd lost the whole thing. And I'm angry because I thought I blew it."

"You are the fastest man in the world, Lindy," Thane said.

Lindy shared what Parry O'Brien, Thane's apartment mate, said to him. "Lindy, you don't realize what you've done. You've just won a gold medal, and that's going to change your whole life. You don't realize how important that is."[23]

"Parry's right," Thane said. "Have a great evening."

"Buddy Davis, you won the first gold medal in these Olympics. I saw you jump on Sunday. I heard you're quitting. How come?" Thane asked the willowy 6'8" high jumper.

Davis's knees came up so high that it looked like he sat in a chair made for a child. According to rumor, he practiced ballet to improve his high jump form.

"Economic reasons. I have this chance to play basketball. It means money in the winter. I have a family. I guess I'll run my ranch in the summer and play basketball in the winter." Davis explained that the Philadelphia Warriors drafted him.[24]

"I hope everything works out for you, Buddy," Thane said before moving on to catch up with Charlie Moore.

"Hey, Charlie, you got a minute? Congratulations on your gold medal in the 400-meter hurdles yesterday."

In the rain, Charlie tied his own Olympic record he set in the preliminaries. He had figured out how to take thirteen steps between each hurdle instead of fifteen like everyone else.

"Thane, the track was wet—not too bad—soggy to a degree,

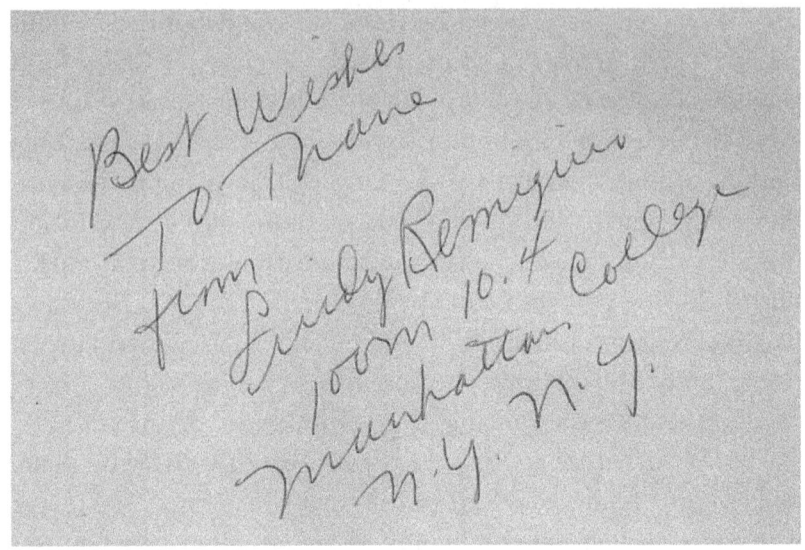

Lindy Remigino's autograph, July 1952. *Courtesy of the Thane Baker Collection.*

but you know that. You ran on it today. It felt so great running that victory lap. Everyone was yelling, 'Charlie Moore! Charlie Moore!' Such a thrill. And I must give all the credit for my success to my dad."

"Why's that?" Thane asked.

"Well, my dad qualified for the 1924 Olympic team in the hurdles."

"I didn't know that."

"He qualified and went to Paris as an alternate. A college graduate himself, he always supported my running, watched me compete in high school and college, and wrote me letters of his expectations."

Thane's own father had watched him compete once in Kansas City. Father had also watched him run when Thane was a youngster riding a horse. The girth on the saddle came loose and slid to one side. Thane kicked his feet free of the stirrups, jumped off the other side, held onto the reins, and ran with the horse until it slowed down. Thane expected to get hurt for sure, then.

Father did not have time to come to Thane's track meets. He worked six days a week until six in the evening. On Saturday nights, all the farmers came to town. While their wives shopped, the men came over to the garage to Father after dinner. He stayed at the garage until after nine most Saturday nights, helping the farmers with their engine problems. If they had a big problem, he would tell them to come back to the garage during the week, but for a minor problem, Father would fix it for free. The garage owner thought it built up good will in the community. Also, Father felt uncomfortable about sports in high school and college, as he only had an ninth-grade education. Thane knew Father supported him as much as he was able.

Charlie Moore nodded to the person sitting beside him. "Thane, have you met Lee Yoder, another American 400-meter hurdler? He placed fourth in the semifinals of the 400-meter hurdles."

"Sure, I know Lee. We met after the ball game in New York." Thane reached out and shook Lee's hand. "Sorry you didn't make the finals."

Lee Yoder responded with a nod, "This Olympic experience has been a whole new world for me. It's so different from Philly. It's much quieter and more organized here. I'm glad to have been a part of this."

Thane asked Lee why he had not seen him on the plane from New York. Lee explained his passport had not come through, and he had to fly to Finland later with the wrestlers.

"Lee and I attended high school together," Charlie rejoined the conversation. "We've known each other for years."

Thane remarked how amazing it was to meet people here they had seen before. He met people from Kansas. Lee Yoder said that he met an exchange student in high school from Finland, who was now on the Finnish gymnastics team. Charlie Moore told of annual meets between Cornell and Princeton with Oxford and Cambridge and how he met those athletes again here at the Olympics. The world of elite athletes was small.

Lee stood up and said, "Excuse me, I want to check out dessert. So much good food here, thousands of athletes, and never a line." Both Thane and Charlie nodded at Lee. He moved away, then turned back to Thane. "Best of luck tomorrow. Hope you make it to the finals."

"Thanks, Lee."

Lee hesitated, looking at Thane. "I got to tell you, Thane, I've seen no one run like you and Dean Smith. People in Philly just don't sprint that fast.[25] You'll do great."

Thane ducked his head. "We'll see."

"One thing from my father I want to share with you, Thane," Charlie said. "Stay focused during your race tomorrow."

"Charlie, I don't know how to be anything but focused. Thanks for the tip," Thane answered. Pre-race tension that he had tried to avoid by collecting autographs crept back into his voice. "Will you sign your autograph?"

"Sure thing, Thane. Good luck tomorrow."

"Thanks, Charlie. I appreciated hearing your story. I better get some more autographs."

The 110-meter hurdler competitor Harrison Dillard sat nearby "Hey, Bones, may I have your autograph?" Thane asked. "Good luck in your heats tomorrow and the finals on Thursday."

"Thank you, Thane. If I win in the finals, it will be redemption for my failure to qualify for the 110-meter hurdles in 1948." Bones said quietly as he reached for the book.[26]

"Thank you, again. Big day tomorrow for both of us."

Thane walked over to Mal Whitfield. "Congratulations on winning the 800 meters again. Makes three gold medals for you, counting your '48 and '52 800-meter victories and the 4 x 400 in 1948. How was your race?"

"I expected the German would set a fast pace, 51 something for the quarter and I'd run with him," Mal said. He shook his head, "It was a slow pace, though, so went out front after about 660 yards, when I had a wind to help me going down the backstretch." Mal explained his coach taught him how to pass his opponents. "When you can take a man, take him fast. It discourages him."

"What's next for you?" Thane asked.

"This is three down and about six to go." Mal explained he still had all his heats in the 400 meters plus the 4x400-meter relay to run in the next few days. Afterwards, "I'm going to run at least once at the 1500 meters before I leave Europe."[27]

"Better you than me, Mal. I don't do that distance stuff. Got to turn in now."

In the prolonged daylight of the north, Thane crawled into bed. Tomorrow he would be in the semifinals of the Olympics, his daydream within reach. Sleep was a long time coming.

Mal Whitfield won the 800-meter race in the 1948 and 1952 Olympics, July 1948. *Photograph courtesy of the National Media Museum of the United Kingdom.*

CHAPTER 10

The Dream Comes True

WEDNESDAY, JULY 23, 1952, HELSINKI, FINLAND

Thane woke up with a start. He had dreamed about today for thirteen years. He picked up a copy of the program for the day. Vendors sold them in the Olympic stadium, but the Finnish Olympic Committee provided free copies to the athletes in the Olympic village.

Thane sat on the big rock in front of his building and worked on his competition shoes the Kansas State Athletic Department provided. The leather sides folded over one another when not in use. He unscrewed his older, more worn-down spikes from the heavy metal plate on the bottom. Thane replaced them with new, half-inch spikes. This scattered red brick dust from yesterday's soggy track onto the ground.

After a light lunch under the tent in Olympic Village, Thane dressed in his Olympic Wilson Sports Equipment Company competition uniform: size 40 singlet and 32 shorts. He had sewn his cloth number 984 onto the front and back of his singlet after borrowing a needle and thread from a team manager. Thane covered his competition uniform with his still damp navy-blue Olympic warm-ups. With the constant rain and humidity in the

One of two cloth Olympic numbers provided to Thane Baker by the Sports Division of the XV Olympia Helsinki, July 1952. *Photograph by author.*

air, his clothes never dried. He pulled up his moist, loose socks and slid his feet in his wet, worn Keds. He wrapped a towel around his neck for warmth, added his shoes with spikes into his PAA bag, and headed out.

Thane rode one of the athletic buses to the stadium. Raindrops slid down the bus windows. The gray sky threatened more of the same. The chill permeated his warmup suit.[1]

"Nervous, Thane?" another competitor asked.

"Anxious."

Under the stands in the warmup area, Thane and the eleven other competitors in the 200-meter semifinals shared the space with thirty 110-meter hurdlers. The six heats of the 110-meter hurdles would begin at 3:00 p.m. with the top two in each heat advancing to tomorrow's semifinals.[2] Thane's group raced next. Thane saw Harrison Dillard warming up–they nodded at each other. Thane murmured a quiet "Good luck," to each of the three American hurdlers.

The hurdlers finished their heats and left the stadium. Javelin throwers and steeplechase runners trickled in the door to start their warmups. Giants mingled with elves, who prepared for their own contests.[3] Thane stood between the two extremes. He set his blocks and verified their position. He continued his warmup.

Thane prepared his mind. He had run 21.2 seconds in the NCAA championships. His personal best came from the Olympic Tryouts at 20.9. Would he qualify for the finals? The top three runners in two heats advanced to the finals.

At a quarter to four, the two other American runners, Andy Stanfield and Jim Gathers, placed first and second, running 21.1 and 21.3 seconds.

Thane's turn arrived. When he stepped out of the tunnel, Thane realized he would run the straightaway into a headwind. He needed to keep his head down and run strongly. He carried and set his blocks onto the wet track.

In this second heat, Thane believed his greatest challenger would be Great Britain's McDonald "Mac" Bailey. Last year, he tied Jesse Owens's record in the 100 meters. This week, Bailey earned a bronze medal in the same event. Like Dean Smith, Bailey equaled the winning time. At twice the distance, Thane hoped his endurance would let him pull ahead.

At the finish line, Thane placed second to Bailey by inches, but tied his winning time of 21.3 seconds.[4] Neither one of them was pushing it. Thane qualified for the Olympic finals!

Later, Thane Baker waited with the other silent athletes in the holding area underneath the Olympic stadium seating. Each performed their warmup alone. Three of his competitors, Les Laing of Jamaica, Gerardo Bönnhoff from Argentina, and Mac Bailey, had run in the 1948 Olympics.[5] The other two Americans in the race, Andy Stanfield and Jim Gathers, attended college plus served in the military, which made Thane, at twenty years old, the youngest runner in the finals.[6] Just last year, Andy Stanfield had set the first official International Amateur Athletic Federation world record running the around-the-curve 220 yards at 20.6.

Stanfield had a couple inches in height and twenty pounds of muscle weight over Thane's six-foot-tall, 160-pound frame.[7] Stanfield always held himself aloof, and he and the Olympic coaches did not get along. Thane never understood what the problem was.

To check the weather, Thane glanced toward the windows. The heavy clouds dimmed the light. Not raining now.[8] Some athletes stood at the wood-framed, multi-paned windows to watch the three heats of the men's 3,000-meter steeplechase. The American Ashenfelter brothers competed in the first and third heats.[9] Thane turned his eyes from the distractions.

Yesterday, Thane had trouble finding a place to stretch and run in the warm-up area. Today, with sixty-five 200-meter athletes eliminated, the space felt empty. Alone with Ward Haylett, his coach, five thousand miles away, Thane drilled himself.

4:55p.m. One hour before the 200-meter Olympic Final.[10]
Focus.
Warmup. Still loose from semifinals.
Indoor warm-up track is too short. Can't extend my stride.
Relax.
Run comfortably.

Thane inspected his thin leather running shoes. His shoes had fourteen grommets, seven on each side, but Thane always left one hole empty on each shoe to allow it to expand where his foot was the widest. Thane checked he had added new spikes. *Good and tight.* He studied the stitching on the outside of his right shoe. Running the curve of the 200 meters placed a tremendous force on that side. The stitches where the top of his shoe met the sole weakened when they got wet. His shoes had been wet since yesterday. What if his foot ripped through those stitches and slid out of the side during the biggest race of his life? He had seen it happen to others.

Lane seven. Worst lane on the track.

He would start in front of everyone. He would not know the other runners' positions until they came off the curve. The outside lane allowed him to run a little straighter. The inside lanes forced tighter turns. During the Opening Ceremonies, thousands of athletes roughed up the outer lanes of the track when they walked around in the driving rain.[11]

Track saturated. The groundskeepers poured kerosene on it after the Opening Ceremony and burned it all night to dry it out.

The track is loose and wet. I'm a pretty good "mudder." I can do this. He would throw dirt with every step.

It is like Kansas in March: wet, windy, and cold. But I'm familiar with this weather. Athletes from California and Texas have complained.

Lean at the finish.

Thane practiced throwing his right shoulder low and forward. A good finish might be the difference between a medal and going home with nothing.

Self-doubt crept in.

Do I belong here? I never placed above third in a national meet before the Olympic Tryouts. I'm just a wet-nosed kid from Kansas. Anyone can see the muscles in my left leg never grew as big as my right.

Stop that. Get your head on straight.

Ignore distractions. Hands on the wall. Stick one leg out behind. Shake to loosen. Switch legs. Shake.

Stand up. Reach high. Bend over. Touch toes. Stretch hamstrings.

Spread legs apart. Touch opposite hand to opposite foot.

Thane visualized his curve running technique.

Turn left foot heel a little away from the inside white line. Swing left arm parallel to left foot. Turn right foot inward at a greater angle than the left foot. Right arm swings parallel to right foot.

Stay less than six inches from the inside chalk line. Cut the distance. Don't cross the line.

Power shorter stride on curve. Lengthen stride on straightaway.

Stretch calves. Easy.

Thane leaned over to push against the wall. He straightened his back leg, keeping his heel down. He switched his back leg.

Pay attention to details.

Bicycle time. Thane moved to the concrete area and lay on his back onto the cold cement. He threw his legs up in the air and supported his hips with his hands, elbows resting on the ground. Thane imitated a bicycle motion in the air.

Long strides.
Back to practice track.
Over stride. Loosen muscles.
Fast feet.
Thane ran in place as fast as he could.
Faster.
Time five-fifteen p.m.. Fifteen-minute rest.

Thane kept moving to stay loose. With relaxation techniques that he mastered during the spring track season, Thane removed himself from the others and stared at the dirt surface.[12] He let his mind drift.

I've made some good friends on this trip.

Thane listened to Dean Smith's voice in his mind. "You are one of the best come-from-behind runners I've ever seen."

Charlie Moore's exhortation from last night appeared. "Focus."

Pastor Bob Richards took me under his wing. He raised me up. "You are a fierce competitor. I'll be praying for you."[13]

I've come a lot farther from home than I've ever been before. This has been such an adventure. I'll remember it for the rest of my life.

His father's voice from that kitchen table long ago resonated deep within him. "Dreams…make you a better man."

I sure would like to win a medal. It would please Mother and Father. I've dreamed, worked, and sacrificed so hard and so long for this moment.

His father's tight words over the telephone when Thane called from Los Angeles struck a chord deep within his soul. "Do your best! Do your best! Do your best!"

Stay calm. Stay relaxed.

"Dear God, please let me do my best. Please let everyone here today do their best. You gave me this chance. Let's see what I can do about it."

Five thirty-five. Rest time's over. Twenty minutes before the race.[14]
Finns run the Olympics on time.
Take off Keds.
Put on spikes. In the silence around Thane, his sock-encased feet whispered as he slid them into each shoe. The cotton laces emitted a sharper sound as he tightened them.
Go to the dirt area.
Stride.
Run sprints. Seven-eighths speed. Smooth.
Stanfield has a wrap on the right hamstring. Affect his running today?
Check starting blocks.
Practice a start. Again.

Thane glanced up to see Andy Stanfield tossing his head back, showing Thane should join him. Thane walked over to Andy and noticed Jim Gathers doing the same. Once together, they whispered and agreed the Americans should win all three medals.

Thane encouraged his teammates, "Let's go one-two-three regardless of who wins. We can do it."[15] Thane was no longer alone.[16]

An official in his deep brown suit, aqua-green tie, and grey hat called the 200-meter finalists to the door.[17] Thane pulled his starting block pins out of the ground and joined the other runners. They wished each other good luck.

The athletes walked through the tunnel and marched in a line to their lanes. Thane scanned his surroundings. Stadium benches are full. More stood to watch.[18] Thane moved to his position in lane seven. As he suspected, the track surface was loose.[19]

Small tailwind on the straightaway. Run tall. Not much wind resistance.[20]

Thane leaned over to set his starting blocks close to the outside of his lane. Next to him, gusts blew in from an entrance where several men stood wearing hats, suits, and overcoats. In the stands, some sat with blankets over their legs. Thane aimed his yard-long blocks toward the curving white line on the inside—to run straight for as long as possible. Previous runners chewed up the middle of the lane with their blocks' three-inch pins at the front and back of each. The power of the sprinters digging their feet into the ground destabilized the track for several yards after the start.

Where's solid ground on this soggy surface? Firm spot. Check the angle of the blocks. Measure distance from starting line to front end of the blocks using my feet.

Need a hammer. There's one on the track. Grab it.

Drive the pins home.

Test blocks. If they slipped, Thane wanted to fix them before the race.

Explode. The officials indicated the athletes could have only one practice start, but they did not complain about a couple more.

Blocks ready.

An official held out a basket.

This is my dream. What I've worked for. I'm in the Olympic finals.

He unwrapped the towel from around his neck and placed it with his shoe bag into the basket.

Keep knees high.

He placed one hand on the official's shoulder for balance.

Unzip bottoms of warmup pants. Don't catch spikes on pants.

He folded and placed his pants on top.

Foot placement.

He took off his USA warm-up top and added it to the basket.

Run the curve strong. Crowd the line.

The official left him.

Concentrate. Powerful stride on the curve.

Thane stood behind his blocks. His lightweight shorts did little to block the swirling dampness. Shaking each leg, Thane stayed relaxed. He shook his arms.

Bönnhoff from Argentina stood in lane two. Andy Stanfield relaxed in lane three. McDonald Bailey moved side to side in lane four. In lane five, Laing from Jamaica adjusted his blocks. Jim Gathers waited in lane six. His wide eyes met Thane's.

Get a fast start. Don't come out too high or too low.

"*Paikoillenne!*" commanded the Finnish starter in his white suit jacket, a pistol in each hand. Thane jumped up and down, tossed his head, shook his arms from his shoulders to his fingertips, then stepped before the blocks and leaned over. His trembling hands, palms down, touched the cold, wet ground before him. Shaking his left foot, he fit it against the forward foot pad. He extended his right foot behind him to loosen it, too, then positioned it on the rear foot pad. He located both feet to verify his toes touched the ground. Thane walked his hands backwards behind the white chalk starting line.

He held still and waited.

The crowd silenced.

The frigid wind blew.

"Dear God," Thane whispered.

"*Valmiit!*"

Thane rose to the set position with his forward body weight on his thumbs and the bones at the base of his pointer fingers. The gun fired.

Thane exploded forward.[21] Each step dug into the soft track surface. His legs powered around the 100-meter curve.[22] He couldn't see or hear anyone behind him because of the screaming swarm surrounding him. With 100 meters to go, Thane glanced out of the corner of his eye and saw Andy Stanfield leading with Bailey close.[23]

Lengthen stride!

Increase speed!

Surge! Passed Bailey.

Surge!

Surge!

Throw arms down. Raise knees![24]

Mouth open, Thane's muscles and desire created a magnificent blast of speed.[25]

Finish line coming!

Thane Baker in the starting blocks, 1951–1952. *Photograph by Laurence Blaker. Courtesy of the Kansas State University Athletic Department and the Thane Baker Collection.*

"Andrew Stanfield Voittaa 200 Metriä" (Andrew Stanfield Wins 200 Meters). Andy Stanfield in foreground with one foot behind the finish line. Thane Baker outside on his right, July 23, 1952. *Photograph # 8305 by Olympia-Kuva OY. Courtesy of the Thane Baker Collection.*

Lunge!

Thane looked back over his left shoulder to determine how he placed. Stanfield finished a yard ahead of him.

Pretty sure. Second.

Mouth wide open, Thane's smile captured his joy. He raised his left hand to cover his mouth in shock.

Gathers got third! We did it! We did it! Americans 1-2-3![26]

Thane grabbed Gathers first and the two of them hugged Andy Stanfield together. Three men together. A team.

"We did it! We won all three medals! A grand slam! Congratulations, Andy. Excellent job, Jim."

"You, too, Thane!"

Thane squeezed them hard and then let go. He could not keep still and danced a few quick steps. All the finishers shook hands

Andy Stanfield steps over the finish line. Thane Baker is second with Jim Gathers third, July 23, 1952. *Photograph by AD Repo**agbild, (illegible) Stockholm. Courtesy of the Thane Baker Collection.*

Andy Stanfield is two steps over the line in lane 3. Thane Baker crosses the finish line in lane 6. Jim Gathers in lane 5 looks to his left to see if he beat McDonald Bailey in lane 4, July 23, 1952. *Photographer from the U.S. Army. Courtesy of Crawford Family U.S. Olympic & Paralympic Committee Digital Archives.*

Thane Baker moments after winning his silver medal in the Men's 200 m, July 23, 1952. *Photograph #7500 by Olympia-Kuva OY. Courtesy of the Thane Baker Collection.*

and congratulated one another.

The electronic scoreboard at the end of the stadium reflected the results of the 200-meter dash. Andy Stanfield tied Jesse Owens's Olympic record with a time of 20.7 seconds. Thane and Jim Gathers shared 20.8. McDonald Bailey held fourth at 21 flat and Laing of Jamaica finished fifth. Considering the track conditions, Thane thought the times fast.

My Olympic dream came true.

While Thane stood there catching his breath, a reporter snapped a photograph of him.

"Everyone, stand together! We need pictures."

Photographers captured the 200-meter Olympic finalists. Five men of different countries and colors stood arm in arm, connected by sport. On his feet, Thane wore the Riddell spikes borrowed from Kansas State College. His sagging, wet socks from K-State completed the picture.

An official joined Thane at the finish line with his basket of clothes and muddy blocks. Thane's heart throbbed in his chest. The chilly wind attacked his sweat-soaked body. He pulled on his warm-up pants and avoided catching them on his dirty spikes. He tugged his warmup top over his head to block the chilly air. The red and white gathered cuffs held in his body heat.

Officials herded Thane and the other two medalists to wait behind the awards stand. Other officials returned the rest of the finalists back under the stadium.

Thane watched the officials set up the track for the semifinals of the women's 80-meter hurdles, the last event of the evening.[27] On top of the covered portion of the stands, enormous speakers projected the announcer's words. He spoke in French to alert the crowds of the upcoming medal presentation.

Metal rods painted beige supported three wooden platforms. The center one was about a meter tall. On its front was a large black number one painted on a white background with the Olympic rings under it. The two side areas, which were about half as tall,

Photographers surround the 200 m finalists, July 23, 1952. Photographer from the U.S. Army. *Courtesy of the Crawford Family U.S. Olympic & Paralympic Committee Digital Archives.*

"200 Metrin Kilpailun Jälkeen" (After the 200-Meter Race). The Men's 200 m finalists. Left to right: Geraldo Bönnhoff (Argentina), Thane Baker (USA, silver), Andy Stanfield (USA, gold), Jim Gathers (USA, bronze), Les Laing (Jamaica), McDonald Bailey (Great Britain), July 23, 1952. *Photograph #8352 by Olympia-Kuva OY. Courtesy of the Thane Baker Collection*

sported a two and three on them. Andy stepped to the wooden top of the stand first. Thane climbed to the second-place position, still wearing his long spikes. The sharp metal points forced him to stand back on his heels. Jim Gathers stepped on the other side of Andy. The three American victors faced toward the covered grandstand. Thane tried to take a deep breath, but his nerves interfered.

The band played a shortened version of the Olympic fanfare. A young Finnish woman wearing a lacy cap and blouse covered by a dark vest with a long, striped skirt and apron held three open medal boxes on a satin pillow in front of her chest. In another language, the loudspeaker said Andy Stanfield's name. A man presented his gold medal.[28]

When they called his name, Thane's chest tightened. He received his medal in an open blue box.[29] Thane leaned over, smiled, and shook hands with the presenter. Nervous and open mouthed, his emotions overwhelmed him. He sucked in the air, searching for oxygen.[30] Thane's eyes watered. Tears formed and rolled down his cheeks. His hand shook a little. He hoped he did not drop his medal.

Thane, Andy, and Jim faced north. The band began the Star-Spangled Banner. Three United States flags ascended their masts above the electronic scoreboard. Feelings overwhelmed Thane.[31] The recognition humbled him.

Why did I succeed? My parents sacrificed. Ward Haylett coached. Dick Towers helped. I worked. Just like Glenn Cunningham from my hometown, I earned a silver medal in the Olympics. Why me, Lord? Thank you for this moment and everything.

Andy, Jim, and Thane stepped down from the awards stand. The same young woman in her Finnish native dress handed each of them a bundle of pink carnations and green plants tied together with ribbon. Thane did not know what to do with his bouquet, but Coach Hamilton had said, "Respect them. It is a token of greatness and bestowed by people with warm hearts."[32] They made him smile.

I can't believe it! A silver medal! My dream came true!

The photographers asked for another picture of the three medalists. The athletes moved onto the track with the stadium seating at their backs. Andy Stanfield stood in the middle. The team members held on to each other as the flashes from the cameras blinded them.[33]

The officials escorted Andy, Thane, and Jim to the stairwell in the infield, which led to the waiting area.

Inside the warmup area, reporters crowded the 200-meter victors. Their pencils poised over their notepads like sprinters set in their blocks. First thing, Olympic-gold-medalist Andy Stanfield lit a cigarette and dragged smoke into his lungs. Hamilton, the head coach, had prohibited Andy from smoking in the stadium where other people could see.[34]

A reporter yelled out. "Did you guys know you made the first sweep in these Olympic Games?"

Andy Stanfield, the new Olympic champion, replied, "Just before we went out onto the track for the race, we talked it over. We didn't care who got what so long as it was USA one-two-three.[35] I think that's the reason we ran so fast."[36]

"What do you say, Baker?"

Thane could not stop smiling. "Old Andy won that gold one. Go talk to him."

"What about Great Britain's McDonald Bailey? He had the same time as the winner in the 100 meters on Monday and was the fastest in the world in the 200 meters last year. Bailey finished a couple of meters behind you."

Andy shifted from one leg to another. "We figured we could take Mac Bailey before we went out. The way we were feeling, I don't think much could have stopped us. Boy, we were all running so fast–the three of us were so hopped up we really moved fast."[37]

Thane added, "All Bailey's fast times were made while he ran alone."

"Andy, how does it feel to win a gold medal in the Olympics?"

Andy clenched his flowers in his hand and shook them in the air. "Whoopie!"

"Thane?"

"We were running all out," Thane said, "and I knew we were going fast. But I don't even feel tired. I think I could do it again right now."[38]

"Jim Gathers, how are you?"

"Very happy."[39]

"Do you plan to run in the 1956 Olympics held in Melbourne, Australia?"

Stanfield, Baker, and Gathers looked at each other. They hoped to be back.[40]

"Andy, are you well enough to compete in the four by one hundred on Sunday?"

"I think if my leg is in good condition, I can run the 100 meters in 10.2, and I sure want to. That's where my heart is."[41]

Just then, Brutus Hamilton, the head coach for the United States Track and Field Team, stepped into the warmup area. The reporters swiveled toward him.

"Mr. Hamilton, did you think the Americans would win all the medals in the 200 meters?"

"I had a lot of confidence in Andy Stanfield, Jim Gathers, and Thane Baker in the 200 meters, but if you had asked me before the race if I thought they'd make a clean sweep of it, I would have said 'Heavens, no.' But they are the three fastest 200-meter men the Olympics have ever seen."

"How did this race today compare with that of Jesse Owens back in 1936?"

"When Jesse set that record, the nearest man to him was timed about 21 seconds, but these two boys were crowding Andy awfully close." Hamilton smiled over at Thane and Jim.

"Is the track in good shape after all the rain we've had?"

"It had to be for running like that," Hamilton answered.

"Mr. Hamilton, what do you think of Andy, Thane, and Jim now?"

"I'm proud of those kids," Hamilton smiled. "You know, everybody wants to get into the act. And so they work hard, and they do get in."[42]

A reporter pulled Thane to the side and introduced himself as from Kansas City.[43] He asked Thane what made him successful. "I give Coach Haylett all the credit."

The reporter had heard Thane watched Glenn Cunningham, another Kansas Olympic medal winner, when Thane was a boy. He wanted to know how that affected him.

"I've met Glenn Cunningham several times. There's a big picture of him hanging on the wall of our high school, and he always was an inspiration to me."

When asked if he wanted to say anything more, Thane thought for a moment, then responded, "I wanted to get first. Of course, everyone did, but second was plenty. I ran the best race in my life. This was a wonderful, unforgettable experience. It was a great thrill to place in the final run." Thane blushed a little before he continued. "Please tell Mother and Father that I'm very happy, and I'll be home soon."[44]

Thane pulled away from the swarm of enthusiastic journalists. Someone asked him when he made his plans for this evening. Thane joked, "Plans for this night were made almost two years ago."[45]

Who would have believed it? A kid from a small town in western Kansas had the opportunity to run track in college, then in the Olympics. Those shoes from K-State carried Thane to his dream.

After Thane walked out of the stadium, crowds of children surrounded him, asking for his signature. His flowers revealed his medal status. Each time he handed a signature to a boy, the young man clicked his heels and bowed his head. The girls bobbed their heads and curtseyed.[46] He signed multiple autographs, but the children kept coming. Thane smiled and pointed to his transportation. He stepped beyond them and headed for the athletes' bus. He worked his way through the crowds streaming from the stadium.

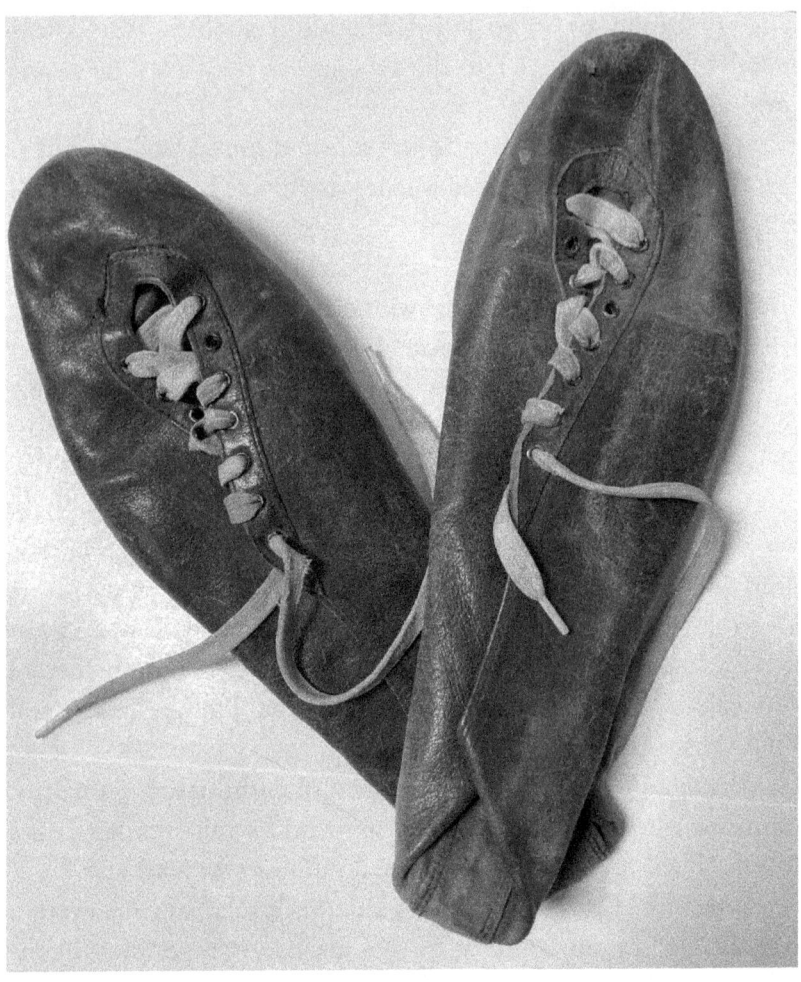

Thane Baker's shoes borrowed from Kansas State that he wore in the 1952 Olympics. *Photograph by Becky Ellis, Director of the Morton County Historical Society Museum in Elkhart, Kansas, and courtesy of the same.*

A large man holding a clipboard stood by the bus. He hunched over from the cold and wore a hat, a clear raincoat, and a pair of glasses.[47] Funny. It looked like Ward Haylett. Impossible! The man turned.

Thane ran up and crushed him in his arms. "Mr. Haylett! What are you doing here?" Thane held on tight. He let go and stood back. He trembled. Goosebumps rose on his arms from seeing his coach.

Mr. Haylett cleared his throat. "Watching you, son."

"Did you see me, Mr. Haylett?"

"Sure did. On that wet track, you beat your best time. Your start is slow, but you do better from behind. I may be prejudiced, but I think you might have won in a middle lane."[48]

"Where were you?"

"I was high in the stands near the 200-meter start. I thought I could do more good for you up there."

"When did you get to Helsinki?"

"I got here Saturday and witnessed all of your preliminary heats."

"Why didn't you tell me you were in the stadium? I'd have waved from the track before my races. We could have gotten together."

Mr. Haylett said he did not want to break Thane's concentration. He reminded Thane that the United States Olympic Committee rules prohibited outside coaching.[49] He was only an interested spectator here.[50] If they had talked beforehand, there might have been trouble.

"I got silver. Want to hold my medal?" Thane retrieved his box out of his pocket and placed it in his coach's hands. Ward Haylett inspected it. Home-bound sports fans peeked over their shoulders to peer at the medal. The crowd pressed in and bumped around them, but Thane focused only on his coach's face.

"That's a mighty fine medal, Thane. You've done well."[51]

"Thank you." Thane stared at his coach. Mr. Haylett never praised his athletes. When he and his K-State teammates excelled in a relay, Mr. Haylett never said a word. His complimentary words today meant the world to Thane.

"You're one of the most interesting competitors I've ever seen, because you had comparatively little high school experience. Of course, after reporting in with me at K-State, you made rapid progress. I told folks Baker's 'a kid you're going to hear about.' They're hearing about you now!"[52]

Thane Baker's 1952 Olympic Silver Medal. *Photograph by author, 2022.*

"You're a brilliant coach, Mr. Haylett. All the guys on the K-State track team appreciate you."

"When you tied the indoor world's record in the 60 yards in March, running 6.1 seconds, that told me this would be an exceptional year for you.[53] You only finished your third year in college, yet here you are, with a medal in the Olympics. You still have another year of college track."

"It's all because of you. You let me run on your team and taught me how to run fast. And you let me borrow these shoes." Thane held up his wet, flattened spikes.

"Keep the shoes, Thane. You ran your last ten yards faster than anyone I've ever seen."[54]

"Again, thanks to you."

"Thane, do you realize you were only a tenth of a second off Jesse Owens' Olympic record? In fact, you just joined a group of only five men in the entire world to run under 20.9 in a curved-track 200-meter race. Three ran with you today, plus Jesse Owens and Mel Patton.[55] Pretty exclusive club. The man who beat you in the 200 had more experience and had been training with athletic clubs with this goal in mind. Thane, this was the biggest thrill of my coaching career, seeing you and those two other Americans on the victory stand."

"Thank you, Mr. Haylett." Thane sniffed.

"I want you to remember something. You may be one of the best athletes in the world, but you're a better man than you are athlete.[56] In life, that's what's more important. Being a good man. That's always been my goal, to produce real men." Ward Haylett handed the medal back to Thane. "A real man is one who has the ability to control himself and to make everything he does a step toward a better life for himself and those around him.[57] And that's you, Thane."

Thane gazed into his coach's wet eyes. His tears that started on the award stand earlier continued and rolled down his cheeks.

Thane shook his head and leaned toward his coach. "Come back to the Olympic Village with me for dinner."

"Thanks. I wish I could. I'm staying with a Finnish family since all the hotels are full. They invited me to dinner tonight. And I still need to buy a decorative plate for my wife to hang on the wall back home before I leave."

"But, Mr. Haylett, you flew twenty-four hours to get here." Thane shivered. Standing outside the stadium near the ocean with the race over, the chilly wind cut into his damp warmups.

"More time than that." Ward Haylett smiled. "I came by steamship from New York to Copenhagen, then flew here.[58] But it was worth it to see you run. Folks back in Manhattan, Kansas, took up a collection to help me. I was at the Olympic Carnival at Triborough Stadium in New York, where you won that 150-yard dash.[59] Now, that's a strange distance for a track meet."

"You were in New York with me? Why didn't you tell me? We could have done things together."

"Rules, Thane. I coached Bob Mathias in the last Olympics, but I'm not part of this team. I didn't want to get you in trouble."

"I've been wishing you were here with me. Your voice coached me. You've been with me this entire time, haven't you?"

"Where else would I be? You did fine on your own. You're a man now, not a boy.[60] If you needed me, I would have stepped forward."

Thane reached out and hugged Ward Haylett again. "Thank you! It means so much to me you were here. I thought I was all alone."

"You were never alone, Thane. You *know* that." Ward gazed at Thane. "Your teammates are here for you. I'll bet you've made lifelong friends. If you'd known I was around, you may not have reached out to others."

"You were so strong, Mr. Haylett, to not tell me you were nearby for my own good."

"Thane, you know I've coached Olympic athletes before, but never one of my own. Your being here, on the Olympic team, fulfilled a twenty-five-year coaching dream for me."[61] Mr. Haylett hesitated and cleared his throat. "You get on that bus now. Get warm. Have a piece of pie for me tonight."

"Yes, sir, Mr. Haylett. I just wish you could stay longer." Thane looked hard at his coach and took a deep breath. "Thank you for everything. If it weren't for you, I wouldn't be here." He shifted his bag on his shoulder.

"You're welcome. Glad to do it. You're one of the most modest boys I've ever seen. You're a fine trainer and very conscientious. One of the best team men in a competitive sport. Never think of yourself and only the team. Son, thank you for doing everything I ever asked of you and your humble attitude."[62]

Thane choked up. It took a moment, but he collected himself. "Have a safe trip home. I'll see you at K-State this fall."

"I look forward to it. You did well, son." Mr. Haylett turned to go.

"Mr. Haylett?" Ward turned back and looked at Thane. "Remember that doctor, who told me to give up athletics, to stop running, when I got that piece of steel under my knee?"

"Yes?"

"Well, guess that doctor was wrong. I'm glad I didn't give up."[63]

Mr. Haylett nodded.

Thane boarded the bus and waved to Mr. Haylett until he faded from sight. Both on the bus and later in the Olympic Village, athletes reached out to congratulate him. Thane thanked them.

Happy, but still in shock, Thane tried to accept what happened. He won an Olympic medal. Mr. Haylett came to the other side of the world to watch him run. Thane shut his eyes and remembered the Olympic scoreboard with his name on it.

My smaller left leg didn't matter. I don't feel worthy. I was never alone. My team was with me. My coach was with me. You were always with me. Thank you, Lord. My dream came true.

That evening, Thane stood in line in the restaurant tent for dinner. If possible, the clamor of voices sounded louder than ever. Jubilant Naval Academy Cadets congratulated one another.[64] Despite the rain, their eight-man crew just won their seventh straight victory in the Olympics, beginning in 1920.[65] The joyful

Thane Baker and Ward Haylett, his coach, on the track at Kansas State, 1952. Credit: Photograph by Laurence Blaker. *Courtesy of the Kansas State University Athletic Department and the Thane Baker Collection.*

noises of exuberant men all around him created a warm glow within Thane's heart. He laughed and joked with the rest of them.

Fifteen days ago, Thane had heard quiet voices and clanking silverware above the cloth-covered tables. As people from diverse cultures became acquainted, they became more comfortable. Now, each successive day of the Olympics freed more competitors from stress. Win or lose, comradery between teams and countries grew.[66]

Before Thane came to Helsinki, he expected to speak only with other English speakers. However, he soon discovered that he connected with people from many countries. He talked with his hands. When all else failed, he found someone who spoke German to facilitate further conversations. Besides English, German was the most common language here.

Now silent, with loud voices all around him, Thane studied the athletes from other countries. The US team members appeared so much bigger and stronger than many of their rivals. At six foot, Thane was of average height on the American track and field squad, but larger than many Europeans. World War II ended seven years ago. Could its hunger have lingered and affected the war-torn childhood of Olympians here today? The Americans earned over half of the track and field medals awarded so far. He felt lucky to be one of them.

Thane looked at the tables where the white and Black Americans sat together. They talked, joked, and swapped stories. Some people back home had a problem with those with different skin tones. Those troubles did not come to Finland. In the 1930s, there used to be a crude sign outside his hometown painted with a setting sun, a half circle with rays coming out of it. The sign meant non-white people stayed out of his town after sunset.[67] The Black American athletes had more hurdles to overcome to train, travel, sleep, and compete than the white ones. But here, in Helsinki, it was better. They traveled, ate, lived, and competed side by side. No one argued with a stopwatch or tape measure. Athletics equalized.

The 1952 United States Olympic Track and Field Team eat together as a team despite racial segregation back home, July 1952. *Photograph by Olympia-Kuva OY. License by CC by 4.0.*

The athletes back at Kansas State College acted the same. Thane lived in the Midwest in the 1950s, not the Deep South. Everyone on the team seemed to get along fine. When Thane's college team traveled to Missouri to compete, prejudice and tradition made race relations more difficult. Those Missouri athletic fields had allowed only whites in the past. Thane thought his K-State teammate, Veryl Switzer, might have been the first Black man to compete on the Missouri track.[68] In the hotels, the managers demanded Switzer go up the back stairs; Thane and the rest of his team chose the back stairs too.[69] When the hotel restaurant said, "Whites Only," Coach Haylett found a private dining room for shared meals.[70] The team trained together, traveled together,

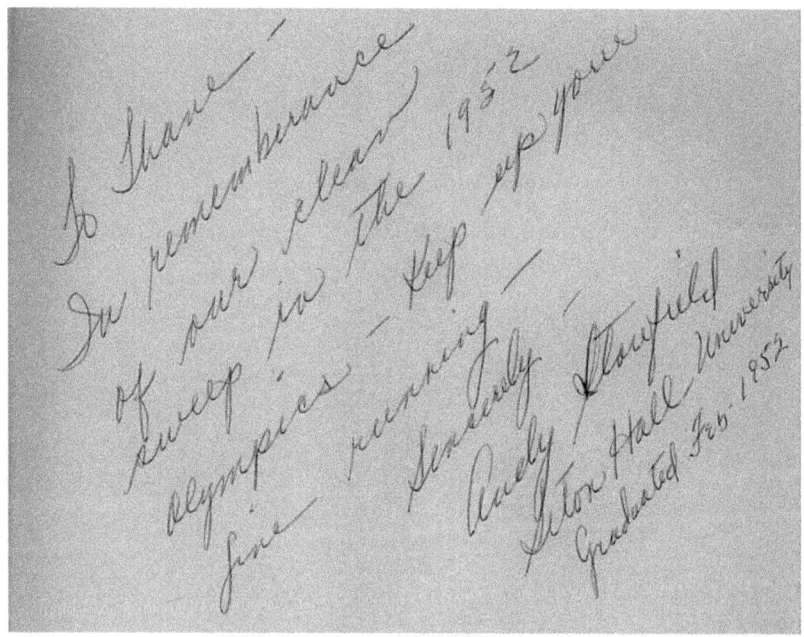

Andy Stanfield autograph, July 1952. *Courtesy of the Thane Baker Collection.*

stayed together, and competed together except at the University of Texas, which only allowed whites.[71]

After dinner, Thane sought more autographs. He stuck a flower from his bouquet in the center of his book.

"Hey, Andy, Jim, we did it! We beat them all!

The head track coach made the rounds, congratulating his team. The coaches and managers lived and ate elsewhere, but Mr. Hamilton often joined his athletes. Thane asked for an autograph and told him that Mr. Haylett spoke well of him.

Despite his exhaustion, Thane asked Bob Richards for a signature. "Bob, you were right. God answers prayers."

Bob reached out to take the notebook. "Thane, next Olympics, folks better watch out for Thane Baker."

"I don't know about that, Bob." Thane laughed.

"Thanks, Bob. How's your friend, Bud Held?"

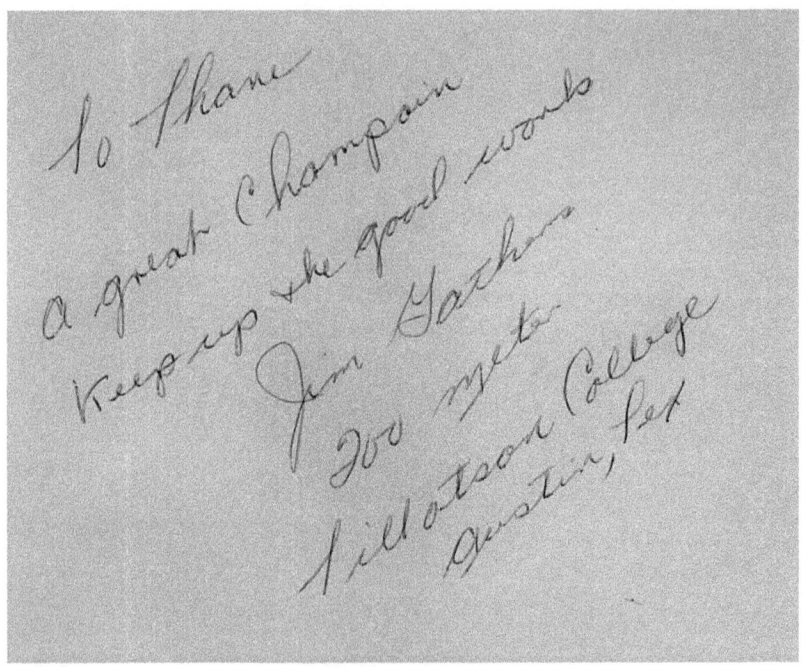

Jim Gathers autograph, July 1952. *Courtesy of the Thane Baker Collection.*

Thane knew Held was one of the world's best javelin throwers and only finished ninth today. The other Americans won first and second. Richards said Held was embarrassed. He had an injured shoulder and was sick. On his last throw, he tripped and slid on his face over the foul line.[72] They both agreed Bud had an off day.

Thane searched for his dessert and found a piece of warm apple cobbler with whipped cream melting on top. He sat down and lifted the first forkful to his mouth. It tasted like pie. Mm.

Thane recalled his own Olympic motivation. He wanted to succeed. When he entered college, his aspirations changed. If he made a name for himself, a young lady might consider him worthy of her interest in him. His foolish reasoning pushed him in every workout to do better than required. If Mr. Haylett asked for six 220-yard dashes in under twenty-four seconds, Thane did an extra

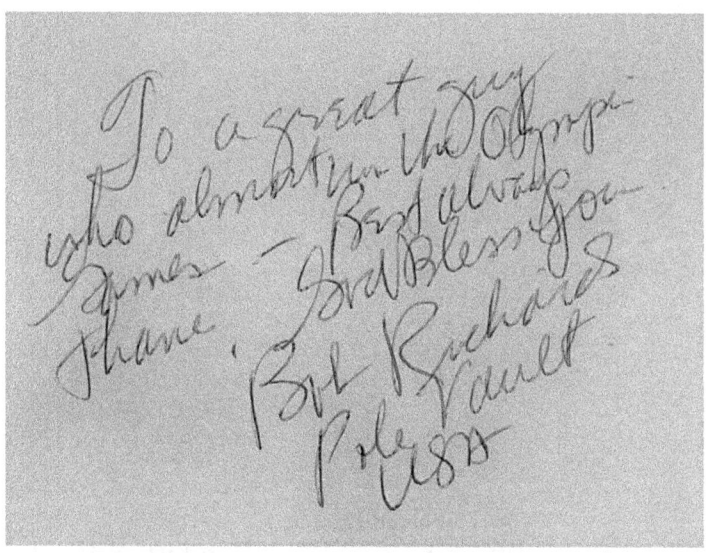

Bob Richards autograph, July 1952. *Courtesy of the Thane Baker Collection.*

one under twenty-three seconds. Even in practice, he tried not to let anyone beat him. His desire for acceptance, recognition, and love brought him to this moment.

The day's excitement faded, and Thane relaxed. Now he need not dream about his goal anymore. He had achieved it.

CHAPTER 11

Exploring Helsinki

FRIDAY, JULY 25, 1952, HELSINKI, FINLAND

At 3:20 in the afternoon, Thane Baker squeezed to stand between Dean Smith and Bob Richards and watch the competitions.[1] The section reserved for the Olympians sat in the southwest corner of the stadium where the first curve of the track began. Thane had an excellent view of the Olympic flag fluttering in the breeze, along with the pole vault and high jump areas. The covered grandstand area sat on their left.

"Hello, Bob, Dean. I went down to the athletes' entrance, where I entered on Tuesday and Wednesday. I didn't realize that entrance was only for today's competitors."

"How did ya find your way over here?" Dean asked.

"Well, you know the Finns. So helpful. One man walked with me from the warmup area all the way around to here to make certain I didn't get lost."

"Didn't I see you writin' on postcards this mornin'?" Dean asked.

"Sure did. I sent out thirty-two postcards to family and friends, plus an aerogram for my folks. I know I missed someone."[2] Thane had received eight telegrams after his race. From Kansas State

Thane Baker in the crowds outside the Olympic stadium, July 1952.
Courtesy of the Thane Baker Collection.

College, the president, the athletic director, the head football and basketball coaches, and the Kansas booster club had all sent messages, along with one of his college track teammates. Thane received one from the Manhattan Chamber of Commerce and a red and gold telegram with loving doves sent by someone named Lisa in Helsinki.

"I've written some," Dean added, "but I'm waitin' 'til after the four by one on Sunday to write again.[3] I want a medal in my pocket first."

Bob Richards encouraged Dean. "The Americans have won that relay every Olympics since 1920."[4]

"I just hope I don't drop the baton."

"You'll be fine. But I'll tell you what, Dean. If you aren't up to running in that relay, I'll be happy to take your place," Thane nudged Dean. The conversation continued regarding who might run the 4x100-meter relay.

Thane said, "The fastest four men in the world can be on a

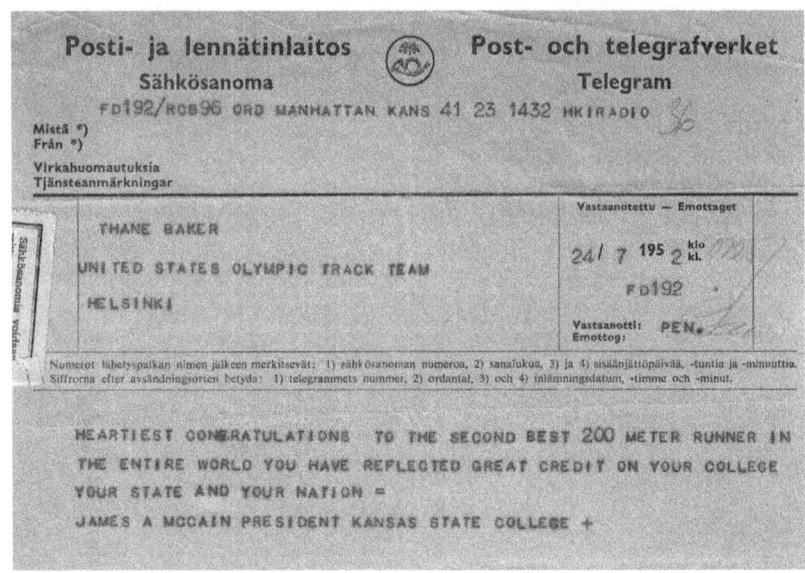

One of the telegrams sent to Thane Baker after his winning an Olympic silver medal in the Men's 200 m, 1952. *Courtesy of the Thane Baker Collection.*

relay team together, but if they can't get the baton around the track smoothly, it doesn't matter."[5]

Turning his attention back to the field, Thane asked, "What'd I miss?"

"The decathletes are putting the shot." Bob replied. "They already had the men's 400-meter semifinal. Mal Whitfield and Ollie Matson from the United States advanced to the finals along with three Jamaicans and somebody from Germany. Those Jamaicans will be tough to beat in the 4x400-meter relay on Sunday." Bob pointed across the field. "You can see in the far corner that the gun will soon fire on the first of seven heats of the women's 200 meters."[6]

"Got it, thanks," Thane checked his program that he picked up in the Olympic Village this morning.

Dean rubbed shoulders against Thane and complained about how cramped it was. They did not have room to sit down. The Olympians got in free but could only be in one section.

Thane Baker often practiced baton handoffs with his fellow Kansas State track runners. This handoff is for a 4 x 440 yard or 1-mile relay. He also practiced blind handoffs where the receiver does not look at the passer of the baton. Runners in the 4 x 100 m relay use blind handoffs, 1951–1953. *Photograph by Laurence Blaker. Courtesy of the Kansas State University Athletic Department and the Thane Baker Collection.*

The gun fired and the first heat started around the curve.

After a while, Thane commented. "It's a lot different being a spectator up here than a competitor down below, don't you think? I know the women must be tense, but I feel removed from it up here. Strange. At least my event is over. I put so much pressure on myself. Now that it's over, I'm happy, but . . . ."

"That's normal, Thane." Bob replied, "I'm thrilled that I won the pole vault, but I'm unhappy my time overseas is ending. I must leave soon."

"But the Olympics aren't over yet. Don't you want to see the other competitions and Closing Ceremonies?"

"I would, Thane, but I have responsibilities at home."

In between the women's heats, Thane, Dean, and Bob turned their attention to the decathlon competitors in the shotput area on the far north side of the infield.

"You're a decathlete, right, Bob?" Dean asked. "How d'ya keep score?"

Bob showed his program to Dean, where he had written numbers on the two-page graph in the middle. The names of the competitors in their assigned numerical order filled most of the left column. Across the top row, an event written in four languages filled each box. "Each part of the decathlon earns points for the athlete from a chart based on how fast he runs, how far he throws, or how high or long he jumps. At the end, the three athletes with the most points win Olympic medals."

"How are the Americans doing?" Thane asked.

"Pretty well. I know Bob Mathias and Simmons from the 1948 Games, of course, where Mathias earned a gold medal and Simmons, a bronze.[7] Milt Campbell is only a kid, fresh out of high school, but he had the best 100 meters this morning. The Americans are all still competitive."[8]

After a time, Thane mentioned, "Looks like Campbell, Mathias, and Simmons wrapped blankets around themselves like you did on Wednesday, Bob."[9]

"I only stayed outside for five hours," Bob said. "Those decathletes will be on the field all day today and tomorrow. They've got to stay warm between their ten events."

"That's rough," Thane replied. "I can't even keep my feet warm. My socks never dry after I wash them. It's cold out here." Thane tucked his gloveless hands into his pockets and raised his shoulders. The towel from his room wrapped around his neck helped retain his body heat.

"At least we've all these warm bodies 'round us," Dean chipped in. "Nobody blocks the wind for those folks on the field."

Thane said, "This is going to sound funny, but I hope my Olympic medal doesn't hurt me or make me change. I don't want to get too proud or anything."[10]

"Don't you worry, Thane. I'll be seein' you at track meets this comin' year. I'll beat the pants off ya' to keep you humble."

"Thanks, Dean, you're all heart!"

"You're going to be alright," Bob said.

The officials set up steeplechase barriers on the two hundred meters unused by the competition. The last set of the women's 200 ran. Several officials placed the last heavy steeplechase barriers.

"Watching them place the hurdles reminds me," Thane said. "Wasn't it great that Bones Dillard won the 110-meter hurdles with a new Olympic record yesterday?[11] That's three gold medals for him in two Olympics. Depending on how the sprint relay goes on Sunday, if he's on the team, he might earn a fourth gold."[12]

"I sure hope he gets his fourth." Dean jumped in. "It will be my first."

"Pray to do your best, Dean," Bob whispered. "That everyone does their best."

"Bob, you giving advice again?" Bud Held, the javelin thrower, looked over his shoulder. "Bob bought a bike the other day and rode it. Well, the Finnish measure measurement for distance differs from the miles in America. Bob ended up going a lot farther than he expected. If he looks tired now, it's because he barely made it back to the Olympic Village before dark. And you know how late the sun sets here."[13]

"I guess winning a gold medal in the pole vault wasn't enough exercise for you," Thane teased. "Doesn't it bother you that Bud likes to tell stories about you?"

"No, Thane, you've got to understand. Bud here and I are batting for the same team. Not only are we on the Olympic team together, but we are also both called to be preachers," Richards answered. "Bud's just practicing for when he'll need to tell a joke during the sermon to keep the folks awake in the pews."

"Heads up," Thane called out at four fifteen. "The finish line judges." Thane pointed to where the uniformed men marched in step onto the field and climbed up the stand, where they settled two abreast. Each sat between the open knees of the man above him.[14] Thane turned to Bob. "You know more than either Dean or I. Help us understand the steeplechase? I've not seen it run often in the United States. I'm afraid I didn't pay attention either."

Bob explained that the five steeplechase barriers are all about one meter tall, the same height as the men's 400-meter hurdles, but topped with a thicker board, so that several runners could land on them simultaneously. Better steeplechase runners never touched the barriers, except at the water jump, where they would use the hurdle to launch themselves as far over the twelve-foot-long waterhole as possible. Just after that hurdle, the water was two feet deep before becoming shallower. The athletes wanted to avoid that deeper water, which would slow them down. Three thousand meters long, the steeplechase combined a distance race, a hurdle race, and a broad jump. The athletes would run the first part without barriers, then the officials would move them into the pole—the innermost side of the track—for seven laps with twenty-eight regular jumps and seven water jumps before the finish.[15]

Charlie Moore, the gold medalist in the 400-meter hurdles, said, "Most people expect the Russian world record holder to win. We have Horace Ashenfelter running in the finals. He's in the FBI. We both represent the New York Athletic Club (NYAC). He's a good distance runner, not great. From what I've seen, he's a determined guy. His family goes to Penn State."

Thane had become better acquainted with Charlie these last few days. Yesterday, they rode a streetcar around Helsinki together. Two Finnish girls sitting nearby had stared at them and giggled.[16]

"Too bad his brother, Bill Ashenfelter, didn't make it to the finals," Charlie said.[17] He reminded them that Horace Ashenfelter collected money from the United States Olympians to fund a scholarship for a Finnish student to attend an American University.[18]

Bob Richards told them some guys were teasing Horace, or 'Nip' as he liked to be called, Tuesday night. He told us, 'I don't care what you say. I believe I can go out there and win that race.' On Wednesday, he surprised everyone in the prelims by beating the old record by almost thirteen seconds and his own best time by fifteen seconds. Nip said he didn't find the track fast, but he said everything went just right. He said he learned a lot in the two weeks he's been here by watching the Finns and even went to the practice track after his race.[19]

"Oh," Thane pointed across the field. "Guns up at 4:20.[20] The Finns always run everything on time." Thane watched the waterfall start, where everyone stood behind a curved line. The gun fired.

Thane paid close attention to the race. "Looks like they are going out pretty fast." He checked his program against the number worn by the early leader. Then, a Soviet and Ashenfelter moved to the front. The Russian ran farther on the outside.[21]

"Think Nip's got a chance?" Dean asked.

"Hard to say," replied Bob. "The Soviet pulls ahead. Ash grits his teeth, and he leads. Back and forth."

Charlie Moore seemed very tense. "He just dogs that Russian. I told you he was determined."

"It will come down to who has the better kick at the end. It's going to be a horse race!" Thane leaned forward and coached. "Come on! Stay focused! You can do it!" Thane clenched his fists.

"Uh-oh," Bob groaned. "It's been five laps. Their legs are starting to wobble. Here's where old Ash is going to quit."

"Come on, Nip! Come on, Nip!" Dean yelled.

The bell sounded. One lap to go.

"The Soviet's kicking, going all out!" Thane bounced up and down. "Nip still has something in the tanks," Thane said. "He's still running relaxed."

"Here comes the water jump; 150 meters to go," Bob said through gritted teeth. "Dig deep, Ash! Come on! Have faith!"

"Jump!" Thane leapt up as Ashenfelter pushed off the water barrier. "Did the Soviet stumble? Ashenfelter passed him like he was standing still! Oh, no! Ash stutter-stepped his last barrier!"

"He still has a good lead," Bob calmed Thane. "Don't worry."

"Nip, don't look behind you!" Thane yelled. "Never do that! Watch out! Someone's standing on the track."

Thane dodged to the side, as if to avoid the official in front of Ashenfelter. "Did you see that? Ashenfelter had to move out to lane two and push that man out of the way! Didn't he realize a race was going on?"

"I think the official tried to bring the finish line string across the track and didn't get off of the track in time," Dean muttered.

Thane jumped up, whooped, and clapped. "Woo-ee! He won!"[22] Dean and Thane hugged and jumped together. Then, Thane reached out and clapped Bob on the back and shook hands with Charlie.

Bob used his preacher voice, "Do you realize an American has never, ever won the Olympic 3000-meter steeplechase? Never![23] Americans just don't do well in distance running."

"He looks thrilled. He's raising his arm and circling his fist in the air." Thane laughed and imitated him.

"Our decathletes are congratulating Ashenfelter down on the field," Bob Richards shared.

"Look at the scoreboard!" Dean yelled. "He set a new Olympic and world record!"

Horace Ashenfelter approaches the finish line of the 3,000 m steeplechase, July 25, 1952. *Courtesy of the National Archives of the Netherlands.*

The Olympic scoreboard announces that Horace Ashenfelter won the 3,000 m steeplechase, July 25, 1952. *Photograph by Thane Baker. Courtesy of the Thane Baker Collection.*

"Did you notice?" Bob asked. "The scoreboard shows the first six runners all beat the 1936 Olympic record!"

"That was a terrific race!" Thane enthused. "It just goes to show you, an FBI man can beat the USSR any day!"

"As the Good Book says," Bob said, "'all things are possible to him who believes.' Nip told us he could bring it home, and he did."

As the top three finishers put their arms around each other for a photo, Charlie Moore nodded with satisfaction. "The New York Athletic Club earned another gold medal."[24]

Thane walked around the stadium to get closer to the board that announced Ashenfelter's win. He took a photograph. Thane wanted to remember the day an American won the steeplechase.

Thane came back to his friends in the athletes' section and looked at his program. "Oh, the decathletes start the high jump next." The cold did not bother Thane anymore.

"Bob Richards, you said the Americans do poorly in distance

races," Dean Smith piped up. "Exceptin' Ashenfelter today. But you hafta admit, we've had a bang-up Olympic Games so far."

Thane rubbed his hands together. "It's good coaching combined with hard work. We aren't the only stars here. For instance, look at Emil Zátopek from Czechoslovakia."

"Back in London in '48, he won Olympic gold in the 10,000 meters and almost had the 5,000, too," Bob added. "He electrified the crowds. The entire stadium chanted Zá-to-pek, Zá-to-pek."

"On Sunday, Zátopek won the 10,000-meter run again," Thane said. "The crowd chanted then, too. People carried him on their shoulders. Yesterday he beat everyone in the 5,000.[25] He set Olympic records in both events."[26] Thane kept his eyes focused on the field in front of him. "There goes Bob Mathias on his approach to the high jump." Thane thrust his chest out as Mathias leapt. "He cleared it!"

"Did you know Zátopek's wife, Dana, won a gold medal in the javelin about an hour after Emil's victory in the 5,000 yesterday?" Bob shared, "After their events yesterday, Emil told reporters his victory inspired Dana to win the gold. Dana told him to go inspire some other girl and see if she could throw a javelin 50 meters!"[27]

"Ha! She's spunky." Thane laughed. "But I don't understand. Why does everybody love him? He doesn't run smoothly. He's from a little Eastern European country."

Bob pondered. "Everybody loves Zátopek, because Zátopek loves everybody. He has a joy about him, a passion for running, people, life."

"Zátopek's that skinny, old, baldin' guy, right?" Dean asked. "He's not what you'd call a graceful runner."

Bob chuckled. "Zátopek said, 'This isn't gymnastics or ice skating, you know.' He just wants to run fast. When you look at him, you don't think he'll be able to finish a lap. He's going to have an appendectomy out on the track. He wheezes, pants. Agony contorts his face."

"Looks like our Campbell's getting ready to jump." Thane focused on the infield. "Got a question about Zátopek. He came

Emil Zatopek leads the 5,000 m with approximately 120 m remaining in the race. He won it with a lead of five yards. Ten yards after this photograph was taken, the two runners behind Chris Chataway, number 180 of Great Britain, passed him. Chataway fell and finished fifth, July 24, 1952.

over to our practice track to workout. He ran slowly, then sprinted, then slow, then fast. All the distance runners I've ever known practice at an even pace. And does Zátopek hold his breath while he sprints? I've seen nothing like his technique."

"Yes, he runs different speeds and holds his breath," Bob said. "Those are two techniques Zátopek's developed."[28]

"Wow! Bob, how do you know all this stuff?" Thane inquired.

"Easy, Thane. I question, and I listen. You young fellas might try that sometime. I've heard that Zátopek might try the marathon on Sunday. He's never run it before."

Thane always thought the marathon was the longest race in the Olympics. An American walker, Adolf Weinacker, set him straight. His event, the 50,000-kilometer walk, was over thirty-one miles.[29] Thane had had trouble finding the walkers for his autograph book. He had never seen them in competition before Helsinki. They seemed older and did not associate with the younger athletes.

"Hey! Simmons's last high jump beat both Mathias's and Campbell's," Thane said. He checked his program. "I want to stay for the final of the men's 400 meters, the next race, but I've got a date." Thane snapped a quick picture of athletes preparing their blocks.

Dean's ears perked up. "A date? How d'ya manage that?"

"A notice on the administration building's bulletin board back in Käpylä offered free tours by local university students. Yesterday, I took a tour of Helsinki. My guide met me at Käpylä's gate. I showed him around the Olympic Village, then we rode all over Helsinki in street cars. He gave me a map of Helsinki. Sometimes, we'd get off and walk around a bit. I remember going into Stockmann Department Store, seeing *The Three Smiths* statue and beautiful buildings around town.[30]

"We even took a boat tour of the harbor on a brand-new ferry. I enjoyed Helsinki by water. Swans, children fishing, it was swell. We stopped at islands with fortifications and cannons. I'd never been on a boat in the ocean."[31]

Thane said, "I have to tell you, I liked the *tivoli* best."

Thane let his last comment hang in the air.

Sure enough, Dean rose to the bait. "What's a *tivoli*?"

"An amusement park!" Thane enthused.

"Did ya ride those rides?" Dean asked.

Thane shook his head. "No, the tivoli boasted bumper cars, a carousel, and lots of other rides, including a large wooden roller coaster operated by brakemen, who rode along with the passengers. But I didn't ride any of them."

"What *did* you enjoy about it?" Bob asked.

Runners set their blocks before the start of the 400 m race. Notice the runner on the bottom right uses a frame to set the block, a technique not used today. July 24, 1952. *Photograph by Thane Baker. Courtesy of the Thane Baker Collection.*

Thane strung them along. "The dance floor!"

"You danced yesterday?" Dean asked in amazement.

"Nope, but I told my guide that I *liked* to dance. He said he would bring his girlfriend and his cousin to meet me at the *Lintsi* tonight. That's the nickname for the *Linnanmäki* Amusement Park.[32] His cousin and I will dance."

"Ya got a blind date?" Dean sputtered.

"Yes, Dean, a date. Something you two old married men wouldn't appreciate. I've got to get back. I've enjoyed the Games with you."

Water view of Helsinki, Summer 1952. *Photograph by U. A. Saarinen. Courtesy of National Board of Antiquities. License by CC by 4.0.*

"Good luck." Dean said. "What will she look like? This year's Miss Universe came from Finland. Hope your date speaks English."[33]

"Me, too. But we won't need to talk too much while we're dancing." Thane's eyes sparkled. "Besides, haven't you paid attention? All the women here are beautiful."[34]

Back at the Olympic Village, Thane stopped in the restaurant tent for dinner before his date. The Americans crowded around Horace Ashenfelter to congratulate him on his amazing victory. Thane pulled out his autograph book and requested a signature.

Thane took back his book, said goodbye, and headed out. He wanted to dance. A friend took a picture of Thane, ready for his date.

Thane stepped off the streetcar and entered the *Linnanmäki* Amusement Park. Smelling of Old Spice After Shave, he wore what his meager wardrobe offered: his belted, dark-blue, high-waisted, wash and wear pants with a crease down the front, his Olympic uniform shirt, tie, and blazer.[35] He wore his black leather, lace-up shoes and carried several *markkas* in his wallet.[36]

The park did not charge an admission fee, but people paid for their rides with tickets.[37] He walked over to the fenced dance floor where people danced.

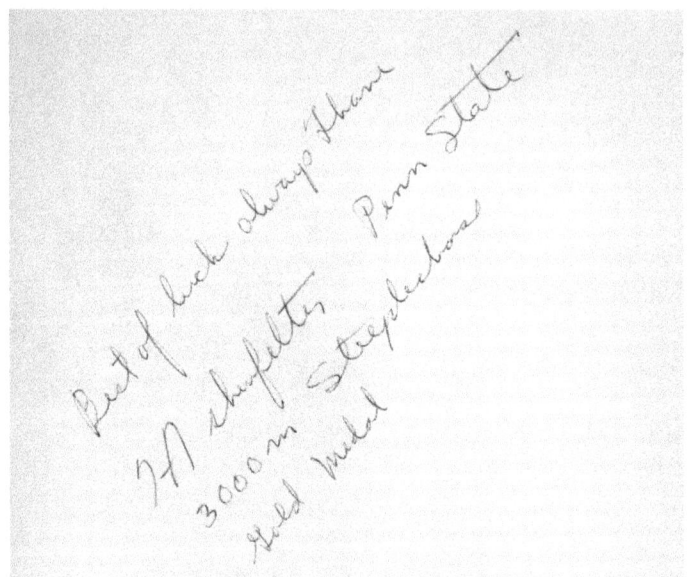

Horace Ashenfelter autograph, July 1952. *Courtesy of the Thane Baker Collection.*

Thane Baker, July 1952. *Photographer unknown. Courtesy of the Thane Baker Collection.*

Just then, his guide stepped out, accompanied by two young women. Thane saw his guide's date and his guide's cousin, Tuija. Thane greeted the smiling young woman. Her short, light brown curls peeked out from under her hat and framed her face. With her pink and green outfit, she resembled a tulip in springtime. Her cheeks bloomed from the Finnish wind and sun. Lovely.

"Tuija, this is Thane Baker. He's an American runner who earned a silver medal in the Olympics. I gave him a tour of town yesterday. Thane, this is my cousin, Tuija."

Tuija raised her voice. Competing music from the dance floor and multiple rides made it difficult to converse. "What did you do in the Olympics?"

Thane leaned over. "I ran 200 meters. Did you watch any of the Olympics?"

"No, it costs too much money. But I've seen lots of athletes and visitors in Helsinki."

"We're hard to miss. I'm a student at an American university," Thane said.

"I go to school and work in a music shop," Tuija said. "We sell instruments and records."

"Would you like to dance?" Thane asked. "I like to jitterbug."

"Yes, I want to dance."

His guide told Thane, "Go buy several tickets."

"Why so many?"

"Each ticket is only good for one dance."

"One evening of dancing?" Thane asked.

"No, one song. To enter the dance floor, you and Tuija must present one ticket to a gate. The music starts. You dance. When the song is over, everyone leaves the dance floor. Once it's empty, the people at the gates collect new tickets for the next song. This song's just over." The ticket takers enlarged the gates as the dancers exited.

"Who gets the money?" Thane asked.

"A welfare fund to help the children of Finland."[38]

Tuija Timonen Suojärvi mailed this photograph to Thane in Elkhart, Kansas, after the Olympics. On the back of the photograph is the inscription: "To my most beloved friend Thane 1.8.-52," August 1, 1952. *Photograph by Tenhovaara Studio. Courtesy of the Thane Baker Collection.*

"Well, that's worthwhile. How much does a ticket cost?" Thane asked.

"A ticket is ten *penniä*." his guide said.

"One hundred *penniä* to the *markka*. So, a ticket for one dance costs one tenth of a *markka*. Got it."

Thane and Tuija stood in line at the ticket booth with other couples. The dance floor looked huge. He bet a hundred couples danced at the same time. Lights strung over the dance floor brightened the floor below, even though the sun still lit the sky. Music from different rides competed against the voices of the couples. Fried food scents permeated the air. Lots of Olympians and people from other countries mingled, but many Finns did as well.

At the booth, Thane handed over one *markka* and received ten connected tickets. He turned to Tuija. "Ready to dance?"

"Ready!" Tuija smiled. They joined the line forming to enter the dance floor, then went inside. Once all the dancers stood in position, the amplified record player began with Rosemary Clooney's flirty "Botch-a-Me."

Thane and Tuija danced every dance from Percy Faith's "Delicado" to Vera Lynn's "Auf Wiederseh'n, Sweetheart." Tuija did not dance well enough for Thane to lift her off her feet, but they both laughed when Thane twirled her.

When the Mills Brothers sang, "Shine, Little Glow-worm," Thane joked, "Wish we'd had more *SUN*shine this week!"[39]

"Too bad about all this rain," Tuija replied.

"It rained at the last Olympics, too. All part of the adventure."

In between songs, some young men held tickets in hands, but not partners. Eager young women stood nearby, waiting to be asked to become part of a couple. Before each dance started, most found matches. Thane spent his entire time with Tuija.

After Thane and his tour guide spent ten tickets, Thane turned to Tuija. "Would you like to walk around the *Lintsi*?"

"I would be happy to." Tuija slipped her hand around Thane's elbow. They strolled by the *Kummitusjuna,* or "ghost train." The wooden rollercoaster rattled past.

"What is that called in Finnish?" Thane asked, pointing to the rollercoaster.

"That is a *vuoristorata*," Tuija answered.

Thane tried to repeat the word with little success. "You speak English well."

"I speak many languages," Tuija said. "I learned in school."

"My high school didn't teach any foreign languages. I didn't take any in college. I didn't think I'd have any use for them," Thane replied.

Tuija nodded her head. "I need those languages for work."

"How did you decide which languages to study?" Thane asked.

"Well, the students with better grades studied whatever languages they wanted. The poor students took Russian because the other language classes filled. Nobody wants to study Russian."

"Why not?" Thane asked. "Finnish is a tough language. Is Russian hard to learn, too?"

"No one wants to learn Russian because we don't like the Russians."

"Because they are Communist? Lots of people back home don't like Communists."

"The Russians invaded us. They wanted our land, ports, and minerals. They bombed Helsinki. We fought them."

"Helsinki bombed?" Thane was shocked. "It looks great today."

"We fought the Russians twice and then the Nazis."

"America was fortunate not to battle on our home soil."

"You are. Because of wars with Stalin and Hitler's armies in our own country, half a million Finnish people became refugees. We are lucky to still be an independent country."[40]

"And yet, here you are, hosting the Olympics!" Thane said in amazement. "I appreciate what your country has accomplished in the seven years since the war ended!"

Tuija forced a smile. "Let's do something happy."

Thane grinned in response. "Would you like a Coke?"

"You mean Coca-Cola? Yes, please. I'd like to try one."

"Try one? You've never drunk a Coke before?" Thane asked.

"No, the Olympics brought athletes and Coca-Cola to Finland."

"And chewing gum," Thane added.

"I'll try that someday."

Thane grabbed a few foil-wrapped sticks of gum from his pocket and handed them to Tuija.

"Thank you!"

Thane bought two six-ounce Coke bottles at a stand and inserted a paper straw into each one. He purchased some of his favorite Finnish cheese packaged in little triangular wedges. He did not understand what the label said, but he liked it.[41]

Tuija sniffed her drink, then took a sip and held it in her mouth. She swallowed and looked surprised.

"Do you like the taste?" Thane asked.

"I think so," Tuija said with a smile. "It is a little . . . sharp, I guess. I feel the bubbles."

Thane and Tuija unwrapped their cheese and sipped their drinks. They walked around the amusement park, past a fun house, a Roll-O-Plane, and two Tilt-A-Whirls.[42] Thane told Tuija that he enjoyed this evening. He asked her if she wanted to get together tomorrow, walk around Helsinki, take a boat in the harbor, then return for dancing. She agreed, and Thane walked her to her streetcar. Thane said goodnight and slipped the triangular-shaped cheese label into his pocket to remember his blind date.

As he traveled to the Olympic Village, Thane noticed that even late at night, the cars did not turn on their headlights. The drivers did not need them, because the sun still shone.[43]

Back at his apartment, Thane felt too excited to sleep. He waited until after dark to observe the Aurora Borealis.[44] After eleven thirty, Thane walked out to the middle of the practice field. He looked north. Something glowed against the sky. Did he spot the Northern Lights? Maybe. Other times of the year and farther north would be better for viewing.[45] Thane ambled back to his dorm to go to bed.

Cheese label that Thane Baker brought home from Helsinki, July 1952.
Courtesy of the Thane Baker Collection.

Now that the pressure of his competition finished, he enjoyed these Olympic Games as a tourist, a spectator, a dancer, and even as an amateur astronomer. He could not wait to see what would happen next.

PART
THREE

European AAU Exhibition Meets

CHAPTER 12

Nightmare

THURSDAY, AUGUST 7, 1952, VIENNA, AUSTRIA

Holding his breath, Thane Baker shrank into the darkened doorway. His heart pounding, he pressed his elbows to his sides to make himself as small as possible. The Jeep full of armed guards rolled slowly past his hideout. As soon as the headlights passed, Thane backed away in the opposite direction. He was lost after curfew in Occupied Vienna.

The city of Vienna extinguished all her streetlights at midnight, leaving the streets illuminated by the full moon.[1] The few people who remained awake hid behind blackout curtains. Through a maze of narrow, shadowy streets, Thane walked block after block, searching for safety. His rapid breathing and his footsteps on the cobblestones sounded loud in the dark. A cat caterwauled. A dog barked.

Thane glanced sideways. He looked behind. Someone might attack him. If the military police (MPs) captured him, he feared he might disappear into a communist prison forever.

A door slammed. Thane flinched.

Burned-out buildings stood as empty husks against the moonlight. Thane dodged around piles of used bricks.[2] He tripped over sidewalks in disrepair. The Nazi occupation of Vienna hurt her. The Soviet Army liberation left yet more scars on this city by the Danube River.[3]

Headlights cut the night from another Jeep. Or was it the same one? Thane hunkered down behind a row of bushes, his heart racing. Footsteps pounded the cobblestones. Rocks rolled. A tree shook and protested as someone scrabbled up its trunk. Others slunk in Vienna's streets tonight.

Thane carried a leather box with his latest award inside it. Each time he ducked into an archway, lay next to a parked car, or hid behind a wall, he scratched it. At least he still held it.

In the pocket over his heart, his Olympic medal weighed against his chest. If the Communists arrested him, what would happen to it? Would both he and his medal vanish behind the Iron Curtain? Who would keep it from the Soviet MPs? After they passed, he crept away.

Earlier today, or maybe it was yesterday now, employees at the Vienna City Hall taught Thane and his fellow American athletes Viennese history. After conquering Germany in World War II, the four Allied countries of Great Britain, France, the United States, and the Soviet Union divided the country of Austria, one of Germany's former possessions, into four zones. Because Vienna, former home of the Holy Roman Empire and the heart of Austria, lay in the Soviet zone, the Allied powers divided the capital city into five zones with each country governing their own section, but rotating control of the *Innere Stadt*, the city center.

Thane heard another motor and dodged in a doorway. He froze.

Rubber wheels thumped down the brick street. In the small light remaining, a two-way radio antenna, taller than a man, danced on the Jeep's back. Exhaust fumes filled Thane's nostrils. Four military police officers, one from each occupying country, rode in the Jeep, which flew their small respective flags as a hood ornament. How could a Soviet combatant ride in a Jeep with a British, French, and American soldier while their countries fought against one another in the Korean War?[4] Those four men searched for scofflaws. They searched for him.

Thane considered himself a law-abiding citizen. Well, there might have been a couple times back in Elkhart during his high school years when he engaged in questionable activities. He and his friends visited a ranch where someone's dad raised calves for the market. They tried to rope the calves and ride them. That made the dad hopping mad. He claimed upsetting the calves "took the weight off them." Another time, they appropriated watermelons from a farmer's field. Of course, Thane "paid" for his watermelon. First, a birdshot pellet from the farmer's shotgun stung his cheek as he peeked over the side panel of the fleeing truck. Second, a store clerk tattled to his mother that a farmer shot her son the night before for stealing watermelons. He got into trouble for that! Thane learned his lesson. Since then, he walked the straight and narrow. Yet, now, he hid from MPs acting under their commandant's instructions.

They passed. Thane darted away.

Thane walked until he smelled the stables of Vienna's famous white horses. He figured out where he was in the *Inner Stadt.*[5] Now, he needed to cross the ring street that marked where the old city wall used to be.[6] Districts radiated outward from the center like spokes. Which direction should he go? He belonged in Neubau, the seventh district of Vienna, which operated under US jurisdiction. If he went the wrong direction, Communists might seize him.

How did Thane lose a five-story hotel that faced a large, open street? The ground floor possessed tall ceilings with brick arches over every window. The top floors boasted tall, narrow windows with the occasional stone balcony. Despite the rough-looking neighborhood, his hotel possessed an elegant quality that reflected her better days. It reminded him of the Paramount Hotel back in New York City. Much to Thane's dismay, every other building in this area also lifted five stories from the street. They formed a maze of solid walls and prevented Thane from gaining a perspective to discover his position.

Photograph of Vienna looking west from the top of St. Stephen's Cathedral. Note the war damage and that most buildings are the same height, August 17, 1945. *Courtesy of the American Commission for the Protection and Salvage of Artistic and Historic Monuments in War.*

Hearing a car, Thane hid in a dark archway. Across the street, Thane saw the glowing tip of a cigarette. Guttural voices whispered, then more footsteps.

Thane's hands trembled. He wiped the sweat off his forehead with his sleeve. Exhausted from hours of hiding and dodging, Thane backed himself into a corner. He shut his eyes, leaned his head against the brick wall, and remembered the last week and a half. How did he get himself into this fix?

CHAPTER 13

A European Tour

JULY 27–AUGUST 4, 1952, TURKU AND LONDON

Sunday morning, July 27, Thane woke up smiling as he remembered yesterday. Tuija and he had spent the day together, then danced their second night at the *Lintsi*. He hoped they would see each other soon.

The thrilling sprint and mile relays would run later today.[1] Thane looked forward to seeing them.

As he dressed, Thane heard a knock on the door. With seven men sharing his small two-bedroom apartment, someone else would answer it.

"Thane, it's for you," a voice called out. Thane left his bedroom.

"Pack your bags, Thane. You're leaving on an exhibition tour this morning," a manager called from the doorway.

"Excuse me?"

"You're costing the Olympic team eight dollars a day. It's time for you to leave. You will travel with an AAU team now. They'll take care of your bed and meals in the future."

"Will they give us expense money?" Thane wanted to know.

"Don't think so. You signed paperwork agreeing to do this back in New York.[2] Hurry and get packed. Your train leaves soon."

Luggage sticker from Helsinki, Finland, 1952. *Courtesy of the Thane Baker Collection.*

"I thought I was supposed to stay here until the end of the Olympics," Thane said. "They still have a week to go."

"Nope. Your event is over. It's time to get on the road." He glanced around. "You other boys will move out soon. Get packed. Thane, meet me downstairs in thirty minutes."

Thane stared at his roommates. They stood in various stages of undressing, looking as confused as Thane felt. He packed his suitcase and added some free Olympic luggage stickers.

At the last minute, Thane dashed off a postcard to his former boss at the Ford garage. He told him of his travel plans with other United States Olympians. Thane asked for work from the time he arrived back in Elkhart until he started his senior year at Kansas State. He could use the money. About his losing to Andy Stanfield in the finals, Thane told his old boss, "I got beat by a good man, so I haven't any kick coming." Thane mailed the postcard on his way.[3]

As he boarded the train, Thane realized he could not say goodbye to Tuija, nor did he know her address. What would she think of him when he skipped town?

The train pulled out of the station. Thane regretted that he missed the final Olympic week and the Closing Ceremonies. They would have made glorious memories.

After a time, the west-bound train stopped. Looking out the window, his train crew strolled past. Another set of train personnel took their place. Alarmed, Thane watched Soviet soldiers patrolling a border. "Why are men in Russian uniforms here? The USSR is to the east."

Someone called out, "We are going to pass through the Porkkala district. The Soviets gained control of this area during the last war." Lights turned on inside the train and metal shutters covered the windows. The train started moving again.

Once they exited the Soviet area, the process reversed itself. The Russian crew stepped off. A Finnish one took over. The shutters came off the windows, and Thane relaxed as the Soviet guards faded into the distance.

Five hours after they left Helsinki, Thane and seven other American Olympic athletes arrived in Turku, which lay in Finland's southwest corner.[4] Like Helsinki, forests and water shaped the city. Turku contained oak trees, plus evergreen and birch, like Helsinki.[5] The signs announced both *Turun* and *Åbo*.[6] Why did the same place need two names? The Americans soon settled into Turun Hospits, their hotel.

Everywhere the eight American athletes walked, the people of Turku stared at them. In Helsinki, the locals became accustomed to seeing the American muscle-bound giants.[7] Jim Fuchs, with two bronze medals in the shot put from the '48 and '52 Olympics,

Finland with Turku in the southwest corner, 1952. *Distributed by Helsingin Osakepankki-Helsingfors Aktiebank.* © *National Land Survey of Finland and courtesy of the Thane Baker Collection.*

Luggage sticker from Turku Hospits, 1952. *Courtesy of the Thane Baker Collection.*

and Marty Engel, who qualified for the finals in the hammer throw, both showed superior upper body strength.[8] The Chicago Cardinals football team drafted broad-shouldered Ollie Matson, with a bronze medal in the 400-meters and a silver in the 4x400-meter relay, to play for them in the fall.[9] Even the lean Americans beat the average Finn in height. Jack Davis stood a lanky six feet, two inches tall. He earned a silver medal in 110-meter hurdles, finishing with the same time as Bones Dillard.[10] From Cornell, glasses-wearing basketball player Walt Ashbaugh won fourth in the hop, step, and jump in the Olympics.[11] Arnold "Arny" Betton, with his relaxed bent knees and curved back, won seventh in the high jump.[12] Lee Yoder placed fourth in his heat of the semifinals of the 400-meter hurdles.[13] These Olympic athletes represented some of the best men produced by the United States. Since Ollie Matson and Arny Betton had Black skin rarely seen by the fair-faced Finns in Turku, their group drew constant attention.

Thane became well acquainted with his Turku teammates. Not only did they tour, compete, travel, and eat together, but they also slept two to a bed in short and narrow double beds, much smaller than American beds.

In the Olympic Village, the coaches sorted who would stay in which apartment by skin color. On the AAU tour, not so. Thane squeezed next to the muscle-bound Ollie Matson. The adage, "You can't argue with someone you share a double bed with," applied. What would people back home say about him sleeping with Ollie? It did not matter to him. Worn out, Thane fell asleep as soon as his head hit the pillow on his share of their little bed.

Monday, an English-speaking guide took the small exhibition team to see the Market Square, and then the Turku Cathedral. Afterwards, he led them on a path down the Aura River toward the sea. They stopped at a huge stone windmill that looked like it had been there for centuries.[14]

"I've seen windmills before," Thane said to Jim Fuchs, "but in Kansas, they're just spindly old things. Never saw one this massive before. Too bad you had such a bum hand and bad ankle during the Olympics. How's your throwing arm now?"

"Not much use. This is the one thing I wanted to win. I couldn't even feel my heaves. My hand was numb, clear up to my elbow. I put that shot in it and shoved; that's all."[15]

"You earned the bronze medal, at least," Thane sympathized. "I'm sorry we missed the last day of track competitions. My friend, Dean Smith, got a gold medal in the 4x100-meter relay. He would have been as pleased as punch about that." Thane thought it was too bad that the American 4x400-meter relay team lost to the Jamaicans by a tenth of a second. But he was glad the American

Jim Fuchs, in the Olympic Village. Notice his bandaged right hand, July 1952. *Photograph by U. A. Saarinen. Courtesy of the National Board of Antiquities. License by CC by 4.0.*

women surprised everyone by coming in first in the 4x100-meter relay and setting Olympic and world records. The women had not placed better than sixth individually.[16]

"Another thing we missed," Thane added as their tour continued, "Zátopek won the Olympic Marathon on the last day. Can you believe it? Three races, three gold medals, three records."

"I got to know him pretty well." Jim nodded. "He is only happy on his two legs, running and running very hard. Emil Zátopek is one of the most remarkable men I ever met. He can talk to you in English, in German, French, Spanish, Russian—in any language you might choose. He's a brilliant scholar."

Thane shook his head. "With his wife, they earned four Olympic Gold medals. And he's smart, too? How 'bout that? You would know. You went to Yale."

"But he doesn't look to be very much physically," Jim replied. "When he runs, you think that each step may be his last. There is no running form. He seems to be almost staggering. You would be willing to bet that he couldn't travel 400 yards. But he can keep running the same for five miles, ten miles, or twenty-six miles."

Lee Yoder, Charlie Moore's friend and 400-meter hurdler, joined the conversation. "You talking about Zátopek? When he ran, he would shake a little. His body wasn't in sync. He ran ugly."

Jim Fuchs remained firm. "He is the most amazing athlete I ever saw."[17]

"And we've seen some great ones," Thane nodded. "I'll give you that Zátopek was the best *runner* at the Olympics. But best *athlete* overall? I don't know. Our decathletes earned the title of best all-around athletes. This was Bob Mathias's second gold medal in two Olympics. He broke his own world record."[18]

Thane and the rest of the team walked along the river until they reached Turku Castle. Thane expected something fanciful, but the masons built this sturdy stronghold to last. Architects designed Nichols Gym back at Kansas State to resemble a castle. Turku boasted the "real McCoy."[19]

On July 29, 1952, the Turku Comrades and the Turku Athletic Union, who hosted the meet, handed out an unusual schedule. Track meets in the United States presented a vertical list of events with their start times written beside each. This schedule was horizontal.

Thane competed in the 200 and 400-meter dashes and raced on two relays against all comers. Unlike the ribbons and medals that he won back in the states, his awards earned Thane four cups and a copper teapot donated by local businesses.[20] The other athletes received similar prizes.

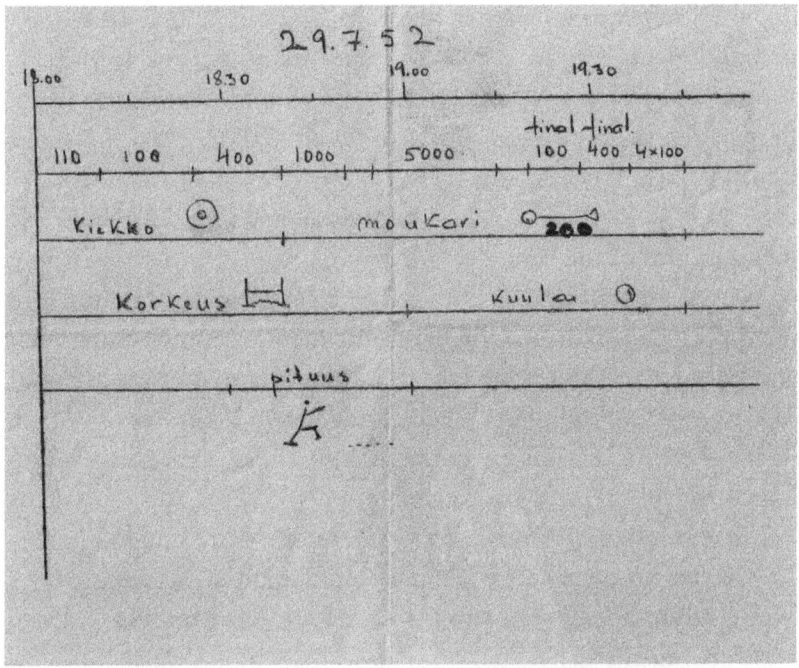

Turku Comrades and Turku Athletic Union track and field meet schedule, July 29, 1952. The top line shows the time with 18.00 being 6:00 p.m. The next line lists the running events (in meters). They line up vertically with the timeline above to indicate their start time. Rows three, four, and five show field events. The drawings help identify the following: kiekko=discus, moukari=hammer, korkeus=high jump, kuula=shotput, and pituus=long jump.
Courtesy of Turun Toverit r.y. and Turun Urheiluliito r.y. athletic clubs and the Thane Baker Collection

"I'm grateful that they gave us these nice awards." Thane said to Lee Yoder as they left the field that night. "But how are we going to carry them all over Europe?"

"Maybe we can have a tea party, Thane!"[21]

"That would work out well," Thane joked, "since our next track meet is in London!"

The Turku team arrived back in Helsinki on August 1.[22] There, they joined other traveling American teams and flew on a KLM

Royal Dutch Airlines charter flight, leaving Helsinki at 10:00 AM to London on August 2.[23] Thane reset his watch on arrival. He appreciated being able to read street signs and newspapers. Even though the people spoke with a different accent, everyone spoke English.

Thane walked around London with his Olympic friends. He took pictures of the sites.

On August 3, the date of the closing ceremonies, one American Olympian met six British flight attendants who also stayed at their hotel: Cadogan Court Hotel, Queen's Gate Gardens, Kensington.[24] The ambitious young man asked all the lovely ladies out to dinner, then asked his friends to come along. Thane and Dean Smith joined the group for a jovial evening.

At the restaurant, they all sat on either side of one long table. The servers brought boiled potatoes and lamb for everyone.

"I surely do miss all those steaks I ate back in Texas," Dean Smith complained.

His dinner companions laughed.

A British flight attendant responded in a haughty, high-brow voice. "We would have more beef here if we hadn't shipped it all over to the *Colonies*." Hoots and hollers went around the table.

Not to be outdone, Dean bounced back. "Heck, I have more beef back on my ranch in Texas than you have on this whole dang *island!*"

And that's when the table fell into hysteria. Thane laughed until tears ran down his face. At the end of the meal, with everyone digging deep and chipping in, they covered their meal tab.

On August 4, Thane's group joined other exhibition tour groups for the United States versus the British Empire Games at White City Stadium on a rain-soaked track. Built for the 1908 Olympic Games, this massive stadium held 50,000 spectators, who stood in a thunderstorm to watch the Americans compete against the English, Australians, Canadians, Jamaicans, and the rest of the British Empire.[25]

Tower Bridge, August 1952. *Photograph by Thane Baker. Courtesy of the Thane Baker Collection.*

In this meet, competitors worked as teams. The winning team tallied the best total score for their three athletes. For example, the three American broad jumpers, including Flash Gourdine, whom Thane met at the baseball game, won their event, even though none of them jumped the farthest that day.[26]

Before the events started, Flash Gourdine, Gene Cole, J. W. Mashburn, and Thane warmed up together in the deluge. They would run the mile relay together later. Thane yelled over his shoulder, "Gourdine, you're a broad jumper. How come you're running the lead-off leg of the mile relay?"

"Back at Cornell, I almost always ran the first leg of this relay," Gourdine called back. "My good friend Charlie Moore was on our team. Our coach always said he could never find a good fourth man for our relay team."

"My coach always says that, too," Thane replied. "This relay is something I do back home."

"Don't worry, Thane. My nickname is 'Flash' from the *Flash Gordon* comic book. I do well when I have a crowd to perform for, like today. Plus, Andy Stanfield has been working with me on my block starts to make me faster."[27]

"Andy's a good starter," Thane replied. "At least in England, we'll be competing in yards again instead of meters." The runners slogged on through the rain and mud. "Cole and Mashburn, I guess you ran this same relay against the Jamaicans a few days ago in Helsinki."

Cole stayed silent.

"No, Thane." Mashburn, the high school student from Oklahoma, cleared his throat and hesitated. "I did not run the four by four in Helsinki."

"What happened?" Thane asked. "Did you get injured?"

"I was supposed to run it," Mashburn said. Unlike the other slender gazelle-like athletes surrounding him, Mashburn's body resembled a grizzly bear. "Saturday night, the night before the race, a coach told me they pulled me out."

"Why?"

"I don't know. They substituted Charlie Moore in my place. Charlie didn't even try out for the 400 meters. We didn't have a runoff between us. They never gave me a reason."[28]

"What did you say to the coaches when they removed you from the relay?" Thane asked.

"I told them I was in the best shape of my life. They said I was just finishing high school and I may be at the next Olympics. After they pulled me, I walked all night, all over Helsinki. My race ran without me. Hopefully, I'll get a good split time today. I've got today and next Saturday on relay teams against the gold medal

Jamaicans. I believe they made a mistake when they took me off the Olympic relay team."

During the 4x440 relay race, Mashburn ran the third leg. He started a yard and a half behind Jamaica's Rhoden, the gold medalist in the 400 meters, and splashed into a lead of two yards by the time he handed off the baton to Thane. The deluge did not discourage Thane as he ran anchor on the mile relay team. Herb McKenley pulled ahead of him. Rainwater got in Thane's eyes, making it hard to see. His feet splattered puddles, and the mud stuck to his spikes and the back of his shirt and shorts. The cheers of the crowd continued, but some officials hid under an overhang off the track. Despite his best effort, Thane couldn't beat McKenley. The Jamaicans set a British all-comers and national record that day. The Americans came in second.

After the race, Thane spoke to J.W. "I'm sorry I couldn't hold him off for you."

"Don't worry about it, Thane," J.W. answered. "I'll get 'em next week."[29]

Later that afternoon, spraying water with every step, Thane sprinted 220 yards on a mile-medley-relay team. Jim Gathers, recent bronze medalist in the 200 meters, ran the other 220-yard leg of the relay. Reggie Pearman, a great relay runner from New York University and new world record holder in the two-mile relay, carried the stick for 440 yards. Mal Whitfield, the two-time gold medalist in the 800 meters, glided through 880 yards. Their relay team set a new British record.

Also, on that miserable, rain-filled day, Charlie Moore won and tied his own world record in the 440-yard hurdles. However, because the British Empire Games tabulated team scores instead of individual places, the British Empire earned first place in Charlie's event.

Overall, the United States won eleven of the sixteen events.[30] On the awards stand, the officials gave Thane two small wooden plaques with enameled flags representing the British Empire and the United States.

Thane Baker's awards from the United States vs. the British Empire games, August 4, 1952. *Photograph by author. Courtesy of the Thane Baker Collection.*

Back at the hotel, Thane washed his mud-splattered competition uniform in the bathroom sink, wrung out the excess water, and hung it and his shoes up to dry. He showered and crawled into his shared bed to sleep.

CHAPTER 14

Vienna

VIENNA, AUSTRIA, AUGUST 5–7, 1952

At 7:50 a.m. the next morning, Thane waited with his new AAU team at 194/200 High Street, Kensington, London, Town Terminal for a bus to transport them to the airport for their 9:20 a.m. flight to Vienna, Austria.[1] They wore their Olympic uniform suits.

Thane looked at his new teammates. Arny Betton, the high jumper, joined Thane in Turku.[2] Wes Santee, distance runner from the University of Kansas, and Thane shared a history.[3] Bones Dillard, with his four Olympic gold medals, planned to compete in the 110-meter hurdles and the sprints in Vienna.[4] Roland Blackman flew over the 400-meter hurdles in the Olympics but did not advance out of the semi-final round.[5] Bill Miller threw the javelin in Helsinki for silver.[6] Don Laz earned his silver in the pole vault behind Bob Richards.[7] Gene Cole ran the 4 x 440-meter relay with Thane last night and placed second in the Olympic four-by-four.[8] Discus thrower Fortune Gordien possessed a bronze medal from the 1948 Olympics and took fourth in Helsinki.[9] Olympic assistant coach Larry Snyder from Ohio State led the AAU Vienna squad.[10]

Thane stared at a rose bush sheltered near a doorway. Black dust coated its blossoms like the pollution-covered roses in the park. Both color and scent failed to escape their dingy coats. Cars, buses, and chimneys belched smoke. Haze hung in the air.[11]

"At least with all the rain last night, we didn't have to breathe in this London smog while we ran. I miss the clean air of Helsinki." Thane commented. "Anyone been to Vienna?"

"I've gone to Frankfurt, Germany, for a track meet." Bones replied. "I'd assume Vienna would be similar."

"When did you travel to Germany?" Thane asked.

"1945," Bones responded. "Turns out General Patton competed in the 1912 Olympic Games. He wanted to host a G.I. Olympics. The Mediterranean Theater competed against the European Theater." The rest of the AAU athletes crowded around to listen to the story.

"How did you do?" Thane asked.

"Now, remember, I experienced competition in the past, not like some of those other boys."

"And?"

"I won four events.[12] Patton was there, all spit and polish. He told the Stars and Stripes, that military newspaper, that I was the best athlete he'd ever seen."[13] They shared a friendly laugh.

"What should we expect in Vienna?" Thane asked.

Bones sobered. "The Allies bombed Frankfurt. Bridges out. Buildings, empty shells without roofs or glass in the windows. Piles of rubble littered the streets. I'm hoping that in the seven years since the war, Vienna will be in better shape."

The team quieted. Roland Blackman told them the army had him stationed in Germany.[14] He would be a resource for the team.

Thane had a copy of the August 5 *London Daily Telegraph* stashed under his arm. He wanted to read the results from last night. He carried his damp competition clothes and shoes in his Pan Am bag. Everything else fit in his suitcase. His Olympic medal rested in his inner coat pocket. He and the rest of his team boarded their bus at 8:20 a.m. The London traffic was heavy. The double-decker buses competed with motorcycles, bicycles, trucks, and cars.

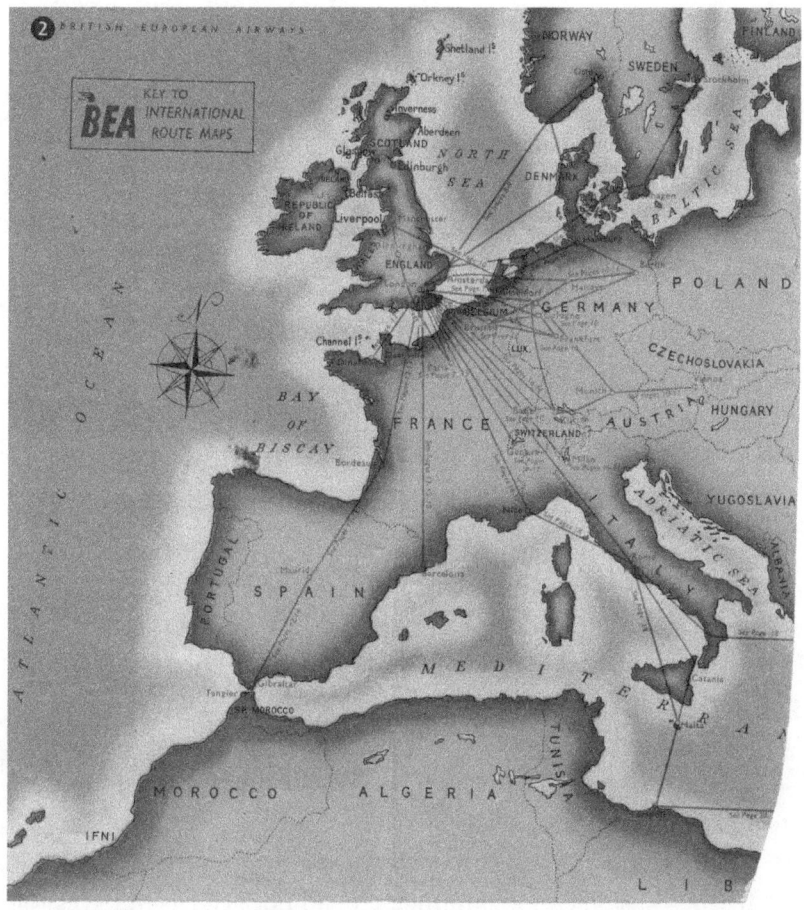

British European Airways flight paths, May–September 1952. Published by (unknown word) Bacon & Co. Ltd. London Edinburgh for British European Airways. *Courtesy of British Airways and the Thane Baker collection.*

Pedestrians dashed between cars that refused to slow down. On every street corner, police guided traffic and tried to create order out of chaos.[15]

On the plane, Thane traced his path on a map the airline provided through stops in Zürich, Switzerland, and Munich, Germany, until the airplane reached Vienna, Austria.[16]

During the flight, another US Olympian approached Thane. "Thane, got a minute?"

"Sure, what can I do for you?" Thane asked. The other fellow looked uncomfortable.

"How did you like London?" He stalled.

"Well," Thane replied, "I'm glad I got to stay for a few days. Didn't care for the smog. You have something on your mind?"

"Well, it's like this," he cleared his throat. "I've run out of money. Flat broke. Would you be interested in buying this revolver and a box of flash shells? Brand new."

Thane manipulated the gun. He dry-fired it to check the trigger action. He opened the gun and investigated. Thane closed it and spun the chamber. The gun appeared clean, well oiled, and never fired. The box of shells was full.

"This gun's in decent shape. Where'd you get it?"

"I bought it in Finland. Those stores sell sporting equipment."

Thane nodded. He noticed the same thing. "How much for the gun and shells?"

"Twenty bucks?"

Thane sucked in air through his clenched teeth. "That's mighty steep. How about ten dollars?"

"Fifteen and you've got a deal."

Thane considered for a minute. He did not need a gun. This was a starter's pistol for an official to start a race, and the blank shells were appropriate for it. Mr. Haylett needed a gun during track practice. Plus, he wanted to help his teammate out of a tight spot.

"Everything looks 'Even Steven.' You got yourself a deal." They shook hands. Thane took out fifteen dollars from his wallet and exchanged it for the pistol and shells. He placed the handgun and shell box in his suit jacket pocket.

Thane and the eight other Americans arrived at Hotel Höller, their home for the next few days, on VII Burggasse 2.[17] Thane set his watch to correspond with the time in Austria. He unpacked his wet competition uniform and hung the clothes out to dry.

Left to right: Arnold Betton, Wes Santee, and Roland Blackmon stand in front of their Vienna hotel, August 1952. *Photograph by Thane Baker. Courtesy of the Thane Baker Collection.*

On Wednesday, August 6, the United States military invited Thane and his fellow competitors to the United States Forces–Austria Headquarters, a wide building seven or eight stories tall. The Olympians learned that the American occupation force in Austria supported the establishment of a democratic Austria and desired a healthy economy for its people. The military personnel explained about the Marshall Plan and how the Austrians recovering from war and starvation benefited.[18] This month, the Soviet Union controlled Vienna's city center. One soldier from France, the Soviet Union, the United States and Great Britain patrolled Vienna together in American jeeps to keep the peace.

After the orientation tour, military personnel brought the team to the European Exchange Service or EES and invited them to shop. The exchange provided nice items at low prices.[19]

Thane whispered to Bones, "I thought only military personnel shopped here."

"Are you complaining?" Bones whispered.

Thane shook his head. "Nope, not me."

"I'm going to look for some new shoes," Bones shared.[20]

"I want a present for my mother," Thane replied. After searching, Thane bought Chanel No. 5 perfume and a marcasite butterfly pin for his mother. Silver metal held the black stones in the two-part pin.[21]

Thane also picked up *Stars and Stripes*, a newspaper for the US Armed Forces in Europe. Of course, he always looked for the report on his race first. On its front page, it declared that the United States beat the Soviet Union in team standings in Helsinki. The Russians also claimed the team victory in the Olympic Games in *Pravda*, their Communist Party newspaper, using a difference point system.[22] Keeping points and scoring the Games by country struck Thane as a new idea. Individual events made up the Olympics.[23] In Helsinki, athletes broke more world records than any previous one. Thane agreed with the newspaper's last comment. The Finns triumphed with their "flawless performance of efficiency and courtesy."

Thane and the AAU competitors did not arrive in Vienna to sightsee, shop, or read. They came to compete in a two-day event.[24] The team rode on a bus to the track. While everyone in Vienna had been nice to Thane, he witnessed a startling sign outside his bus window. It said, "AMI GO HOME," along with other words in German. Some Austrians did not want the Americans in Vienna.

Later, Thane saw a giant Ferris wheel missing cars. He pointed it out to Bones, who told him they were in the Communist section of Vienna.

"The USSR controls this area?" Thane asked.

Thane took a photograph from his bus of this sign, which told the Americans to go home for a free, independent Austria, August 1952. *Photograph by Thane Baker. Courtesy of the Thane Baker Collection.*

Bones nodded. "Remember, at the Olympics, Thane? The Soviets were just as nice as they could be. Good sports. It's gonna be okay."

The Austrian Athletic Association and Austrian Olympic Committee held the event at the Wiener Athletiksport Club, or WAC.[25] Before the meet began, all the athletes lined up on the side of the track facing the stands.[26] Fifty-four men and thirteen women from multiple cities, universities, and a military base in Austria joined nine Americans and three men from Switzerland.[27] Photographers took pictures of athletes on display in front of the spectators.

At 6:15 p.m., Thane set starting blocks behind the starting line of the 100-meter race. Four-time Olympic gold medalist Harrison

The United States Olympians stood with athletes from other countries by the track at the Weiner Athletiksport Club (WAC) prior to the beginning of the meet. The Americans, left to right: Roland Blackmon, Bill Miller, Harrison Dillard, Thane Baker, Gene Cole, Fortune Gordien, Arnold Betton, Wes Santee, and Don Laz. Each autographed his picture on this photograph, August 6, 1952. *Photograph by Franz Votava/brandstaetter images/picturedesk.com and courtesy of the Thane Baker collection.*

"Bones" Dillard lined up against Thane.

Thane reached out his hand. "Good luck, Bones."

"You, too, Thane. Watch out. That track's pretty soft."

Thane and the other competitors exchanged handshakes. He looked down the straightaway. On his right, spectators stood on old cement steps on the side of the track.

"Auf die Plätze!" The starter flung his arms out straight and yelled something incomprehensible. Every starter spoke the language of the host country. Thane learned to keep the starter in his field of vision. He stepped into his blocks.

"Fertig!" The starter barked and pointed his gun at the sky.

Thane rose to the set position.

The gun fired. Thane charged out of the blocks. Bones Dillard led halfway. Thane bounded forward as fast as a pronghorn antelope from Kansas. Bones disappeared from his field of view. Thane won the 100 meters against one of the most preeminent sprinters in the world!

Shocked, Thane looked back to see that pain seized Bones's face as he grabbed his right thigh.

"Hey, are you hurt bad, Bones?" Thane asked after the race. "I would rather have beat you in a fair race."

"You beat me today because you were faster, a better runner." Dillard said in his friendly yet reserved manner.

Thane shook his head. "Thanks, Bones. You take care of yourself, okay?"

Mr. Snyder, the American coach, hustled over to check out his injury. Thane pulled his warm-up suit back on to await the next race. Mr. Haylett would sure get a bang out of hearing that Thane beat Dillard in a race.[28]

At 7:15 p.m., Thane ran in the 4 x 100-meter relay, which the Americans won. Afterwards, the bus brought the team back to the hotel. While on the bus, Thane passed around his program and asked everyone to sign it.

On Thursday morning, Vienna leaders invited the Olympians to Das Wiener Rathaus, their elegant city hall.[29] On the outside, four smaller towers flanked an enormous center tower. A guide told the athletes that the statue on the center tower brought its height to over 100-meters tall.

Inside the Rathaus, sumptuous chandeliers hung in high-ceilinged rooms swathed in damask silk. Beautiful wood combined with lovely mosaics to create a church-like atmosphere. Elaborate moldings decorated the walls and ceilings. A stairway rose forever. Thousands of people worked here. The dignitaries gave Thane and the others a booklet with six postcards and a map showing the important landmarks of Vienna's inner city. Written on the inside covers, four

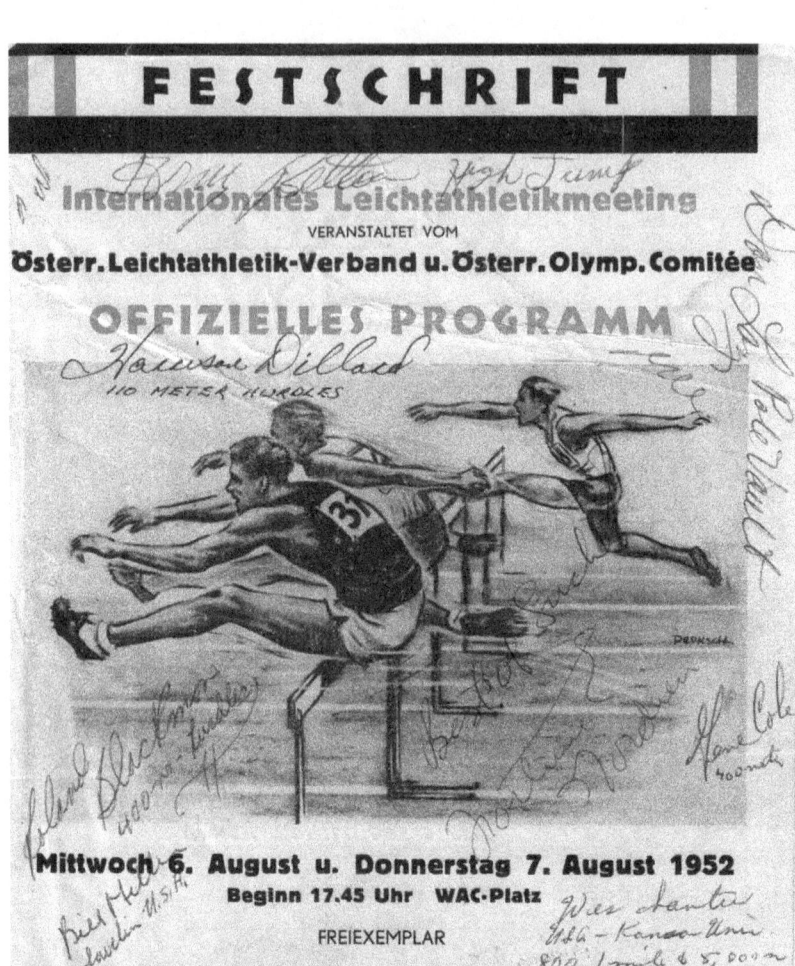

Front cover of the Vienna program with autographs from Arny Betton, Harrison Dillard, Don Laz, Gene Cole, Fortune Gordien, Roland Blackmon, Wes Santee, and Bill Miller, August 6–7, 1952. *The American Information Service for United States Forces in Austria published the Wiener Kurier. Also courtesy of the Österreichisches Olympisches Comité and the Austrian Athletics Federation.*

Rathaus in Wien, Vienna City Hall, 2006. *Photograph by Gryffindor. Converted to black and white. License by CC by 2.5.*

languages described the city hall to visitors.[30] They also gave each member of the team a picture book of famous sites in Vienna with captions written in four languages.[31] After their tour, the team gathered outside the Rathaus. Once again, the team, dressed in their formal Olympic suits, collected stares from all around. But unlike in Turku, the people of Vienna were more accustomed to seeing Black men, because of the United States' military presence.

After their time at the courthouse, the American athletes wanted to go back to the hotel. Thane studied the map in his hand. "We didn't get enough sleep last night, what with the meet running late and having to get up so early this morning. But I want to go exploring. I don't want to waste a minute of my time here. When will I ever be in Vienna again?"

"By yourself?"

Thane Baker's hand-drawn map of Vienna's First District. The road marked "Ring" is part of the Ringstraße. The word "Bristol" stands for the Hotel Bristol. "Opera" indicates the Vienna Opera House. Kärtner Straße (written "Kaernterstrasse" on the map) runs perpendicular to the Ringstraße. "St. Stephens" is the cathedral, and Springer is a gun shop, Johann Springer's Erben, formerly located at Graben 9 (or 10). August 1952. *Courtesy of the Thane Baker Collection.*

"Sure, I've got a map," Thane lifted his little booklet. "I'll see you back at the hotel later." Thane also carried a hand-drawn map on scrap paper, which indicated how to find the cathedral and Johann Springer's Erben gun store on Graben Straße.

"Bye, Thane. Don't get lost," his teammates said.

With a month of international travel behind him, Thane toured Vienna's brick-covered streets. None of the other cities he visited prepared Thane for the opulence of Vienna's architecture, which contrasted against the ruined buildings still rotting after World War II. Construction sites inspired hope that Vienna would soon recover from her wartime devastation.[32]

This was the city of Mozart, Beethoven, and the Strauss family![33] In this city by the Danube River, Thane walked on Burgring Straße away from City Hall. He passed a park with well-tended formal gardens on his left, along with a magnificent palace. On the other side of the street stood impressive museums. The street made a slight left and became Operning Straße. Past the Opera House, but before the Bristol Hotel, he turned left onto the narrower Kärtner Straße and continued toward the rebuilt St. Stephan's Cathedral. As he walked, Thane peered into shops and watched the surrounding people. New York overwhelmed a Kansas boy, as did London. The buildings in Vienna took ornamentation to a much higher level.[34]

An enormous bell rested in the courtyard of St. Stephan's Cathedral. It had to be ten feet tall and ten feet in diameter. Multiple towers pointed to heaven.[35] This building must be taller than the Vienna City Hall. Back home in Elkhart, the Methodist Church only had two stories. Thane felt very insignificant.

From the cathedral, Thane walked to Graben 9 to visit the Johann Springer Gun Shop. Thane walked by churches, museums, palaces, and private homes that looked like palaces. Graben Straße had a great column to commemorate the end of the plague and many markets.

Eyes wide, Thane wandered back toward his hotel. He did not want to miss anything. The Hofburg Palace housed the Holy

St. Stephan's Cathedral, August 1952. *Photograph by Thane Baker. Courtesy of the Thane Baker Collection.*

Roman Emperors. The Catholic history of Vienna contrasted with the Protestant countries he stayed in earlier. He stopped at an outdoor café and enjoyed Sacher-Torte, a delicious chocolate cake with apricot jam in the middle smothered with chocolate icing and served with whipped cream on the side.[36] He watched a man playing his organ on wheels. The day was getting late. He still needed to compete that night.

That evening at six thirty, Thane won the 200-meter dash with a time of 21 seconds.[37] Roland Blackman came in second. Bill Miller

Don Laz signs an autograph for boy wearing lederhosen on a WAC field, August 6–7, 1952. *Photograph by Thane Baker. Courtesy of the Thane Baker Collection.*

threw the javelin six inches farther than the winning Olympic gold medal throw in Helsinki.[38] Wes Santee won the Hermann Wraschtil Memorial Challenge Trophy for the English mile run in 4:10.2, setting an Austrian record by over nine seconds. Dillard did not compete that day because of his injury. Don Laz won the pole vault.

The photographer from yesterday gave Thane a copy of the group photograph. Thane asked his fellow Americans to sign their pictures. An older gentleman, who only spoke German, came up to Thane and showed that he wanted to write on the back of the picture. Thane handed it over. The man's pen did not write well. From what Thane discerned, this man had been a champion in races from the four hundred meters to the marathon at the end of the last century and the start of this one. Thane shook hands and said, *"Danke,"* the German word for thank you. The senior man smiled and strolled back to the stands.

Exhibition meets combined strange events, and athletes competed outside their specialties. The *Schwedenstaffel für Männer* or Swedish relay claimed the last spot on the program. Bill Miller, the javelin thrower, dashed the 100-meter leg. Thane sprinted the 200. Gene Cole, a 400-meter runner, claimed the 300-meter length, and Roland Blackman, a 400-meter hurdler, ran the 400. Because the teams could put their runners in whatever order they wanted, no one knew who was ahead until the end. Their baton handoffs may not have been the smoothest possible, but Thane thought it was a lot of fun.[39] The American relay team won. In fact, the Americans earned victories in all seven events that evening, which disappointed local spectators.

Felix Kwieton autograph. Felix Kwieton wrote that he had records from the 400 m to the marathon from 1897 to 1913. Kwieton placed 20th in the Men's Marathon in the 1912 Olympics, August 7, 1952. *Courtesy of the Thane Baker Collection.*

They returned to the Hôtel Höller, cleaned up, and dressed in their Olympic suits.

Thane asked Bones. "Think you'll be able to run in London in a couple of days?"

"Not with this leg injury. I'm done for the season. I got five new pairs of track shoes while I was in Europe, and I'll run next year."

An Austrian guide led the American team to their dinner located about five blocks from the hotel. Once inside the building, Thane and his teammates joined various dignitaries and other athletes who performed in the meet for a multiple-course meal.

As everyone finished their last course, an announcer stood up to distribute awards earned during the last two days of competition. Servers distributed small cookies with coffee. The speaker recognized Thane for his four victories. He had enjoyed a good track meet.

After the officials distributed the awards, Thane hoped to leave. He ate too much and just wanted to go to bed. Just then, an unknown man stood up. He had thick, dark eyebrows. Large, black-rimmed glasses sat on top of his prominent nose. He had combed his short gray hair away from his receding hairline. Everyone quieted and treated the leader with respect. Thane thought he must be someone important, like the mayor.[40] The man spoke in German, then called out, "Thane Baker."

Stunned, Thane stood up. By gestures, he understood he should go stand next to the speaker. Thane walked around the end of the table, with everyone smiling and clapping. He felt a knot in his stomach. The speaker opened a brown leather-covered box which held a silver plate with a gold branch attached to it. The speaker gave the box to Thane. They shook hands. Smiling, Thane held up the box to show everyone the plate inside. Thane closed it and walked back to his seat. Their guide told Thane he had won the special prize because he scored the most points in the competition. His fellow Americans reached out to congratulate him. Bones made a point of encouraging him. Still in shock, Thane shook hands with everyone.

Best Athlete Award presented to Thane Baker by Karl Waldbrunner, Federal Minister of Transport and Nationalized Enterprises. Award reads:

Internat. Leichtathletik–Meeting
Wien 1952
Ehrenpreis
Des Bundesminister
F. Verkehr und Verstaatl Betriebe
Dipl. Ing. Karl Waldbrunner.

Courtesy of the Thane Baker Collection.

Left to right: Unknown, Wes Santee, Roland Blackmon, Thane Baker, Gene Cole, Don Laz, Harrison Dillard, unknown Swiss athlete, Bill Miller, Arny Betton, unknown, Diplom-Ingenieur Karl Waldbrunner, Coach Larry Snyder. Fortune Gordien not pictured, August 7, 1952. *Photograph by US Information Service Pictorial Section Vienna. Courtesy of the Thane Baker Collection.*

Everyone stood for one last photograph. The important man posed with Thane and other Olympians. Who would have dreamed that Thane would be the outstanding athlete among all these Olympians?

CHAPTER 15

Night Terrors

AUGUST 7–8, 1952, VIENNA, AUSTRIA

Once outside, the Americans huddled in a circle. Most wanted to check out the local taverns. Their Austrian guide promised to return them to the hotel.

"Hey, Thane, we're going to grab a beer. Check out these *Kneipe*s around here. You wanna come?"

Thane smiled but shook his head. "It's only ten o'clock, but I'm so tired I can hardly stand up. You folks go ahead. I'll just head to the room a few blocks from here."

"You sure? We don't have to stay out late."

"I'm sure. You go on." Thane disliked bars where the air hung heavy with cigarette smoke and stunk like stale beer.

"See you later."

Thane left his teammates and headed back. He carried a luggage sticker in his pocket to remind him of the name and address of his hotel.

Thane soon discovered a flaw in his plan. He did not speak German. How could he request directions? If someone told him where to go, he would not understand what they said. The shady characters under the streetlamps unsettled him. Perplexed, he

Luggage stamp from the Hotel Höller, August 1952. *Courtesy of the Thane Baker Collection.*

walked and walked, seeking his hotel. During the daylight, Thane navigated Vienna with ease. The darkness distorted his sense of direction.

Women sauntered. Men ogled. Thane moved away.

Two hours later, curfew descended. Without light, the night prevented his reading of the address on the stamp or the street signs. If he worried about appealing for directions before, Thane worried twice as much now.

Jeeps filled with MPs circled.

Thane ducked and dogged along. His stomach clenched.

The tall, dark buildings bewildered him. He missed the flat openness of his small hometown on the prairie. Where did the hotel go?

Thane walked on.

The church bells bonged one in the morning. He had to leave for London in a few hours.[1]

Bright headlights aimed at Thane. He lunged into a doorway, only to find three other men already there. Thane's legs weakened.

With the vehicle coming closer, Thane feared if he left his spot, the MPs might see him and give chase. Thane wrinkled his nose at the odor of alcohol. One man smoked a cigarette. Thane watched the small circular glow of the cigarette get brighter as its owner inhaled. He pushed his prize box behind him as he leaned into the wall. The stranger blew smoke into Thane's face. Thane held his breath. No one said anything. The Jeep came closer.

The men barraged Thane with growls. *"Wer sind Sie? Warum sind Sie hier? Woher kommen Sie?"*

Thane's breath rasped in and out. They questioned him. What they wanted; he did not know. These strangers must not discover he held an American passport. What if the Soviets caught him?

Thane crouched and peered around the corner. He pretended to focus on the Jeep and not on his fellow criminals.

"Dies ist unser Platz! Jetzt! Gehen Sie!" The anger in their voices escalated.

Thane acted drunk and grunted. Staggered. He did not want them to know he did not speak German.

The Jeep crawled past their hiding place.

Thane stepped away. He did not run because he did not want to give himself away as a visiting athlete. In the darkness, he faded against the stone.

Thane hurried up and down the side streets. He kept going and going, faster, slower, faster, slower. He felt like Emil Zátopek during one of his workouts. Thane plodded with one foot in front of the other over. Then he propelled himself in an adrenaline rush.

However, Zátopek was different. An underlying joy bubbled up from inside of him as he ran.[2] Not Thane. Tonight, even though he had earned the outstanding athlete award and beaten Harrison Dillard in a race, Thane fought despair.

Thane dodged around corners until at last, all his energy drained away. He leaned over and panted. Thane's knees folded, and he plunked down on the ground with his back against a building. After hours of walking over bricks and cobblestones in his thin-soled dress shoes, bruises hurt his feet.

Like that greased pig that Thane and the other children chased to exhaustion back in Elkhart, Thane's body and spirit quit. His feet stopped.

Muscles shaking, Thane rested his head in his hands and prayed for God's help. He should have hit the bars with the other guys. He tried to live a clean life. Look where that got him!

The bells tolled at two o'clock. Thane had wandered the streets of Vienna for four hours. If he were going to find his hotel, he should have found it by now.

Last night, officials recognized Thane for his athletic excellence. A great triumph! Now, disoriented, his nightmare closed in around him. His head spun. That fancy meal upset his stomach.

Thane needed to compete in London in thirty hours. What if he missed his flight? Would the MPs take pity on him and return him to his hotel? Not likely. The American, French, and English service members might sympathize with his troubles, but the Soviet soldier could have a different idea. Would they detain him at their headquarters?

He finally decided what to do and nodded his head. He would turn himself in and take his lumps. After he shared his award, would they understand?

Like an old soldier, Thane got to his feet once again. He looked across a wide street at the archways. Before, the blinding Jeep headlights dulled his vision. Now, in the moonlight, his eyes adjusted. Thane stood up and trudged across the wide brick street beneath his feet. He examined the building before him. Narrow, tall windows. Wait! A stone balcony? Could this be his hotel? He crept along the wall until he found the front door. The curtain-covered glass did not hint at the building's interior. Thane opened the unlocked door to discover a bright lobby with its tall ceiling. He found it!

Thane nodded at the surprised-looking desk clerk and climbed two flights of stairs holding onto the iron pipe handrail. He turned down the hallway to his room. He turned the doorknob and slipped inside the wooden door with its frosted-glass window. The snores and lumps in the bed showed his teammates had returned. Thane poured water from the pitcher over his hand into the bowl below. He washed his face and hands in the dark and stripped down to his skivvies. Thane reached out for an iron bed frame. He found an open spot and slipped into it so as not to wake his unknown bed partner. Tears leaked from his eyes. Thane took a moment to thank God for his deliverance before falling asleep.

CHAPTER 16

All Dreams Must End

SATURDAY, AUGUST 9, 1952, LONDON, ENGLAND

Friday afternoon, August 8, Thane, tie rumpled and its clasp askew, stood with his other American teammates beside his British European Airways plane for one last photograph in Vienna. Thane's BEA luggage sticker was in his suitcase. He hoped he would sleep on the way back to London through Munich and Zurich. Tomorrow, he would run again in another track meet.

On Saturday, August 9, the News of the World presented the post-Olympic British Games for over two hundred athletes from Great Britain, the United States, Australia, Canada, the Gold Coast, Jamaica, New Zealand, Nigeria, and South Africa at London's White City Stadium.[1] Thane collected a program printed with blue ink.[2]

At 1:55 p.m. on Saturday, Thane stood in the "J" section reserved for athletes in heavy rain. The "A Invitational 440-yard Dash" ran with only three entries. Mal Whitfield, Gene Cole, and Herb McKenley held ten Olympic medals between them. Mal Whitfield won in a time of 47.2 seconds.[3]

Thane began his warmup. A little after three o'clock, Lindy Remigino won the 100 yards and proved his Olympic victory was

United States Olympic Team athletes boarding British European Airways (BEA) flight from Vienna to London. Left to right: Gene Cole, Roland Blackmon, Harrison "Bones" Dillard, Arny Betton, Wes Santee, Thane Baker, Fortune Gordien, Bill Miller, and Don Laz. Not pictured: Larry Snyder, coach. On the back is an autographed note written in German. "Zum Andenken an die schönen Stunden in Wien." This translates to "In memory of the beautiful hours in Vienna." The ink has faded, and the signature is unrecognizable, August 8, 1952. *Photograph by Franz Votava/brandstaetter images/picturedesk.com and courtesy of British Airways and the Thane Baker collection.*

British European Airways luggage sticker, August 1952. *Courtesy of British Airways and the Thane Baker Collection.*

White City Stadium, London, 1960. *Photograph from the RJRowe Collection.*

not a fluke. Britain's McDonald Bailey placed behind Remigino with an identical time.[4] Dean Smith finished after them both.[5]

Stocky J. W. Mashburn, excluded from the Olympic relay, competed in the open 440-yard race at 3:10 p.m. The rain sheeted down, but Mashburn burned to prove himself to his coaches and the world. The officials assigned lane two to Mashburn. Lane one, which held the most water, remained empty. The thin men, George Rhoden, Olympic gold medalist in the 400 meters, and Arthur Wint, the silver medalist, started in lanes three and five. On the second curve, Rhoden pulled ahead of his Jamaican teammate. The wind driving the rain hindered the runners. On the final straightaway, Mashburn pumped his arms, pounded the track, and left Rhoden and Wint in the mud. Mashburn won his race in 47.2 seconds, the identical time to Mal Whitfield's win in the 400-meter Invitational held earlier that day.[6]

After the race, Thane waited his turn to congratulate Mashburn. "You did it! You showed everybody! You ran that lap as fast as

Front cover of the program from the British Games, August 9, 1952. *Reprinted with permission from News Licensing, London, and the Thane Baker Collection.*

anybody in the world!"

His lungs still blowing like bellows, Mashburn leaned over with his hands resting on his knees. He nodded his head at Thane.

When Mashburn stood up, he told Thane, "Wait 'til after the relay."

Mashburn's legs wobbled beneath him. Thane walked alongside with an arm around Mashburn's waist. Thane believed Mashburn should keep moving to avoid cramping. Head thrown back, Mashburn stumbled and tripped on the infield grass. The buckets pouring from the sky mingled with Mashburn's sweat.

"Still hafta prove I should have been on Olympic four by four. Lake out there," Mashburn huffed. After walking together about 100 yards, Mashburn turned to Thane. "Thanks for the support."

"Happy to help. I've got to finish my warmup for my 220-yard race."

Thane joined other 220-yard hopefuls in the dressing room at White Stadium to meet with the Chief Competitor's Steward. Thane knew most of the athletes and their abilities. Andy Stanfield and Jim Gathers from the United States stretched. Les Laing from Jamaica, who placed fifth in the Olympic 200 meters, stood nearby. Some of the 100-yard dash runners tried their luck at the longer sprint. The 220-yard heats started at 3:40 p.m. Thane, Andy, and Jim eased through their heats to the final.[7]

At four thirty, Thane discussed with Andy and Jim how Charlie Moore broke the world record in the 440-yard hurdles on the messy track in the outside lane.[8]

Then Thane inhaled. "Guys, listen. I'm exhausted. Vienna wore me down." Thane endured some good-natured teasing about whether Thane's exhaustion involved any hijinks. Despite Thane's denial, he experienced more ribbing. "Let's be serious. My gas tank is empty. I'll do my best. Let's go one-two-three again."

The officials put Jim Gathers in lane four, Thane in five, and Andy Stanfield in six. Multiple runners had torn up the muddy track surface. Each time a foot hit the ground; it left a divot. Unlike

Helsinki, these officials did not smooth the track between races. Patches of standing water did not help.

After the 4:40 p.m. gun sounded, the 220-yard sprinters flew around the turn. Thane fought through his race and came on strong at the end.[9] The finish judges awarded Andy first, Jim second, and Thane third.[10] Mashburn came over to check if Thane needed any assistance and stayed to stabilize him as Thane yanked on his sweats and switched his spikes to his Keds. Mashburn told Thane that Bud Held, who fell during the Olympics, won the javelin with a meet record. They watch Flash Gourdine, silver medalist in the broad jump, run and win the 220-yard hurdles.[11]

"I got to get over to my mile-relay team." Mashburn said, "We go next."

"Go on, go! Get!" Thane waved J. W. away. "I can take care of myself. Appreciate the help."

Dean Smith joined Thane in the infield from where he had been sitting in a dry corner under the stands.

"I gotta support Mashburn in the relay," Dean said. "He's an Okie. Regularly, you understand, Oklahoma and Texas folks are at each other's throats during competition."

"Like K-State and Kansas University," Thane said.

"Exactly. You and Wes Santee from KU are enemies of each other and mine back home," Dean said. "But today, we celebrated his mile run victory twenty yards in front of his nearest competition." They both knew this was Mashburn's last chance at redemption after the coaches removed him from the Olympic 4x400-meter relay.

"Mashburn's second leg. Let's spread out and encourage him." Thane suggested. "I'll be at the start of the second turn."

At five o'clock, the starter shot his gun. Arthur Wint of Jamaica and American Gene Cole ran lead-off legs. They looked even. As the runners neared Thane, he cheered for Cole. From Thane's position across the track, he could not tell which of the second stage runners received the handoff first.

"Come on, J.W!" Thane shouted. Mashburn ran against Les Laing. "Run! Run! Run! Lift your knees!" Thane screamed himself hoarse. Water collected in pools on the track shredded by previous runners. Despite the conditions, a husky Mashburn powered through his race, finishing ahead of the smaller man and leaving the American third leg, Reggie Pearman, in an excellent position against Jamaican George Rhoden, the Olympic 400-meter gold medalist. At that point, Thane thought the race might be all over. Both Rhoden and Herb McKenley, the last two Jamaican runners, were extremely fast. But Pearman beat Rhoden and passed the baton to Mal Whitfield, the two-time Olympic champion in the 800 meters, a yard before McKenley.

"Come on, Mal, leave McKenley behind," Thane rooted.

When the runners reached Thane, Mal's powerful stride placed him about five yards ahead of McKenley. With 100 meters to go, McKenley pulled up even with Whitfield to pass him. Whitfield dug deep and sprinted home first. The Americans beat the Jamaicans with Mashburn on the team![11]

Thane ran across the field to congratulate his friends. Mashburn sat on the judges' stand to put on his sweatpants. Whitfield pounded the mud off his spikes against the side of the stand. Thane paid his respects and stood back.

The announcer shared some surprising news. The American team, with Mashburn's aid, set a new world record in the 4 x 440-yard relay! On this soggy track, they broke an eleven-year-old record![12]

Head track coach Brutus Hamilton came out onto the field, swimming against those struggling to leave. He crossed the track, stood in front of the relay team, and stared at the close-knit group. Mr. Hamilton admitted the coaches made a mistake when they took Mashburn out of the Olympic relay. He apologized. Mr. Hamilton congratulated the relay team on their new world record and for beating the 1952 Olympic gold-medal-winning Jamaicans.

J. W. Mashburn thanked Mr. Hamilton and promised him he would continue to train to prove Mr. Hamilton wrong. "You can expect me in the '56 Olympics," Mashburn told him.

Mr. Hamilton said he hoped so.[13]

After cleaning up in the hotel, Thane, Dean, and J. W. walked into The Dorchester, invitations in hand, dressed in their formal dress uniforms and smelling of various aftershaves. A green-liveried door attendant directed them to the ballroom where Mr. W. Emsley Carr, Chairman of News of the World, hosted a banquet for the British Games athletes and officials.[14] They walked through the hotel, past the striking marble columns, parquetry floors, beautiful curtains, and hothouse flowers.

"We're getting pretty good at cleaning up after a track meet," Thane contributed.

"We almost look like we belong in this fancy place," Dean added.

At a quarter past seven that evening, Thane sat at a round, cloth-covered table with Dean Smith on one side and J. W. Mashburn on the other. Their table also included Harrison "Bones" Dillard with his sore leg, Charlie Moore, new world record holder in the 440-hurdles, and his Cornell teammate, Flash Gourdine, silver medalist in the broad jump.

A folded cloth napkin stood on top of each porcelain plate. Heavy silverware flanked it. Two stemmed glasses stood at the top right of the plate. One held water and the other, wine. Standing by each plate, an open gilt-edged program announced the menu and toasts.

A man went to the podium and asked the guests to please find their seats. Once everyone had a place, he welcomed the guests to dinner. He told them that The Dorchester often hosted royalty. During World War II, General Eisenhower planned the D-Day invasion of Normandy here.[15] The Americans looked much more impressed by the second fact. The announcer asked that everyone please stand and continue standing through the invocation. A

Postcard from The Dorchester, London, mid-twentieth century. *Courtesy of the author.*

fanfare played as distinguished gentlemen walked into the room to stand at the head table. The band then played "God Save the Queen." Soldiers in uniform brought the British flag into the room and posted the colors. Afterwards, an Anglican priest opened with prayer. Everyone took their seats.

Once again, the announcer stood and ordered the gentlemen to charge their glasses. Thane looked at Dean, who shrugged his shoulders. By the servers scurrying around with wine bottles and topping off wine glasses, Thane assumed "charge" meant to fill the wine glasses. The announcer asked everyone to stand again.

Mr. Carr raised his glass. "To Her Majesty the Queen," he called out.

All cheered, "To the Queen." Everyone sipped their wine glass. Thane drank water.

Another man announced, "To our guests."

Thane and his friends got the idea. They answered, "To our guests."

Two speakers, one from the United States and another from New Zealand, made official replies.

Another man raised his glass. "To the winners."

By now, the athletes at Thane's table joined the spirit of the event. In rowdy voices, they yelled, "To the winners." One winner offered an official reply on behalf of all.

The toast came for "The News of the World." Since they hosted both this afternoon's track meet and tonight's dinner, the shouted response deafened Thane. "To News of the World."[16]

The announcer invited everyone to please take a seat.

"How come didn't they toast President Truman?" Dean whispered.

"Because we're in England?" Thane murmured back.

Once the formal introductions ended, the noise level rose as the table conversation began.

"These Brits sure know how to throw a fancy party," Flash said.

"They only earned two Olympic bronze medals in track and field," Charlie said.[17] "But they couldn't be nicer to us this evening."

"Of course, their Empire did all right. Take the Jamaican men and Australian women, for example," Thane contributed. "They set lots of new records at the Olympics."

The servers brought out mint-flavored melon, one small bowl for each plate. Dean took one bite and pushed his bowl away. "What's everybody doin' when they get home?"

J. W. said, "I'll go to work on a drilling rig to earn a little money."[18]

Dean nodded. "I've got a gold medal, but not one quarter to my name. I'll go into the Texas oil fields and haul pipe."[19]

Flash Gourdine volunteered, "I've got to talk to the folks at Cornell University. I found out after the Tryouts that I'd lost my scholarship, and I may lose my room and board, too. Where will I live? My father doesn't make much money. My parents provide for four younger siblings and two cousins at home. They can't spare any cash for me."²⁰

"College is a means to get ahead in this world," Thane responded. "I hope everything works out for you, Flash."

Everyone else at the table nodded. Life would be more difficult for Flash because he was a Black man.

Thane returned to the question at hand. "I'm going to visit a girl in Waco, Texas, then work at the Ford garage back home, doing oil changes and such."²¹ Hoots and hollers began. Thane received far more advice than he wanted about the young lady in question.

Thane shut down the kidding. "Some of our team members are on active duty in the military. They'll go straight to their assigned bases. They might fight in Korea."

"Did the military pay their salary while they trained and competed in the Olympics?" J. W. asked.²²

"I believe so," Thane replied.

The fish course arrived. Dean grabbed a roll instead. "Not that I'm complainin,' but we lost money bein' on the Olympic team this summer."

They discussed athletes who turned their athletic prowess into dollars. Ollie Matson, a bronze medalist in the 400 meters, was now in training camp for the Chicago Cardinals football team.²³ Of course, Walt "Buddy" Davis, gold medalist in the high jump, would be playing professional basketball this fall.²⁴ Bob Richards, a preacher since the mid-forties, would bring people into the pews because of his gold medal.²⁵ That would not hurt the collection plate. But they were the exceptions. They all agreed the strict amateur code kept them from earning money as track and field athletes. They did not think it was fair that the Soviet government supported their athletes.²⁶

Thane shared, "That reminds me of something Fortune Gordien, the discus thrower, wrote when he signed his autograph for me, *'Make up your mind now! A great track man or a good living!'*"²⁷

"I have an idea about earnin' a livin'," Dean said. "J. W. and I went to watch *Gone with the Wind* at the movie theater. They dubbed the movie in Finnish."²⁸

"It was terrible," J. W. jumped in. "They served warm beer, and everybody puffed cigarettes. The movie screen hid behind a smoky gray wall."

"You like warm beer, Dean?" Thane teased.

"Nah, but it made me think about doing Westerns in Hollywood. They need stunt men. I run fast and ride a horse better than anyone. I grew up on a ranch and used to rodeo. Plus, I'm a looker," Dean posed.

"I was with you, Dean, 'til you started bragging about your pretty face," Thane joked.

"It's somethin' to consider," Dean replied.

The servers delivered the main course. Thane looked down at his plate.

"It's duck. In Western Kansas during the Depression, we used to go out hunting for dinner that evening."

"How's life in the Dust Bowl now?" Flash, the New Yorker, asked.

"We're doing all right. At the end of the War, those farmers who held on to their land 'got well' with several good harvest years."

"The cattle on my grandma's ranch have done pretty good these last few years," Dean nodded. "It's amazing what a healthy rainfall can do for grass."

J. W. lifted his fork and captured a few peas. "Back at the Olympic Village, the amazing food filled me. We ate all we wanted. In Cologne this week, they had little. They haven't recovered from the War."

"Vienna was rebuilding," Thane added. "I had one meal where they presented simple food in a fancy way. London's further along in their postwar recovery."

"Yes," J. W. agreed. "But London is still rationing food. You can't get milk or steak here unless you buy it illegally."[29]

"And what would you know about that, J. W.?" Thane inquired, his eyebrows rising.

J. W. threw up his hands. "I'm repeating what I heard."

Bones spoke in his soft, measured voice and told them about the 1948 London Olympics, the 'Austerity Games.' Athletes had to bring their own towels. Everything was basic.[30] They used White City Stadium from the 1908 Olympics. Destroyed homes and bomb craters were everywhere. The United States athletes lived and ate in eight separate places. Their Olympic Committee flew food in from the United States daily.[31]

"It sounds like Helsinki was much better," Thane commented. "We don't appreciate how good we lived back in the States.[32] We should be grateful. Thanks for the perspective, Bones."

Everyone focused on their food until Charlie Moore broke the silence. "J. W., I just wanted to congratulate you on setting the world record today. You had a great run."

The table turned to J. W. since Charlie replaced him in the 4x400 in Helsinki. "Thanks, Charlie. We all worked hard today. Congratulations on your new world record, too."

"Old McKenley beat me in the Helsinki relay. I ran the fastest time of my life on my relay leg, but he ran almost two seconds faster. He wanted that gold medal. When he took that baton, nothing was going to get in his way, including me. I let the team down. I am absolutely devastated." Charlie slumped down in his seat, rested his elbows on his legs, and looked at the floor.

"Don't feel bad, Charlie," Dean jumped in. "I watched you run. You left it all on the track. Your team broke the existing world record."

Charlie glanced up.

J. W. said nothing for a moment. "Charlie, the coaches made the call to pull me out and put you in my place."

Thane took a forkful of his chopped green apples with diced mint leaves. "This is our last night together. Tomorrow, we will take a plane to New York and scatter."

The servers removed the dinner plates and distributed a decorative dessert with peaches, pineapples, cherries, and cream.

"Who's coming to Melbourne in '56?" J. W. asked.

Thane spooned some whipped cream with a bite of peach. "I would love to run in '56, but I don't understand how it could be practical. How can we Americans afford to train for the next Olympics? We need jobs to support ourselves. I only have one more year of college, and I'm in Advanced ROTC. Who knows where the military will send me after that."

"I'm getting too old," Bones said. "This is my second Olympics. I'm twenty-nine. It takes longer to loosen up and recover than it used to."

Charlie Moore contributed. "I set a world record today, and I've got Olympic gold and silver medals. When I took my shoes off today, I said, 'That's it. I'm done.' I've won every individual race I've ever run, NCAA, AAU, Olympics. Why should I keep running? To lose?" Charlie shrugged his shoulders.

"But what will you do?" Thane asked.

"I'll work for my father. He needs me in the family steel business."[33]

"That sounds like a good plan." Thane said. "I don't want this to end," Thane cut into a piece of pineapple with the side of his spoon. "I kept my eyes as wide open as possible, not wanting to miss anything. The Olympics are the most amazing thing that has ever happened to me."

"Right ya are, Thane," Dean added. "We might not carry any money in our pockets, but this was one of the best experiences of our lives. The friendships we've made here will last forever. I also appreciated the father-son relationship with my coach. What did the rest of you like about the Olympics Games?"

Thane spoke again. "My coach, Ward Haylett, followed me to the Olympics. I can't tell you what that meant to me," Thane choked. "He came all that way just to watch me. So special."

"All those beautiful women and the crowds cheering for me," Gourdine joked with a wicked smile to lighten the mood. Everyone else laughed, too. Gourdine straightened in his chair. His face transformed into a sadder and older man. "Helsinki was a slice of heaven for me. A few folks might act rude to me because of the color of my skin, but it rolled right off my back. With the Olympic team, we were safe. At home, I must be constantly vigilant—how I act or how people treat me is a matter of life or death."[34]

Bones nodded. Everyone at the table sat silently.

"Worst time it ever was. Fort Greene Projects race riots. I was out with a Puerto Rican guy that night. Coming through Fort Greene Park, near the tower, there were wall-to-wall white boys. Whites from Coney Island and Eastside and a long way away. They came to get us. Some white guy got killed. The Navy Street boys, some white guys I used to hang out with, escorted us home. We never would have survived otherwise. From my apartment, I called people outside and warned them to hide. They said thanks but didn't react. The whites showed up like locusts. Everyone scattered. Two killed. Outnumbered." Gourdine paused. "I've been lucky in my life. Had lots of opportunities."[35]

"I didn't realize things were that bad in New York," Thane said quietly. "I thought it was only bad in Dixieland."

Everyone sat silently until Bones changed the subject to something lighter. "Back to what Dean said. Friendships are an important part of the Olympic Games."

"Remember that saying that they put up on the electronic scoreboard during the Opening Ceremony?" Thane asked, "'Great is to triumph. Greater far noble combat.'[36] I didn't understand that, but I do now. We came to do our best and to belong to something bigger than ourselves. We represented the athletes back home who tried to come but didn't qualify. For a lot of us, the stiffest competition in the world is back in the US. We are here for our country." Thane stopped for a moment and looked around the table. "I'm sorry this is over. I'll miss you guys."

"Now don't get all sad, Thane. You'll get to stare at the back of my uniform next year when I whup ya in the 100." Dean chipped in.

"We'll see about that!" Thane tossed back. "The college athletes, if we don't run into each other at the local meets, we should see each other at the NCAA meet next June. J. W., you'll be at the Big Seven events. For athletes out of college but still competing, we'll meet at the AAU National Championships.

"One thing about the Olympics surprised me," Thane added. "Back home, we heard about the Russian Communists, the German Nazis, and the Japanese, who attacked Pearl Harbor, all those *bad people* from other countries. I expected to find different nationalities, who looked evil, different from the people on the Kansas State campus. But they didn't. Everyone in the Olympics looked just like you and me. Without their uniforms, I wouldn't even recognize their home country.

"I spent some time talking to Levan Sanadze from the USSR. He raced in my first heat of the 200 meters. We both advanced to the second round, but other runners eliminated him. He spoke English, and we talked about the weather, the track, and the race. But he held back, and I didn't talk about politics with him. Sanadze was just an average guy like us."[37]

"That's one purpose for the Olympics, Thane," Bones said.[38] "To break down prejudice and bring people together to meet in friendly competition and not war."[39]

Thane finished his dessert. The servers offered more coffee.

"I almost wish we could stay."

"Sorry to break it to you, Thane, but our servers want to leave." J. W. stood up and stretched. "We need to get back to the hotel. Our plane home leaves tomorrow."

"So, you're telling me, J. W., that we have to wake up and join the real world?" Thane joked. "I don't think I'm ready."

PART
FOUR

Return to Kansas

CHAPTER 17

Return to Reality

SATURDAY, AUGUST 16, 1952, ELKHART, KANSAS

West of Liberal, Kansas, Thane walked down the portable stairwell next to his small plane and toward the airfield building.[1] The summer sun beat down on his Olympic hat. He carried his PAA bag over his shoulder. His suitcase waited by the doorway into the terminal. Thane adjusted his load, collected his custom-stamped suitcase, heavy with memories, and walked inside.

Mother waved with one hand. She yelled, "Thane! Thane! Over here!" Her other hand gripped Father's hand as she jumped up and down with excitement.

Thane rushed over to them, set down his baggage, and picked his mother up in the air. He spun her around and sniffed. Home.

"Thane!" Mother gasped. "Put me down."

Thane laughed and complied. He turned to Father and hugged him. Father squeezed Thane back until he gasped for air. He inhaled the scent of White Owl Cigars mixed with motor oil. Father released him and shook his hand hard.[2]

"This has been a grand summer, but I missed you both so much," Thane said. Thane threw his arms around both parents again. "You are the most wonderful parents in the world, and I

United States custom stamp, 1952–1953. *Courtesy of the Thane Baker Collection.*

wouldn't trade you for anyone."[3]

"You can't trade us in," Mother chortled. "We've missed you, too."

"Let's go home, son." Father grabbed Thane's suitcase. "Need to beat the weather."

Father led the way out of the terminal building. Thane held his arm out for his mother to wrap her arm around, and they followed.

Father called over his shoulder. "Hot as blazes this week. Temperatures over one hundred. This evening promises to be cooler. A front's moving in."

In the parking lot, Thane looked up at the sky. Clouds angled upward where the warm southern air met the cooler air from the north. The wind whipped through the tall grasses like waves on the ocean.[4]

After Father loaded the bag in the trunk, Thane opened the door for Mother to sit in front. "Oh, no, Thane! You sit with Father. I'll sit in the back and listen." Thane glanced at Father over the car. Mother? Listen? That would be the day!

Thane nodded, walked around, and pulled the front seat forward on the driver's side. Mother slid into the back. Even though his parents had left the windows cracked, the August heat converted the car into an oven. Everyone rolled down their windows. Once the car moved, warm air flowed in and offered some relief.

Mother squeezed Thane's shoulder. "It seems like forever since we've seen you.[5] After you were home that first weekend in June, you started traveling and kept going."[6]

"Tell me about it! I expected I'd be right back. I lived out of that suitcase for two months. The Olympic Committee gave me uniforms, which filled out my wardrobe."

Father cleared his throat. "That's why Bing Crosby and Bob Hope raised all that money for your team, for uniforms."[7]

"Plus, almost five hundred people traveled, stayed in hotels, and ate food," Thane said. "But the AAU paid for living expenses and transportation for the exhibition meets after the Olympics."[8]

"Well, I guess that cost an arm and a leg."

"Good thing Mr. Haylett let me hold on to those athletic shoes and socks I borrowed from K-State. Some guys got new shoes in Europe. But who wants to break in new shoes?"

Mother asked from the rear, "How did your trip back home go?"

Thane laughed, "Long, Mother, extremely long."

"We've got an hour's drive before we reach Elkhart. Why don't you tell us about it?" Father suggested.

"Alright." Thane said. He reached into his PAA bag and pulled out a map that PAA distributed with the airline route marked in red. Thane had covered the lines with his own markings and arrows, pointing to the way he flew. Thane passed the map back to Mother in the backseat. He experienced so many adventures. Where should he start?

"I stayed in London with the last of our US team still abroad. We left England about ten o'clock on Sunday evening. With stops for fuel, we arrived at New York City's La Guardia the next day."[9]

"That was quick!" Mother exclaimed.

275

Pan American World Airways Routes, 1952. Printed for Pan American World Airways, by C.S. Hammond & Co. *Courtesy of Brown Dog 2, successive owner, and the Thane Baker Collection.*

"A ship would require least a couple of weeks." Thane smiled. "The people of New York welcomed us when we returned. While our plane taxied on the runway, someone mounted the US and Olympic flags outside the pilot's windows, one on each side of the plane. Reporters greeted us and took our photographs.[10] I spent Monday night in the Paramount Hotel with my remaining Olympic team members. Some already left earlier in the day. I got closer to my teammates than I expected. I've got their addresses in case I want to write.

"Tuesday morning, I flew to Dallas. I caught a small plane to Waco, Texas."

"Didn't you go to meet a girl?" Mother asked, leaning forward from the backseat.

"I did. She was never more than a good friend." Thane explained when he arrived in Waco, he got to meet her new boyfriend. But the local radio and newspapers interviewed him while he was there.[11] Thane wanted to come home earlier, but today was the first day he could catch a flight from Waco to Liberal. He explained that the US Olympic Committee covered the cost of his journey. They said the athletes could fly wherever they wanted if it wasn't farther than their home.

Thane looked out the window. A meadowlark sat on a barbed-wire fence. Without trees or tall buildings to interfere, the sky flowed on forever. After the crowded cities of London and Vienna, and the trees of Finland, Thane enjoyed the surrounding plains.[12]

Kansas.

Home.

"With this break in the weather, we'll get a cool spell for a while," Father commented.

Thane shuddered. "Don't talk to me about cold. The Olympics were cold, windy, and wet. It rained seven of the eight days of track and field competition like a wet, early spring at home. I swear I was never dry. I hung my wet clothes up every night, and I put them on, damp, the next day!"

"In July?" Mother asked, shocked.

"Helsinki sits on a bay that connects to the North Sea. The northern third of Finland rests in the Arctic Circle. Between the wind and water, it was cold. After the Olympics, we competed in exhibition tours in Turku, Finland, London, Vienna, and back to London. Finland was my favorite. You've never seen a sky so blue. I saved pictures, menus, maps, and papers from everywhere to show you."

Thane could smell the distant rain. Summer in Kansas, with its dirt, wheat, sorghum, alfalfa, weeds, and cattle, reminded Thane of Dorothy's saying, "There's no place like home."[13] Even though he traveled to almost mythical lands far away, the warmth of home beat weeks of track meets.

Mother cleared her throat. Thane turned around to face her.

"What is it, Mother?"

"I don't know, Thane. I can't quite put my finger on it. But you've changed."

Father turned his face from the road ahead to glance at Thane.

"For the better or worse, Mother," Thane teased.

"Better," Mother laughed. "But you're not the boy who left here. You've grown up."

"Isn't that what I'm supposed to do?"

"Yes, but it happened overnight."

"Travel will do that to a person, Mother. The important parts of me remain unchanged."

"Of course. I'm just being silly." Mother rested her hand on Thane's shoulder. "Everyone here has been so excited about all your adventures."

"Folks sent me telegrams. I appreciated the support."

"The Federated Store kept all your trophies and medals in their window display all summer long. I used to walk by them on my lunch break to look at them." Father added.

Mother said she and Father had driven to Hugoton, Kansas, to watch a newsreel showing Thane in the Olympic Tryouts in Los Angeles and then boarding the plane for New York.[14] Friends from all over cut out newspaper articles for the family.[15] Thane looked forward to reading them.

Father joined in. "We learned of your winning a silver medal in the Olympics on the day of your event. Moon Mullins, the athletic director from Kansas State, called us and congratulated us on your achievement. A fifteen-minute, long-distance, telephone call!"

The length and expense of the telephone call shocked both his parents. They told him the athletic director also sent a telegram to the mayor of Elkhart congratulating him on producing an "All-American boy." Mother told him the local paper printed Thane's high school graduation picture, and the *Wichita Beacon* had a photograph of Thane crouching down and setting his blocks.[16]

Thane leaned his head back toward Mother. "The photographer staged that one. He asked me to pretend to fix a set of blocks."

"How did it feel to win the Olympic medal?"

"Unbelievable. So much to share. Where do I start? My dream came true. Overwhelming."

The first heavy drops of rain fell. Father turned on the windshield wipers. Everyone cranked up their windows. Thane left an opening at the top. He loved Kansas in the rain.

Mother leaned forward again. "When can I see your medal?"

Thane laughed. He pulled it out of his pocket. "Here you go, Mother. I hope this is my medal. We passed them around, looking at them after our competitions.[17] Who knows? I might have someone else's silver medal, and he holds mine. But they all look the same."

"It's heavy." Mother turned the medal over in her hands. "These men aren't wearing many clothes."

Thane chuckled. "Mother, not only did we wear clothes, but as soon as our race finished, we put more clothes on as fast as possible to warm ourselves. I always kept the medal close, so I wouldn't lose it."

Mother moved closer behind Thane. She almost bounced in her seat. "I have news for you. The businesses in town got together and planned a barbeque for the entire town in your honor. Friday night up at the high school. It's in the newspaper. Everybody wants to hear about your trip."[18]

"That's nice of them." Thane sat in silence for a time. "I'm grateful. These people are so nice, but I almost dreaded coming home. I want to say hello to everybody, of course. But I prefer no one notices me. I want to go fishing, drown a worm. Sit by the fireplace and think about the last two months. School starts on September 1, and I have so much to do. It's time to earn money at the Ford garage." Thane sighed. "I wouldn't have missed my Olympic adventures for anything. I tried to appreciate every moment, to listen to everything, to absorb as much as I could. I'll never have that opportunity again. Everything leading up to my race, running in the Olympics, and afterward." Thane paused for

Reverse of the 1952 Olympic silver medal. *Photograph by author. Courtesy of the Thane Baker Collection.*

a moment. "They were the greatest experiences of my life. I never expected this to happen to me, especially since the doctor told me I couldn't run anymore."

The rain stopped as suddenly as it began. Father pulled the car into the driveway. He patted Thane's knee. "We'll have more moments to share this. Maybe we'll go fishing and drown a worm with you."

As Thane stepped out of the car, his sister, Ruthene, bolted out of the house, ran down the steps, and hugged him. "I'm so proud of you, Thane. You did it! Earned a medal in the Olympics!"

Thane laughed. "It's good to be home." He hugged Ruthene back. "What are you doing in town? Is Larry here, too?"[19]

"He couldn't get away," Ruthene answered with a sparkle in her eyes. "Let me go." Ruthene wriggled out of his arms. "We have something important to do. Close your eyes." Ruthene stood beside him. She held Thane's elbow with one hand and covered his eyes with her other.

"What's this all about?"

Ruthene led Thane across the grass. "Open your eyes."

"Why's this car here?"

Father cleared his throat. "A 1946 Ford Business Coupe. Straight-six engine."[20]

"I figured that out, Father, but why is this car in front of our house?"

"It's yours, son."

"For me?" Thane's jaw dropped open. He swung around and grabbed Father. "Thank you, thank you!"

"Well, I figured with you spending your summer running all over the place, you didn't earn any money. Knew you'd been trying to set aside enough to buy a car."

Mother bragged. "Father found this tan-colored coupe sitting next to a fence row in a farmer's field. He paid cash and brought it back to the Ford garage. Every night after dinner, he'd go back to the shop to fix it up for you."

"The coupe only has the one bench seat in front. Three people can sit acrost. No radio or clock. Could use a paint job." Father said.

"My own car!" Thane huffed. "It's perfect!"

"Happy to do this for you, son." Tears flowed from both Thane and Father's eyes.

Thane walked around the car under the cottonwood tree. He touched the large fenders over each wheel. The raised front hood and large grill made it look powerful. Thane turned to Father. "I'll think I'll sit in her for a spell."

Father chuckled, "Well, I'd expect you to."

Thane opened the driver's side door. Ruthene got into the passenger side. The evening rain had cooled off the air.

Ruthene rolled down the larger window and opened the triangle-shaped window next to the front windshield. "Mother said Father worked so hard on this car."

Stunned, Thane just sat and looked through the divided windshield. He glanced at the small oval back window through the rearview mirror. His father cleaned the car both inside and out. Everything shone. If Father fixed up this vehicle, Thane knew the motor would purr. He rested his hands on the large, thin steering wheel. His feet shifted between the accelerator, brake, and clutch. He tested the thin stick shift that came out of the right side of the steering column. His own automobile! An Olympic medal and a car!

"As much as you want to stay in that car," Mother smiled, "let's get inside and wash up. Ruthene picked green beans and tomatoes from the garden. She fixed the beans with bacon while we went to pick you up. We killed a nice, plump chicken that I'd been saving for your return. Now that you've finished training, you can eat the strawberry-rhubarb pie I made just for you. I know it's your favorite."

Mother led them back into the house. Thane glanced back at his car. He would take it to college. Plenty of time to get acquainted.

CHAPTER 18

Sharing the Dream at Thane Baker Day

FRIDAY, AUGUST 22, 1952, ELKHART, KANSAS

"Breakfast's ready," Mother hollered as she knocked on the stairway wall that led to Thane's basement room. Already awake and dressed, Thane grabbed a thick white envelope and left his cool room. As he climbed the stairs to the kitchen, the temperature increased. The coffee percolated as he entered the kitchen.

"Good morning, Mother."

"Morning, Thane. Sleep well?"

"Like a rock. I can't imagine why I'm still so tired." Thane set the envelope beside his plate, poured his Wheaties, and added milk.

"I'd guess it feels good to be in your own bed. You can relax." Father joined them and poured his corn flakes.

"You may be right. Remember that thick envelope I received in the mail yesterday?"

Father nodded. Mother asked, "Was it about the Olympics?"

"In a way. I met a nice girl in Finland named Tuija. We went dancing twice. The coaches ordered me to leave Helsinki before I said goodbye. I didn't know where she lived. She figured out that I came from Elkhart. The address says, 'Mr. Thane Baker, Elkhart, Kansas, USA.' The post office found me."

"What's in the envelope?" Mother asked.

"A magazine. I've already shown you the other material I picked up while overseas. I'm on page 19." Thane turned the magazine around for his mother and father on the other side of the table.

"But, Thane, what do these words mean on top of the picture?" Father asked.

"Well, that's written in Finnish: '200 m' and 'Andy Stanfield,' who won first place. I assume it says something about the race." Thane described the six finalists, including how he lost to McDonald Bailey in his semifinal race. He pointed out the photographs of the 100-meter finish, where his friend Dean Smith tied the winning time and finished fourth. In a photo, Dean stood with Bones Dillard, Lindy Remigino, and Andy Stanfield after their gold-medal-winning, 4x100-meter relay. He showed Bob Mathias and the two other Americans, who won gold, silver, and bronze in the decathlon.[1] In another photograph, Dillard and Jack Davis shook hands after winning first and second in the 110-meter-high hurdles.[2] Thane told them how he beat Bones, a four-time gold medalist in Vienna, but said that Dillard suffered an injury in that race. A picture of Bob Richards flying high over the pole vault impressed his parents, especially after Thane showed the wrap around Bob's hamstring and how he suffered to compete. Thane shared stories of the other athletes, including Emil Zátopek, who covered the front of the magazine.

Someone knocked at the door. Father answered. After a burst of excited conversation, Father brought back a full-page newspaper advertisement with Thane's name on the top. The businesses of Elkhart bought an ad in his name.

"I can't believe they'd do that. Spend all that money on me," Thane said.

"Folks here are all kinds of pleased for you, Thane. You're the best news we've had in a long time," Mother said.

Father said, "On my way home from work yesterday, I stopped by the open pit folks dug north of the school building. The meat

Full page honoring Thane Baker, signed by businesses in Elkhart, Kansas, August 22, 1952. *Courtesy of the Elkhart Tri-State News and the Thane Baker collection.*

rested on poles laid over a burning pit. They started the fire about noon. By the time this evening comes around, the Junior Chamber of Commerce and Lions Club members will have roasted that meat for close to thirty hours. Rain or shine, the food will be delicious."[3]

"I'll need to fix my hair nice for this evening." Mother patted her head.

"Don't worry, Mother," Thane smiled. "You're beautiful. I'm the one who must give a speech."

Father cleared his throat and looked at his 1951 Kansas Relay watch, which Thane gave to Father last year. He was so proud of that watch.[4]

"Time to leave for work," Thane said. "We can talk more about these photographs later. The best news is, when Tuija sent this to me, she included her address. Now I can write her back. What will we do at the Ford garage today, Father?"

"Whatever rolls in the door."

Thane smiled at Father's old joke.

Thane drove Father downtown in his new-to-him two-door coupe. They kept the windows open. Early in the morning, the breeze made the summer heat tolerable.

"Funny thing about you being home from the Olympics, Thane. Seems like everyone in town wants to come into the shop. They say want to talk about their car, order a part, or get their oil changed. They just hope to talk to you, son. Shake your hand. Even though you're only here for a few weeks, the boss will make money having a celebrity around."

Thane grinned. "It's nice to see everyone. I recognize people everywhere I look. Back in early June, I joined Mr. Haylett and other K-State athletes to head west for competitions. He never missed a significant sight. Unfortunately, I was the only K-Stater who qualified for the Olympics. Traveling, I only knew my American teammates. I like to be in a country where I can read the street signs and understand what people are saying. I've heard many languages, but mostly Finnish and German."

"Too bad you never learned German from your grandparents, Thane."

"Might have helped in Vienna."

"What happened in Vienna?"

"Let's discuss that later." Thane parked the car downtown. "We better get to work."

That evening, Thane, Mother, and Father sat on folding chairs to the right of the microphone. Although the mercury climbed into the nineties today, the evening wind made it tolerable.[5] The townspeople erected a temporary wooden podium in front of the door to the high school. Thane wore a white, short-sleeved shirt, tan pants, and his Olympic white buck shoes, still stained pink. The enormous wooden stand built in front of New York City Hall honored the Olympians. This low 8x10-foot platform in front of his hometown school welcomed him better.

Dr. Buckmaster, emcee, shared the stage with them. He introduced the superintendent of schools, who gave the welcome.

Glenn Cunningham, the man who inspired seven-year-old Thane to try for the Olympics, surprised Thane by his appearance and spoke next. He drove three hundred miles to honor Thane on his special day. Mr. Cunningham said rarely did a town the size of Elkhart generate two Olympic medal winners in such a brief time. He claimed the confidence, courage, and clean living of the Elkhart citizens created an environment designed to produce greatness.[6]

Thane spoke at the microphone next. "I want to acknowledge the businesses of Elkhart for putting on this great barbeque for the entire town. You could've knocked me over with a feather when I opened the Tri-State News today. I am so honored that you got together and took out a full-page newspaper advertisement congratulating me and welcoming me home.[7] Thank you so much.

"We've smelled that barbeque cooking all day long. I won't speak for long. Some folks here are hungry. I sure appreciate all of you coming out." Thane looked back at his mother. Her face glowed with joy.

Glenn Cunningham, silver medalist in the 1936 Olympics and Thane's inspiration, speaks to the town, August 22, 1952. *Photographer unknown. Courtesy of the Thane Baker Collection.*

"Glenn Cunningham," Thane continued. "Did you have any idea when you visited Elkhart on your special day in 1939 that you would inspire another Olympic runner? If it weren't for you, I wouldn't be here today. We share another connection. Brutus Hamilton coached you at the University of Kansas all those years ago and served as head coach of the United States Track and Field team in Helsinki this summer. Talk about a small world! Glenn, thank you for inspiring me. And I'm grateful to you and your two daughters for driving all the way from Peabody to visit us today. You have always been my hero.

"Now, I want to introduce two more of my heroes. Walter and Susie Baker, please stand up. As most of you know, these are my parents." Everybody laughed. "My father has worked hard every day of his life. He inspired me always to do my best at whatever I

Thane Baker delivered his speech to Elkhart with Susie and Walt Baker, his proud parents, watching, August 22, 1952. *Photographer unknown. Courtesy of the Thane Baker Collection.*

do. He told me if I dug a ditch, to dig it deep and dig it straight. My mother timed my running for years using an old alarm clock without a second hand. Quite a trick. She told me to practice as hard as I could, because someone, somewhere, was coming around the corner, and might be just a little bit better. Well, one person ran faster than me during the 200-meter finals at the Olympic Games. I can live with that. Father, Mother, thank you for everything."

Both his parents were crying as he shook hands with Father and kissed Mother on the cheek.

"Although he's not here today, Ward Haylett, the track and field coach at Kansas State College, allowed me to walk on his team two-and-a-half years ago.. He taught me form, training, and speed. Mr. Haylett always said, 'You're going to win more races above the shoulders than you are below.' He meant to run smart. And I'm

Thane Baker introduces his parents and holds his mother's hand, August 22, 1952. *Photographer unknown. Courtesy of the Thane Baker Collection.*

going to train with him this year with an Olympic medal that he made possible."

Thane looked out over the crowd. Cross-legged children sat on the grass on either side of the sidewalk, penned in by low stakes connected by string. The adults sat behind them in folding chairs or stood. "This part is for you kids out there. Find something you want to do. Find people who are good at that. Imitate, listen, and learn from them. And never give up.

"You kids are too young to remember. When Glenn Cunningham was young, he burned his legs badly. He couldn't walk for months. But he didn't give up. He walked, then he ran. Glenn Cunningham earned a silver medal in the 1936 Olympics. I watched him when I was young, like you. He ran with amazing grace and power. Because of him, I set my goal, to run in the Olympics.

"At fourteen, a piece of steel stabbed under my kneecap. Two different doctors operated but couldn't remove the steel. One doctor told me to quit athletics. It took some time before I could run. But I got the doctor's permission to try again. I stand before you today and with that metal in my knee." Thane choked. His eyes watered. He had to clear his throat. "I didn't quit." Thane inhaled a deep breath and blew air through his lips. "I earned an Olympic medal." He swallowed and blinked. With a hoarse voice, he continued. "Maybe one of you will win an Olympic medal or do something else as wonderful. Never give up." Thane sniffed. He cleared his throat.

"Finally, thank you, my friends and family, for your support over the years. From my neighbor, who mowed a track for kids to run on in a nearby vacant lot, to my friends who raced against me, words cannot express how grateful I am to all of you. Your telegrams meant so much while I traveled far from home. Thank you for your support.

"I want to thank the cooks who prepared the meat, barbeque sandwiches, potato chips, and soft drinks. Thank you all for coming. Let's eat."

Everyone clapped and clapped. Thane ducked his head and raised one hand to wave, embarrassed by the attention.

Thane spent the evening shaking hands, talking, hugging, and laughing. As he mingled, Thane compared the meals he ate at New York City's Waldorf Astoria, Helsinki's Olympic Village restaurant tent, Vienna's multi-course meal, and London's The Dorchester against the paper plate he held in his hand. Those meals he experienced happened once in a lifetime, but he enjoyed this meal at home more, with the people who shared his life from its beginning.

A great deal had changed in the last thirteen years for the citizens of Elkhart. During the Depression, people hardly had enough money for food and clothing. The families around him today looked comfortable. And the businesses donated a full meal for over six hundred people.

As the evening advanced, Thane's confidence grew.

Lit by one bulb stuck high on a pole with a wire leading away from it, the party progressed late into the evening. Friends who had

The Thane Baker Day picnic begins, August 22, 1952. *Photographer unknown. Courtesy of the Thane Baker Collection.*

The party lasted late into the night, August 22, 1952. *Photographer unknown. Courtesy of the Thane Baker Collection.*

known each other in tough times and better times came together to celebrate one of their own.

Thane ambled over to Mother and Father. He wrapped an arm around each of them. "I did it. I set a goal and completed it. Remember when you said if I followed my dream, I would go on a long journey full of adventure? I sure did. Without you two, I wouldn't have made the Olympic team. Thank you."

"Believe it, Thane," Mother answered. "You earned this."

Father cleared his throat. "Proud of you, son."

APPENDIX 1

Thane Baker's Autographs of the 1952 United States Track and Field Olympians[1]

100 METERS

To Thane
From Lindy Remigino
100 m   10.4
N.Y. N.Y
Gold medal (100m)
Gold medal (4x100)

May our friendship last forever and may this trip and competition make us better friends in the future.
Dean Southpaw Smith
100 meters, Univ. of Texas
I still think you have the fastest finish of any boy I have ever run against.
Gold medal (4x100)
4th place (100m)

Best of luck always
Arthur Bragg
100 meters 10.4
Morgan State College
6th place (semi-finals, heat 1)

200 METERS

To Thane,
In remembrance of our clean sweep in the 1952 Olympics—
Keep up your fine running.
Sincerely, Andy Stanfield
Seton Hall University
Graduated Feb. 1952
Gold medal (200 m)
Tied the Olympic Record with Jesse Owens
Gold medal (4x100)

To Thane—
A great champion
Keep up the good work.
Jim Gathers
200 meters
Tillotson College
Bronze medal

400 METERS

It has been nice being on the same trip, and I know that in the next one, you will do better. I know that you can because you seem to have the heart to win.
Ollie Matson 400 meter
Bronze medal

To an Olympic winner,
My best always.
Gene Cole
400 meters
1600-meter rel.
Ohio State University
Silver medal in the 4x400
400 m: Semi-Finals
4th place (heat 1)

To a big seven sprinter and a great guy. The best of luck in years to come. See you next year in the big seven. Best of luck always. Take care of the women at K.S.
J.W. Mashburn
400-meters USA, 1952 Olympics
Oklahoma University
Did not start.

800 METERS

Best wishes to you.
May the hinges of our friendship shell never rust.
Mal Whitfield
U.S.A. Olympian
Gold medal, 800 meters,
Olympic Record
Silver Medal (4x400)
6th place (400 m)

Here's to a series of 20.4s.
Reggie Pearman
800 meters
7th place

Thane,
Your running in the Olympic Games was a thrill.
Sincerely wish you every success in the future,
John Barnes, 800 meters run.
4th place (semi-finals, heat 2)

1,500 METERS

To a great sprinter and a great guy.
It's been a pleasure to be your teammate.
Bob McMillen
Occidental College
1500er-3:45.2
Silver medal
American record

Hi there Thane,
Best of luck in all things.
Warren Druetzler
1,500,
Formerly of Michigan State College
12th place

Hope you win them all!
Next year-1953.
J. Montez
1500 m
T.W.C., formerly of Michigan State College
[Texas Western College, now the University of Texas at El Paso]
6th place (first round, heat 5)

5,000 METERS

To Thane,
I wish you the very best of luck in your future running, and I am sure that you will do your very best whenever you compete.
May God Bless You Always,
And may you never let Him down.
Sincerely,
Charlie Capozzoli
5,000
7th place (heat 1)
Curtis C. Stone
5,000 & 10,000 m.
New York A. C. [Athletic Club]
Penn State '47
8th place (5,000 m, heat 3)
20th place (10,000 m)

Thane,
It has certainly been great being a teammate of yours in these 1952 Olympics. I shall always remember these days and of course the great battle between
ole K.U. and K-State.
Best of luck in the future.
Wes Santee
Univ. of Kansas
5000 meters
13th place (heat 2)

10,000 METERS

Best wishes to a great sprinter and a fine fellow.
Sincerely,
Fred Wilt, Indiana
21st place

MARATHON

Vic Dyrgal
USA – Marathon
Univ. of Idaho
13th place

Tom Jones
Marathon
Earlham College
West Grove, Pennsa.
36th place

Theodore Corbitt
USA Marathon
University of Cincinnati
44th place

110-METER HURDLES

Good luck & best wishes,
Harrison Dillard, 110-meter hurdles
B-W [Baldwin Wallace College]
Gold medal and Olympic record (110 m hurdles)
Gold medal (4x100)

Best Wishes
Jack W. Davis
110 M HH 1952-1956
Silver medal

Art Barnard
110 m and at La Jolla, Calif.
Navy-ex. USC
Bronze medal

400-METER HURDLES

Best Wishes
Charlie Moore
400 m. hurdles
Cornell U.
Gold medal
Olympic record

Thane Baker—
One of the Olympic greats who came through in great style. Don't stop now—
You are just starting.
Lee Yoder
400 M. Hurdles
U of Arkansas
4th place in semi-finals, Heat 2

To a real great guy
A team member
Lots of luck, Thane
Roland Blackman
400 m-hurdles
U.S. Army
5th place in semi-finals, heat 1

3000-METER STEEPLECHASE

Best of luck always Thane
H. Ashenfelter Penn State
3000 m Steeplechase
Gold medal
Olympic record

Browning Ross
Villanova College Steeplechase
12th place (heat 2)

Bill Ashenfelter
3000 m. Steeplechase
Pennsylvania State College
1952
Did not finish

10-KILOMETER RACEWALK

To a great athlete and swell guy—
Best wishes and lots of luck in future competitions.
Henry Laskau
10,000-meter walk
Disqualified

To Thane
With best wishes for future success
Price King
10,000-meter walk
Univ. of California
9th place (heat 2)

50-KILOMETER RACEWALK

To Thane!
Best of luck & success in everything you may do.
Sincerely,
Dr. Adolf Weinacker
50-kilo Walk   4 hr. 47 minutes
Michigan State '51
22nd place

Best Wishes.
See you in 1956.
John M. Deni
50-Kilo Walk
London 1948 Helsinki 1952
Pgh. Pa. [Pittsburgh]
Did not finish

Leo Sjogren
50,000-m Walk
4313 9th Ave
Brooklyn, N.Y. U.S.A.
Did not finish

HIGH JUMP

Walter Davis
High Jump
Texas A & M
Gold medal
Olympic record

Congratulations on your performance. Good luck.
Marquette Univ.
Ken Wiesner
Hi Jump
Milwaukee
Silver medal

To a real friend & a great competitor. May only the best be yours.
I am Arny Betton
Drake U.
7th place

POLE VAULT

To a great guy who almost won the Olympic Games—
Best always Thane.
God bless you.
Bob Richards
Pole Vault
USA
Gold medal

Don R. Laz
Univ. of Illinois
2nd Olympic Pole Vault '52
Silver medal

Best of luck to a great guy & a terrific athlete.
George Mattos
Pole vault 14' 5 3/8"
Ex-San Jose State
9th place

LONG JUMP

May success always follow you.
Jerome Biffle
Broad Jump 24.10 ½
University of Denver
Gold medal

Best of luck.
Meredith Gourdine
Broad Jump 1952
[Cornell Univ.]
Silver medal

To Thane Baker,
I think that your performance in the Olympic Games and the Olympic Trials was one of the greatest exhibitions of determination I have ever seen.
George Brown,
Broad Jump,
U.C.L.A.
12th place, tie

HOP, STEP, AND JUMP

Best of everything in the future.
Walt Ashbaugh
Hop, Step, Jump- 50' 8¾"
Cornell University
4th place

To Thane, a great sprinter now, and a boy whom I think will be the greatest sprinter in the world.
Jim Gerhardt
Hop-Step-Jump
Rice Institute
11th place

Best of luck to the '56 200 meter Champion.
George Shaw
Hop, Step, and Jump
Columbia U.
Did not qualify for the finals

SHOT PUT

Thane:
It's been a pleasure traveling with you.
Sincerely,
Parry O'Brien
Shot Put
SC [University of Southern California]
Gold medal
Olympic record

Best Wishes Always, Thane!!
Darrow Hooper
Texas A & M College
Shot Put
Silver Medal 1952
17.39 meters

It certainly has been a pleasure to have been on this team & associate with you, Thane. Best wishes always from your friend.
Jim Fuchs
Shot put Yale
Bronze medal
World record holder

DISCUS THROW

Sim Iness
Discus #1
USC (University of Southern California)
Gold medal
Olympic record

To the best
Jim Dillon
Alabama Poly
Discus Bronze Medal
174' 10"
Bronze medal

Thanks.
Good luck.
Fortune Gordien
1952
USA Olympics
4th place
World record holder

HAMMER THROW

Sam Felton
Hammer
Harvard-NYAC (New York Athletic Club)
187' 7¼"
11th place

Good luck, old man!
Bob Backus
Hammer
Tufts College-NYAC
176' ¾"
13th place

Martin Engel
Hammer 182' 5"
N.Y.U. [New York University]
Fouled three times in finals

JAVELIN THROW

To a great guy!
Cy Young U.C.L.A.
Javelin Champ, 242'1"
Gold medal
Olympic record

Best of luck to you, Thane.
Hope you have continued success in life
and in your athletic career.
Bill Miller
Javelin, U.S.A.
Silver medal

Thane,
To a pool player in Princeton.
Bud Held
B.S. Stanford 1950
M.S. Univ. of Calif. 1952
Entering San Anselmo Theological Seminary,
Javelin, 249' 8 ½" [1951 US record]
9th place

DECATHLON

Best Wishes
Bob Mathias
Stanford
Gold medal
World record
Olympic record

Milton
Campbell
Decathlon
Plainfield High School
U.S.A.
Silver medal

Thane, a real pleasure knowing you
and being on the same team.
Floyd M. Simmons
Decathlon
Bronze medal

UNITED STATES COACHES

To Thane who represents his country and Mrs. Hamilton's
Alma Mater so nobly and well. Every good wish.
Brutus Hamilton
University of California
Head Coach

To a great fellow
Clyde Littlefield
Coach U.S.A.
The University of Texas

Larry Snyder
Coach USA 1952
Ohio State U-

Best wishes always to a great fellow. Nice going, Thane.
Chic Werner
One of the coaches '52
[Penn State]

UNITED STATES MANAGERS

*To my good friend, Thane—a fine fellow & a helluva sprinter—
best always.*
Bob Kane
Manager
Cornell University
Ithaca NY
Head Manager

*Congratulations to a mighty fine athlete and a sterling gentleman.
May you have continuing success in your future years.*
Larry Houston
Assistant Manager
Los Angeles, Calif.
U.C.L.A.

*To Thane Baker
For the fondest memories of a most memorable trip.*
Pincus Sober
1540 Broadway
New York 36, N.Y.
C.C.N.Y. – 1926
Fordham Univ. – 1929

*To Thane Baker—
a wonderful guy to have along on the greatest Olympic Team ever
fielded by the United States.*
Harold Berliner,
Assistant Manager
10 Crown Terrace
San Francisco
Helsinki, Finland
July 27, 1952

UNITED STATES TRAINERS

Congratulations on your success on the Olympic team. It has been a pleasure to work with you and we will meet again.
Ken Howard
Trainer A.P.I. [Alabama Polytechnic Institute]
Auburn, Alabama

When your pains are aches
Be sure to think of
Eddie Wojecki Trainer
Rice Institute Houston Texas

Ike Hill
Trainer
U of Illinois

UNITED STATES DIVING

You sweet thing—
What a great team we had.
With Love & Hugs
Pat McCormick
Gold medal (3 m Springboard)
Gold medal (10 m Platform)

Rx
Good Health
Sammy Lee, M.D.
Gold medal (10 m Platform)

UNITED STATES ROWING

Thane: The Best of Luck.
Tom Price
Rowing '52
Gold medal (Coxless Pairs)[2]

APPENDIX 2

Fiftieth Reunion of the 1952 United States Olympic Teams

On Tuesday, March 26, 2002, the 1952 United States Summer and Winter Olympic Teams gathered at the New York Athletic Club in New York City for their fifty-year reunion.[1] That evening from six to nine, the NYAC hosted a reception in their Hall of Fame room on the second floor. Thane and Sally, his wife of forty-eight years, checked into the reception together.[2] The hosts prepared name tags for the Olympians, but not their spouses. Thane thought some of his friends looked the same as they did in 1952. Others he would not have recognized without their name tags. Thane brought his 1952 Olympic autograph book and asked the athletes to sign their name again on the same page that they signed fifty years earlier.

> *50 years later, I repeat the wish-Harrison Dillard 3/26/02.*
> *Great being with you J.W. Mashburn '02*
> *To my best friend at Helsinki: Thane Baker Lindy Remigino 3-26-02*
> *All the best Bob Mathias March 26, 2002, NYAC*

A handout that evening stated that men must always wear a jacket and tie inside the NYAC. The club would not permit women to enter the club wearing pants or pants suits. Sally Baker, the fifteen other wives, and the female Olympians just looked at each other. Many of them were in their seventies and had not packed a skirt to come to New York City in March. No one enforced the rule against the women wearing pants.

That night, the track and field Olympians, with twenty-three athletes, far outnumbered the participants from other sports. They also formed the largest contingent during the 1952 Games. Eight swimmers, four divers, two water polo athletes, three rowers, and one kayak/canoe racer represented aquatic sports. Two Modern Pentathletes (horseback riding, fencing, shooting, swimming, and running), one gymnast, and one wrestler completed the Summer Olympic contingent. From the 1952 Winter Olympics, four members of the Ice Hockey team, two skiers, and one speed skater came to the event. Fourteen women and thirty-nine men composed the fifty-three Olympians who visited New York to celebrate their fiftieth.

Wednesday morning at ten, Thane and Sally Baker joined the other 1952 Olympians with some of their spouses for a press reception at the NYAC. After getting their coffee and donuts, the organizers asked everyone to please find a chair. On Thane's left sat Dr. Sammy Lee, an ear, nose, and throat doctor, who had won back-to-back gold medals in platform diving in 1948 and 1952 and served as an Army doctor during the Korean War.[3] Sally sat on Thane's right next to Congressional Representative Bob Mathias. After decathlon gold medals in 1948 and 1952, Mathias had worked in the Marine Corps, Hollywood, the US House of Representatives for four terms, and was the first director of the US Olympic Training Center in Colorado Springs.[4]

Some athletes gave speeches.

Photographers took pictures of various groups of athletes. Thane stood by Darrow Hooper, Lindy Remigino, Horace Ashenfelter and Dean Smith for one picture.

Before the event finished, a reporter asked the spouses to discuss what it was like to be married to an Olympian. Bob Mathias and

The 1952 United States Olympians at New York City Hall, March 27, 2002. Credit: Photograph by Sally Baker. *Courtesy of the Thane Baker Collection.*

Thane nominated Thane's wife, Sally, for the impromptu speech.

At noon, the Olympians and their wives enjoyed a buffet lunch of a broth soup with cabbage, bread, lunch meat, and brownies. Sally and Thane Baker sat with the Director of the NYAC. During lunch, someone announced that the wives could not go on the tour of New York City because there was not enough room on the bus after seating the athletes and press. Sally talked to the NYAC Director about this problem.

At one o'clock, everyone boarded the bus. Somehow, everyone fit. Some wives sat in their husbands' laps, and several members of the press stood in the aisle. The first stop was the New York City Hall. Fifty years ago, the athletes visited this building. The Olympians posed on its steps in the 53 degree weather. Dean Smith wore his white cowboy hat. Lindy Remigino and Sammy Lee wore their 1952 Olympic dress uniform blazers. At 1:30 p.m., Deputy Mayor Dan Doctoroff greeted the Olympians and took them on a tour of City Hall.

Next, the bus took the Olympians, wives, and press members

Thane and Sally Baker enjoy the 50th Reunion of the 1952 Olympians, March 27, 2002. *Courtesy of the Thane Baker Collection.*

to the VIP area of Ground Zero, where the World Trade Center buildings fell six months earlier. Mementos of those who died, flowers, and one note that said, "Mommy, we miss you," covered the walls. A chaplain for the New York Fire Department delivered a heart-wrenching prayer. The bus returned everyone to the NYAC a little after 3:30 p.m. for the riders to prepare for their evening event.

At 5:30 p.m., the 1952 Olympians and their spouses boarded the bus again. That night, they gathered for a black-tie event at the Waldorf Astoria, the site of the luncheon the Summer Olympians enjoyed on July 7, 1952. Thane wore a purple cummerbund and tie in honor of his alma mater, Kansas State. The tabletop flower arrangements in the foyer stood five feet tall. Beautiful crystal chandeliers hung from the ceiling. Someone took Thane and Sally's photograph on Sally's camera as they entered the hotel.

Escorts took the Olympians to the Conrad Suite on the fourth floor to meet Ian Thorpe and former New York City Mayor Rudolph Giuliani. Sally took a picture of Thane and Rudy.

The Olympians then progressed to the West Foyer on the third floor for the VIP reception. Charlie Moore, gold medalist in the 400-meter hurdles, and Thane caught up there. Charlie had entered his family's steel business, then became CEO of several international manufacturing companies. He served on the US Olympic Committee as public sector director and chair of the audit committee. Charlie said he donated his Olympic medals to his high school because he could not divide his two medals among nine children.[5]

J. W. Mashburn went into real estate in Oklahoma and did well for himself. His family joined him in the business. Wes Santee sold insurance, and he still bragged. This time, he told everyone how much he paid for a Broadway show. The old friends continued to tease each other, just as they did fifty years earlier.

Mal Whitfield had triumphed in the 800-meters in both the 1948 and 1952 Olympics, along with gold and silver in the 4x400-meter relays in those two Olympics. He spent years working in Africa on behalf of the United States Information Service. He coached, mentored, and promoted good will during his tenure there.[6]

Dean Smith went to Hollywood, where he worked as a stuntman in ninety-two film projects and an actor in sixty three.[7] Lindy Remigino told Thane that he married after his two gold medals in the 1952 Olympics, started his family, and coached high school

Charles H. Moore Jr. and Thane Baker, March 27, 2002. *Photograph by Sally Baker. Courtesy of the Thane Baker Collection.*

Left to right: Dean Smith, J. W. Mashburn, Thane Baker, and Wes Santee at the Waldorf Astoria, March 27, 2002. *Photograph by Sally Baker. Courtesy of the Thane Baker Collection.*

Mal Whitfield and Thane Baker, March 27, 2002. *Photograph by Sally Baker. Converted to black and white. Courtesy of the Thane Baker Collection.*

track and field in Hartford, Connecticut.[8]

Thane discovered the seating chart placed him on the dais for honored guests, perhaps because of his gold medal in 1956. The 1952 gold medalists processed in from the back to join Thane at the raised table. Dinner included a tart filled with cheese sauce and cooked vegetables, Parmesan crusted chicken breast with asparagus, and risotto. For dessert, they ate chocolate cake, cookies, and candy.

The program honored Ian Thorpe, a seventeen-year-old swimmer from Australia. He received the American-International Athlete Trophy because he won three gold and two silver medals in the 2000 Sydney Olympics. Someone loaned him a tuxedo jacket for his acceptance speech. Former Mayor Giuliani received the American Global Award for Peace for his work after 9/11. The speaker introduced all fifty-three Olympians. Everyone agreed the 1952 Olympic Team needed to get together soon.

At ten o'clock, the long program ended. Thane and Sally took the elevator downstairs and joined the others back on the bus. Someone stuck their head out and announced that the reception would continue for another hour. Everyone could either sit on the bus until eleven or come back and join the party. After he got off, the bus driver looked at his tired passengers in their seventh decade of life and announced he would leave for the NYAC now.

Thursday, the Bakers walked around New York, finished their fourth roll of 35-millimeter film, and flew back to Dallas. Thane and Sally were glad they visited Thane's old friends, many of whom Sally met for the first time. The 1952 United States Olympic Team never met again.

APPENDIX 3

Thane Baker's Lifetime Accomplishments

Thane Baker loved to run and enjoyed the friendships he formed on the track, but those composed only part of his history.

Thane Baker earned gold, silver, and bronze medals in the 1956 Olympics held in Melbourne, Australia. His gold came from the 4x100-meter relay, which set an Olympic and world record of 39.5 seconds.[1] His silver medal in the 100 meters, which tied Bobby Morrow's winning time of 10.5 seconds, surprised the world.[2] In the 200 meters, Andy Stanfield, who beat Thane in 1952, once again finished ahead of him. But Bobby Morrow finished in front of both.[3] Thane Baker returned home in 1956 with an Olympic medal of each color. He entered four Olympic events in his life and medaled in all four.

Stopwatches recorded Thane Baker's best times before electronic timers and artificial tracks. Colleges in the United States and the British Empire ran in yards rather than meters. While attending Kansas State, Thane Baker twice tied the indoor 60-yard world record at 6.1 seconds.[4] On June 18, 1953, Thane held the best college times in America in three events: 100 yards at 9.4 seconds, 220 yards at 20.4 seconds, and the 440 yards at 47.1 seconds.[5] At the NCAA national championships in 1953, Thane won the

220 yards and placed second in the 100 yards.[6] At the Ohio State Relays in 1956, Thane set a new world record in the 300 meters, at 29.4, which broke a ten-year-old record.[7] Thane Baker beat Andy Stanfield, the 1952 gold medalist, at the 1956 National AAU Championships and tied his world record time by running the 200 meters in 20.6.[8] Contemporary newspapers also reported that Thane tied the world record in the 100 meters at 10.2 seconds, but his name is not in the record books.[9] On December 5, 1956, after the Melbourne Olympics, Baker and three others set a world record in the 4 x 220-yard relay in Sydney, Australia.[10] After that Olympics, family and work commitments ended his running career.

At age forty, Thane laced up his spikes again. In 1971, he and others began the Masters Track competitions. He traveled to Europe for a month in 1972 with men from the United States, Canada, and Australia to encourage others over forty years of age to run. Thane's name lives in the Masters world records in the 100 meters for men ages 40-44 at 10.7 seconds, which was only five-tenths of a second slower than his personal best in 1956. His world record in the 45-49 bracket was 10.8 seconds. In the 50-54 category, his world record 100-meter time slowed to 11.4 seconds. In the 55-59-year-old group, he returned to Melbourne, Australia to run 11.65, which was only three-hundredths of a second off the world record for that age group.[11]

With the 200 meters, Thane established Masters world marks in the 40-44-year age group at 22.2 seconds and for 50-54-year-olds, 23.4 seconds.[12] He competed in world championships in Germany, Italy, Canada, Australia, Puerto Rico, and the continental United States. He also set a record at 220 yards and ran on record-setting relays in 4x100, 4x200, 4x400-meter relay teams, and the sprint medley relay.

Thane Baker married Sally Baker in 1954, who stayed by his side for sixty-six years. He also joined the Air Force and served in Germany. He retired after thirty years as a colonel and squadron commander in the Air Force Reserve. Thane Baker worked for

Thane Baker set the world record in the 100 m for the over-forty men age category in 10.7. seconds in Cologne, Germany, 1972. *Courtesy of the photographer Inéz Kissels-Pohley.*

thirty-nine years and fifteen days, first for Magnolia Petroleum Company, then Mobil Oil Corporation, and finally for Mobil Research and Development Corporation, where he retired as a Material and Transportation Manager with recognition as a Certified Purchasing Manager.

From 1959 to 2015, Thane shot the gun to start other runners in their races. The Texas Relays, where he officiated for almost fifty years, NCAAs, National Federation, Border Olympics, US versus the Soviet Union, Texas Christian and North Texas Universities,

Texas high school championships, college conference meets, and others kept him busy during the spring and early summer. He also helped organize Masters meets in Dallas for several years. These activities led to other volunteer commitments.

In the late 50s and early 60s, Thane belonged to the Chicago Chapter of the Olympians. Since he lived in Dallas, Thane became the first president and co-organizer of the Southwestern Chapter of US Olympians. He again served a term as their president in the early 70s. In July 2021, the Southwest Olympic alumni held a birthday party for Dean Smith and Thane to coincide with the Tokyo Olympics.

Thane volunteered on the Board of Directors for the US Olympians, the Cotton Bowl Athletic Association, the Dallas Area 2012 and 2020 Olympic Bid Committee, and the Dallas Metropolitan March of Dimes. He functioned as a member of the Dallas All Sports Association, the Mobil Management Association, the organizing committee for the United Way of Hood County, and the committee to bring a YMCA to Granbury, Texas. The Hood County YMCA presented Thane and Sally with the Volunteer of the Year Award. He also served as Rotary Club President, Mobil Lab United Way chair, and in many church offices, in addition to his work for other charities, including delivering Meals on Wheels. When invited, he spoke to organizations and instructed young people about track.

Thane's dedication to Kansas State University never wavered. Thane and his wife, Sally, served as members of the K-State Alumni Board of Directors and the K-State Foundation Trustees. Thane and Sally funded two scholarships at Kansas State.

Awards followed Thane's athletic prowess. The Amateur Athletic Union of the United States picked Thane Baker to the 1952 All-College Track and Field Team for the 220-yard dash. He received a nomination for the James E. Sullivan Award in 1956 and garnered the third highest number of votes that year. Thane belongs to the Kansas Sports Hall of Fame and the Kansas Activities Hall of

Thane Baker starts a race at the TCU Invitational, March 16, 2012. *Photograph by Wayne Dunlap. Converted to black and white. Courtesy of Wayne Dunlap.*

Left to right: Dean Smith and Thane Baker honored at the Southwest Chapter of the U.S. Olympians Opening Ceremony Watch Party held at Fair Park, Dallas, Texas, July 23, 2021. *Photograph by author.*

Fame. KSU inducted Thane into the inaugural class of their Sports Hall of Fame in 1990. In Texas, where he started so many track meets, Thane also is in the Texas Track and Field Coaches Hall of Fame. Given his world records over age forty, the US Masters Track and Field Association also brought him into their Hall of Fame. Among his many awards, Thane appreciated receiving an NCAA Silver Anniversary Award, given to an NCAA student-athlete who "has achieved personal distinction" in the twenty-five years after his graduation.[13] Sally volunteered as well and received a Distinguished Service Award for her outstanding work for the Department of Human Ecology at KSU.

Thane Baker volunteered at an Olympic Development Program offered at Walnut Hills Recreation Center in Dallas, Texas, early 1960s. Courtesy of the Thane Baker Collection.

After Sally and Thane Baker became empty nesters, they took a two-week trip every year for thirty-four years and filled multiple scrapbooks. Thane saw Tuija, his 1952 dance partner, several times, and they continued their correspondence for the rest of Tuija's life.[14] Thane said he visited over fifty different countries in his lifetime and ran races in most of them.

Tuija Timonen Suojärvi and Thane Baker, 2005. *Photograph by Sally Baker. Converted to black and white. Courtesy of the Thane Baker Collection.*

When possible, Thane connected with his 1952 Olympic friends. Dean Smith, Bob Richards, and other Olympians lived in Texas. J.W. Mashburn was nearby in Oklahoma. He met Reggie Pearman, an 800-meter runner. Thane and Charlie Moore, 400-meter hurdles, discussed Dallas as a potential site for the 2012 Olympics. There are few still alive today.

During the 2023 Homecoming weekend, Cliff Rovelto, head track and field coach for Kansas State University, and Gene Taylor, K-State Athletic Director, surprised Thane by dedicating a bronze bust which portrayed his collegiate running days. Overwhelmed at first, Thane rallied to speak.

"I wish there was some way I could express to all of you that K-State and track was the greatest thing that ever happened in my life," Baker told the audience at the K-Club event as he choked back the tears. "It opened doors and made me have opportunities to run in two Olympics and earn four Olympic medals. Without K-State, that would not have been possible. Glenn Cunningham . . . was my hero. . . and he ran down main street after the '36 Olympics, and I said, 'I want to go to the Olympics someday.' That

Thane Baker and Reginald "Reggie" Pearman PhD, seventh in the final of the Men's 800 m in the 1952 Helsinki Olympics. Oklahoma, August 1989. *Photograph by Sally Baker. Converted to black and white. Courtesy of the Thane Baker Collection.*

was my dream." Baker struggled to continue. "That was my dream. Thanks to Kansas State my dream came true."

The following day, Thane and his family and friends went onto the football field where the university recognized his accomplishments with images on the big screens. The sold-out crowd gave Thane a standing ovation.[15]

The world knows Thane Baker as a world record holder and an Olympic Champion, but that is only part of his story.[16] A faithful church attendee, he cried when a man landed on the moon and when he discovered he made Air Force Colonel. He changed his own oil in his cars until his late eighties. Thane likes to say he invested in the future. He seldom bought coffee at work and brown-bagged his lunch to save money. Used cars, bought for a fair price, maintained, and repaired, satisfied Thane. When something needed fixing around the house, he pulled out his tools and got to work. Thane Baker developed yard work into an art form with his sculpted trenches that controlled the water supply to his plants. His powerful hands show his years of effort. He still likes to "do the washing up" after family meals.

Most of all, Thane enjoys his relationships with family and friends. He likes to joke and tease, but he is careful never to harm anyone. If someone upsets him, Thane grabs the marble he always carries in his pants pocket. He thinks three pleasant things about that person before he releases it. He never wants to say something bad about anybody. After ninety-two years on this earth, still exercising and enjoying life, Thane tells anyone who will listen that people and relationships matter the most.

ACKNOWLEDGMENTS

I must thank the incredible generosity of many individuals.

Thane Baker, my father and my hero, shared his amazing story with me. His memory of the details of his first Olympics and the memorabilia that he saved allowed me to reveal this special time with the world. Susie Baker, Thane's mother, and Sally Baker, his wife of sixty-six years, kept records of his successes. Doyle Thane Baker, my brother, and John Patrick Doyle, my uncle, shared their memories of Thane. My husband, Chuck, and my family made this book possible. Thank you to TCU Press for believing in this book.

Interviews from individuals at the 1952 Olympics: (in alphabetical order)

William Harrison "Bones" Dilllard, 1948 Olympics, 100 meters—Gold; 4x100-meter relay—Gold; 1952 Olympics, 110-meter hurdles —Gold; 4x100-meter relay—Gold. Sullivan Award winner 1955.

Meredith Charles "Flash" Gourdine, 1952 Olympics, Long Jump, Silver. (Traci Gourdine, his daughter, shared audio recordings created by her father during his lifetime.)

Franklin Wesley "Bud" Held, 1952 Olympics, Javelin Throw— 9th.

Jesse William "J.W." Mashburn, 4x400-meter relay, 1952 Olympics—did not start; 1956 Olympics—Gold.

Charles Hewes "Charlie" Moore, Jr. 1952 Olympics, 400-meter hurdles—Gold; 4x400-meter relay—Silver.

Robert Eugene "Bob" Richards, Pole Vault, 1948 Olympics—Bronze; 1952 Olympics—Gold; 1956 Olympics—Gold.

Finis "Dean" Smith, 1952 Olympics, 100 meters – 4th, 4x100-meter relay—Gold.

Adolf Weinacker, 1948, 1952, 1956 Olympics, 50-kilometer walk—placed 16th, 22nd, and 7th respectively

Dewey "Lee" Yoder, 1952 Olympics, 400-meter hurdles – 4th in the Semi-Finals.

Neil Ziegler, American spectator

From the United States Olympic and Paralympic Committee (USOPC):

Dana Jozefczyk, Associate General Counsel, Intellectual Property

Amanda McGrory, Archivist and Collections Curator

Cindy Stinger, Alumni Relations Manager

Gwendolyn Swift, Archives Digital Coordinator of the Crawford Family USOPC Archives

Guiselle Torres, Associate General Counsel, Marketing and International Affairs

From Kansas State University:

Veronica L. Denison, Assistant Professor and University Archivist, Morse Department of Special Collections, KSU Libraries

Ryun Godfrey, former Assistant Track Coach and head Cross Country Coach at KSU, now head Cross Country Coach at University of Nebraska

Kenny Lannou, Executive Associate AD for Communications

David Levy, Director of the Collegian Media Group

The Honorable Jerry Mershon, KSC teammate

Amy Button Renz, President and CEO of the K-State Alumni Association

Cliff Rovelto, Director of Track and Field and Cross County

Gene Taylor, AD

Tommy Theis, Manager of Photo Services

Richard "Dick" Towers, KSC teammate and at the 1952 Olympic Tryouts, former KSU AD.

Also from Kansas:

Myrna Barnes, previous director, Morton County Historical Society Museum

Alice Joan "Jody" Billings, Ward Haylett's daughter

Becky Ellis, Director, Morton County Historical Society Museum

Linda Glasgow, Curator of Archives and Library for the Riley County Historical Museum

Frances "Wendy" Haylett, daughter-in-law of Ward Haylett

Lisa Keys, Kansas State Historical Society

Kathy Lafferty, University Archives in the Kenneth Spencer Research Library, University of Kansas

Cindy LeBarge, J & C Images, Manhattan, KS

Greg A. McCune, writer of HighJumpU: K-State Track and Field Blog

Amanda Rupp, Interim Director of the Ellis County Historical Society of Hays, Kansas

From Helsinki, Finland:

Matti Hinktikka, Information Service Coordinator, Sports Museum of Finland

Antti Leskinen, Executive Director of the Turun Urheiluliito Athletics Department

Mika Noronen acting for Taina Susiluoto, Managing Director for the Finnish, Olympic Committee

Sami Savilinna, City of Helsinki

Susanna Sinero, City of Helsinki

Sami and Tom Suojärvi, sons of Tuija Timonen Suojärvi

Vesa Tikander, Researcher for the Sports Museum of Finland

Tuomo Tyllinen of Helsinki, Finland, and Tuija's friend

From Vienna, Austria:

Emily Exenberger, Editor-Content Marketing, City Editorial Office and Newsroom

Dr. rer. pol. Margeret Hall, Assistant Professor, Department of Strategy of Innovation, Wirtschaftsuniversität, Wein University of Economics and Business

Hannes Maschkan, Head of International Relations, Austrian Olympic Committee

Mag. Peter Prokop, Head of Customer Service for the Austrian National Library Image Archive and Graphics Collection

Alfons Stockinger of the Austrian Press Agency

From Germany:

Inéz Kissels-Pohley, photographer

Volker Kluge, former editor of *Journal of Olympic History*

From London, England:

Chris Astbury, Director of Marketing and archivist for The Dorchester, London

Marc Culter, News Corp. UK & Ireland Ltd.

From Wisconsin:

Jennifer Lukomski, archivist for the Congregation of the Sisters of St. Agnes

Writing Coach:

Rebecca "R.J." Thesman

Early Beta Readers:

Laura Goettsche, JD

William Nicholson

Dr. Teresa A. Sullivan, President Emerita and University Professor of Sociology, University of Virginia

Professor Jay Westbrook, Benno C. Schmidt Chair of Business Law, University of Texas School of Law

Dr. Kristine Woods and her husband, Tom

Paula Zwenger, writer

Line Editor:

Thane Baker
Sarah Webster

Other Assistance:

Dan Degrassi, artist
Lori Mellender
Myrle Saunders, Sr.
Ian and Madi Wohlwend

FOREIGN LANGUAGE GLOSSARY

Author's Note: Both Finnish and Swedish are official languages in Finland. French and English are the official languages of the Olympics. The Olympic Motto and the prayer said during the Opening Ceremony were in Latin. Some of the Americans competed in Austria and Germany after the 1952 Olympics, where German served as the primary language.

Ami go home für Ein unabhängiges Osterreich (English and German): Sign posted in Occupied Austria in 1952. A rough translation is "Americans go home for an independent Austria." *Ami* is slang for "Americans."

Åbo (Swedish): The Swedish name for the city of Turku, Finland.

athletiksport (German): Athletic sports.

athlétisme (French): Athletics.

auf die Plätze (German): On your mark, first command from the starter to the runners.

Auf Wiederseh'n, Auf Wiedersehen, (German): Until we meet again, see you later. "Auf Wiederseh'n, Sweetheart" was the name of a song popular in 1952.

bois d'arc (French): Bodark wood, also known as hedge apple wood, obtained its name from the French term *bois d'arc*. The Native Americans used this exceedingly hard wood for bows and clubs. Its formal name is osage-orange or *maclura pomifera*.

Burgring (German): A street which is part of the *Ringstraße* or *Ringstrasse*, a street that circled the old city borders of Vienna where the city walls used to stand.

Citius, Altius, Fortius (Latin): The Olympic Motto meaning "Faster, Higher, Stronger." In July 2021, the IOC changed the motto to *Citius, Altius, Fortius – Communiter*, which means "Faster, Higher, Stronger – Together."

danke (German): Thanks.

Delicado (Spanish): Delicate, the name of a song popular in 1952.

Des Bundesminister (German): Of the Federal minister.

Dies ist unser Platz. (German): This is our place.

Ehrenpreis (German): Prize.

fertig (German): Ready, second command from the starter to the runners.

Festschrift, Internationales Leichtathletikmeeting, Veranstaltet vom Österr. Leichtathletick-Verband u. Österr, Olymp. Comitée, Offizielles Programm, Mittwoch 6. August u. Donnerstag 7. August 1952, Beginn 17.45 Uhr WAC-Platz, Freiexemplar (German): Commemorative, International Light Athletic Meeting, organized from the Austrian Light Athletic Association and Austrian Olympic Committee, Official Program, Wednesday, August 6 and Thursday, August 7, 1952, Beginning at 5:45 p.m. Vienna Athletics Club-Place, Free copy.

Eläintarha (Finnish): Practice field for the female competitors at the 1952 Olympic Games. Also, this served as the staging grounds for the Olympians before they marched into the stadium for the Opening Ceremonies.

Friidrott (Swedish): Athletics, also written Fri-Idrott on the Olympic daily programs.

Helsingfors (Swedish): The name for Helsinki, Finland.

Gehen Sie! (German): Go!

Hofburg (German): The Hofburg Palace, former winter home of the imperial family.

Hôtel Höller Nächst der Wien Ringstrasse VII. Burggasse 2 (German)ː: Holler Hotel next to the Ringstrasse in the seventh district of Vienna on Burggasse Street number two.

hotelli (Finnish): Hotel.

Innere Stadt (German): The old city center of Vienna, the first district.

Internat. Leichtathletik-Meeting, Wien 1952, Ehrenpreis, Des Bundesminister, F. Verkehr und Verstaatl Betrieb Dipl. Ing. Karl Waldbrunner (German): International Athletics Meeting, Vienna 1952, Prize of the Federal Minister, Federal Transport and Nationalization Undertakings, Karl Waldbrunner, with a degree in engineering.

jetzt (German): Now.

Käpylä (Finnish): An area or neighborhood inside Helsinki, Finland. The Americans stayed in an Olympic Village located inside Käpylä. They referred to their housing as Käpylä Olympic Village. Technically, this was the new Olympic Village or *Kisakylä* in Finnish. Previously, Finland had built an Olympic Village, named *Olympiakylä*, for the expected 1940 Olympic Games.

Khorosho (Russian): Good.

Kneipe (German): Tavern or pub.

kummitusjuna (Finnish): Ghost train ride at Linnanmäki Amusement Park in Helsinki in 1952.

Kurier (German): *Messenger*, a newspaper in Vienna, Austria.

Leichtathletik (German): Athletics or track and field.

Linnanmäki (Finnish): The name of an amusement park in Helsinki.

Lintsi (Finnish): A nickname for Linnanmäki Amusement Park in Helsinki.

markka was the currency in Finland. In Finnish, they were *Suomen markka*. In Swedish, *Finsk markka*. In 1952, the conversion rate was 231 markkaa to the dollar. (Note the plural form with an additional "a"). The Americans made the markka plural by adding an "s," markkas. One markka equaled one hundred penniä.

Olympia (Finnish): Olympiad in English, an athletic celebration held every four years.

Olympiastadion (Finnish): Olympic Stadium.

Olympische (German): Olympic.

Olympische Sommerspiele (German): Olympic Summer Games.

Operning (German): Street in Vienna that is part of the *Ringstraße* or *Ringstrasse*, a street that circled the old city borders of Vienna where the city walls used to stand.

Österreich (German): Austria.

Otaniemi (Finnish): Soviet and Eastern Bloc athletes remained in nine buildings at a student hostel, with 1,388 beds.

paikoillenne (Finnish): The first command the starter used during the Olympic races. The Americans understood this to mean, "On your marks."

pankki (Finnish): Bank.

penni (Finnish): One hundredth of a markka, the monetary

currency of Finland in 1952. One markka equaled one hundred penniä.

Rathaus (German): City hall.

Riesenrad (German): Ferris wheel.

Schwedenstaffel (German): Swedish Relay, a relay race covering 1,000 meters in distance, with different athletes running 100m, 200m, 300m, and 400m, also called a medley relay.

stadion (Finnish): Stadium.

stadion or *stade* (Ancient Greek): Distance athletes in the original Olympics raced, about 192 meters, or one stadion in length.

Straße (German): Also seen as *Strasse*, street. May be added to the end of a word.

Suomi (Finnish): Finland.

Suomalaista emmental juustoa kosken laskija (Finnish): A cheese served in Finland.

Turun (Finnish): Turku, a city and former capital in southwestern Finland.

Turun Toverit r.y. (Finnish): The Turku Comrades (located in Turku, Finland).

Turun Urheiluliito r.y. (Finnish): The Turku Athletic Union (located in Turku, Finland).

urheilijat (Finnish): Athletes.

Urheilumuseo (Finnish): Sports Museum.

valmiit (Finnish): Done or steady, understood by the American runners to mean "set," the second command after "on your marks."

vuoristorata (Finnish): Rollercoaster.

Warum sind Sie hier? (German): Why are you here?

Wer sind Sie? (German): Who are you?

Wien (German): Vienna, Austria.

Wiener Athletiksport Club or WAC (German): Club where the Americans competed in Vienna, Austria.

Woher kommen Sie? (German): Where do you come from?

Wiener Rathaus (German): Vienna City Hall.

Yhdysvallat (Finnish): The United States.

yleisurheilu (Finnish): Athletics.

zwischen Himmel und Erde (German): Between heaven and earth.

ABBREVIATIONS

4x100	four by one hundred (in relays meaning four by one-hundred-meter relay), also known as the four by one
4x400	four by four hundred (in relays meaning four by four-hundred-meter relay), also known as the four by four
AAU	Amateur Athletic Union
AD	Athletic Director
AP	Associated Press
BOA	British Olympic Association
IOC	International Olympic Committee
KSC	Kansas State College (prior to 1959)
KSU	Kansas State University (1959 and after), also known as K-State
MP	Military Police
NCAA	National Collegiate Athletic Association
NYAC	New York Athletic Club
Pan Am	Pan American World Airways
NYT	New York Times
T&F	Track and Field
UP	United Press
US	United States
USOA	United States Olympic Association
USOC	United States Olympic Committee, currently known as the United States Olympic & Paralympic Committee
WA	World Athletics formerly known as IAAF (or State of Washington based on context)

Opening Material

1. IOC, "What is the Olympic Creed?"
2. Guest, "Dreams of Youth," *Just Glad Things*, 136-137.
3. Stavropoulos, "The Evolution of Women Participation in Sports Events," Statathon.
4. On the 1952 US Olympic Team, women comprised 11% percent of the American team with 36 women and 287 men. Bushnell, *US 1952 Olympic Book*, 63-66. Title IX refers to Title IX of the Education Amendments of 1972, 20 U.S.C. §1681 et seq. (2020); History.com, ed., "Title IX Enacted." Title IX only applies to educational institutions that received federal funding.
5. Chen, "Finland," World War II Database; Rare Historical Photos, "The Amazing Story of Finland in World War II, 1939-1945."
6. Torsten Santavirta, Nina Santavirta, and Stephen E. Gilman, "Association of the World War II Finnish Evacuation of Children with Psychiatric Hospitalization in the Next Generation," 21-27.
7. Bushnell, *US 1952 Olympic Book*, 27-57.
8. Next Big Idea Club, "David Goldblatt on the Impact of Olympics on the World Stage."
9. Mintz, "Statistics: Education in America, 1860-1950"; Paul Zimmerman, "Makes Plans after Olympics: American Javelin Thrower Held Looks Ahead to Missionary Work; Soft Track," *Los Angeles Times*, July 19, 1952, https://www.newspapers.com; J. W. Mashburn, in discussion with the author, April 2020; IOC, "Milton Gray Campbell."
10. Charlie Dean Archives, "1952 Summer Olympic Games."
11. Tyler Benson, "The Role of Sports in the Soviet Union," Guided History, History Research Guides by Boston University Students directed by Simon Rabinovitch, http://blogs.bu.edu/guidedhistory/russia-and-its-empires/tyler-benson/.
12. Smithsonian National Museum of American History Behring Center, "Separate Is Not Equal: Brown v. Board of Education: White Only: Jim Crow in America"; Brown v. Board of Education of Topeka, 347 U.S. 483 (1954).

13. Loewen, *Sundown Towns: A Hidden Dimension of American Racism*, rev. ed.; History & Social Justice, "Information about Sundown Towns"; America's Black Holocaust Museum, "Sundown Towns: Racial Segregation Past and Present."
14. *Plessy v. Ferguson*, 163 U. S. 537 (1996); History.com, "Plessy v. Ferguson."
15. Redihan, *Olympics and the Cold War, 1948-1968*; Rider, *Cold War Games*.
16. No one should embark on a new training or diet program without first discussing it with their own physician.
17. Frank Litsky, "Avery Brundage of Olympics Dies, Head of Games for 20 Years—Tenure Controversial," *NYT*, May 9, 1975, https://timesmachine.nytimes.com/; Zirin and Boykoff, "Racist IOC President Avery Brundage Loses His Place of Honor."

Chapter 1

1. "The Significance," AAU James E. Sullivan Award, http://www.aausullivan.org/History/Overview; AAU, "AAU Sullivan Award–Past Winners"; "Glenn Cunningham Sets New 1,500-Meter World Record," first published in the *Morton County Farmer* on March 2, 1934, and reprinted in the *Elkhart Tri-State News*, July 5, 2018; Cunningham and Sand, *Never Quit*, 24-65, 116-127; IOC, "Xth Olympiad Los Angeles 1932"; IOC, "The XIth Olympic Games Berlin 1936."
2. Bridwell, *Superman*.
3. Egan, *The Worst Hard Time*.
4. McLaughlin, *Geology and Ground-Water Resources of Morton County, Kansas*.
5. "Rare Dust Storm Wednesday Night," Glimpse Back into History, *Elkhart Tri-State News* (KS), published April 14, 1933, and reprinted July 19, 2018.
6. Associated Press (AP), "Cooler Weather Seen by Monday," *Emporia (KS) Gazette*, September 2, 1939, Evening Edition, https://www.newspapers.com.
7. Associated Press, "World on Brink of Holocaust: Hitler Told to Halt Campaign against Poland or England and France Will Take Action; Thinks U.S. Can Escape Holocaust; President Hopeful Country Can Be Kept at Peace," *Hutchinson (KS) News*, September 1, 1939, https://www.newspapers.com.
8. "Hot Time in Kansas Too: Sun, Not War, Causes Discomfort in Middle West," *Hutchison (KS) News*, September 3, 1939, https://www.newspapers.com.
9. "Big Crowd Here Last Saturday: Cunningham's Talk and Exhibition Is Feature of Day; Big Crowd Sees Events," *Elkhart (KS) Tri-State News*, September 8, 1939.
10. Public Broadcasting Network, "Surviving the Dust Bowl–Timeline: The Dust Bowl."

Chapter 2

1. Jennifer Lukomski (archivist, Congregation of Sisters of St. Agnes) in discussion with the author, March 2020, https://www.csasisters.org/.
2. Blicker, "Ether in Surgery."
3. Gerald Mayer provides information about child workers in the 1930s. "Child Labor in America: History, Policy, and Legislative Issues," *Congressional Research Service*, November 18, 2013, https://fas.org/sgp/crs/misc/RL31501.pdf.
4. Oil-Dri Corporation of America, "History."

5. Smithsonian National Museum of American History, "Beef, Iron & Wine."
6. Morris, "The End is Near for 3.2 Beer."
7. Trees of Texas, "Osage-Orange," Texas A&M Forest Service.
8. Batens and Major, "Class 9 Items: Drugs, Chemicals and Biological Stains Sulfa Drugs."
9. Hays, Kansas, on the map on p. 8 is on Highway 70.
10. US Food and Drug Administration, "Fluoroscopy"; Marsh, "When X-Rays Were All the Rage."
11. Rise of Automobiles After World War II, "During WWII: Automobile Growth Halted."
12. In 1945, Walter Franklin Baker, Thane's father, served on the Elkhart City Council.

Chapter 3

1. Manhattan, Kansas, is west of Topeka, Kansas, and north of Highway 70. See the map on p. 8; Associated Press, "Winter Storms Sweep Out of Rocky Mountains: Warnings Are Issued Throughout Kansas with Freezing Rain and Slick Highways," *Manhattan (KS) Mercury-Chronicle,* December 20, 1949, https://www.newspapers.com.
2. "Today, athletes train all year with better tracks, equipment, and knowledge of the human body." Ryan Godfrey, Assistant Coach and Head Cross Country Coach, KSU in discussion with author, June 2021; "To Show Track Movie," *Kansas State Collegian,* December 19, 1949, https://archive.org/details/KSULKSColl-194950V56N5380/page/n95; Kansas State University, "Nichols Hall History," http://www.k-state.edu/maps/buildings/N/.
3. Richard Towers, in discussion with the author, September 2019, March 2020, May 2021.
4. Judge Jerry Mershon, a KSC track teammate of Thane Baker, reported that Ward Haylett was quiet, effective, respected, and a fine gentleman who never raised his voice. He rarely praised anyone, but if he did, he meant it. Haylett appreciated that his K-State "boys worked their feet off for him." An honest and decent man, people liked him. "Commencement Days: Clay Center, Neb.," *Omaha Daily Bee,* May 26, 1913; "52 Officers, 800 Men Discharged: Total of 283 Officers and about 8,500 Men Have Been Released," *Daily (Little Rock) Arkansas Gazette,* December 15, 1918; "Local News," *Clay County Sun* (Clay Center, NE), https://www.newspapers.com; Homer Socolofsky, "Ward Haylett Chronology, (1895-1990) a Biographical Sketch," October 28, 1993, Vertical Files Collection, Athletic Teams, Track and Cross Country-Haylett, Ward, Morse Department of Special Collections, KSU Libraries; "Kansas Aggies Offer Haylett Job at Track," *Des Moines (IA) Register,* June 26, 1928; Honorable Jerry Mershon, retired, in discussion with author, May 2021; Alice Joan "Jody" Haylett Billings, in discussion with author, February 2021.
5. Freddy Mendell, "K-State's Ward Haylett Is Grand Man of Track, Field," *Hutchison (KS) News,* April 19, 1957.
6. "Will See Olympics," *Manhattan (KS) Mercury,* June 30, 1932.

7. Wilson, "Men's Track and Field: Report of the Committee Chairman," in *Report of the US Olympic Committee 1948 Games*, ed. Bushnell, 74-76, 98-100.
8. While Haylett frequently referred to himself as a "one-man operation," today, multiple coaches work with the KSU track team. Mark Janssen, "Haylett: A Legendary Figure in KSU Track; Inductee Initiated Pattern of Success in the Sport," *Manhattan (KS) Mercury*, October 7, 1990, www.newspapers.com; Godfrey, see note 2 above; "Elmer Hackney" K-State Athletics Hall of Fame, K-State: Official Site of K-State Athletics, https://www.kstatesports.com/honors/k-state-athletics-hall-of-fame/elmer-hackney/18.
9. United States Olympic Committee (USOC), *1952 US Olympic Souvenir Book: Track and Field Tryouts for Men*, 64.
10. Mershon, interview, (see chap. 3, n. 4).
11. "City School Notes," *Clay County Patriot* (Clay Center, NE), March 18, 1910, https://www.newspapers.com.
12. "Baker Races to Records: Breaks Three Records at Cimarron Relays," *Elkhart (KS) Tri-State News*, April 29, 1949; "They Can't Stop Baker: Win Three Firsts at Ulysses," *Elkhart (KS) Tri-State News*, April 15, 1949.
13. Dale Mullen, "Elkhart Youngster Follows Hero's Running Footsteps," Kansans in the Olympics, *Wichita Beacon*, October 10, 1968.

Chapter 4

1. USOC, *Instructions to Athletes: U.S. Olympic Track and Field Try-Outs*; "The Men Who Will Compete for the Stars and Stripes in the Olympic Games," Wirephoto, *Kansas City Times*, July 1, 1952; Los Angeles Coliseum, *The Story Behind the Largest and Finest Stadium in America*.
2. Please note that English speakers use the word "Olympiad" or "Olympics." However, in the Finnish language and concerning the town in Greece, the word is "Olympia."
3. In May 1952, Bob Hope held a telethon and raised pledges of over $1,000,000. David Lobosco, "Bing and the 1952 Olympic Telethon," *Bing Crosby News Archive* (blog), August 3, 2012, https://bingfan03.blogspot.com/2012/08/bing-and-1952-olympic-telethon.html; Bushnell, "Olympic Telethon," in *US 1952 Olympic Book*, 46-51.
4. Bailey, "The Lockheed Constellation"; Wilkinson, "Call Her Connie: The Legendary Lockheed Constellation"; Trans World Airlines, *Skyline New York*.
5. Finis "Dean" Smith attended the University of Texas, where he and his teammates set a world record in the 4x100-meter relay. As he ended his September 5, 2019, telephone interview with Thane Baker and the author, Dean told Thane, "I love you with all my heart." Smith, *Cowboy Stuntman*.
6. In 1952, the event which qualified US T&F athletes for the Olympics carried the name "Tryout." Kane, "Men's Track and Field," in *US 1952 Olympic Book,* ed. Asa Bushnell, 74; USOC, *Instructions to Athletes*; USOC, *1952 US Olympic Souvenir Book: Tryouts* USATF, "US Olympic Team Trials–Track & Field."
7. The IOC refers to all competitors as "athletes" but still refers to the sport of T&F as "athletics." IOC, "Athletes," https://olympics.com/en/athletes/; IOC, "Sports."

8. Robert J. Kane, Men's T&F Manager, reported the final day of the Olympic Tryouts, June 28, 1952, was the coldest day on record. Bushnell, *US 1952 Olympic Book*, 74.
9. Thane Baker to Mr. and Mrs. Walter F. Baker, July 15, 1952, private collection.
10. USOC, *Instructions to Athletes*.
11. Ted Smits, "Can U.S. Produce Another Great Sprinter for '52 Olympic Games," Associated Press (AP), *Lancaster (PA) New Era*, June 12, 1952, https://www.newspapers.com.
12. Ward Haylett brought other KSC athletes to California to compete in June 1952, but only Thane Baker made the Olympic team. Towers, interview, (see chap. 3, n. 3); NCAA, *31ˢᵗ Annual National Collegiate Athletic Association T&F Championships*.
13. Smith, *Cowboy Stuntman*, 53.
14. Amateur Athletic Union of the US, *64ᵗʰ Annual US Track and Field Championships*.
15. AP, "Smith Boosts US Olympic Sprint Hopes," *Austin (TX) American*, June 24, 1952; Bob Myers, "Whitfield Heads List of AAU Champs," AP, *Valley Times* (San Fernando Valley, California), June 21, 1952, https://www.newspapers.com.
16. Thoreau, *1953 Official NCAA Track and Field Guide*, 53; Harold V. Ratliff, "Relays Boosted Olympic Hopes," *Austin American*, April 7, 1952, https://www.newspapers.com.
17. "Baker Ties 60-Yard Dash Record," *Fort Collins Coloradoan*, March 30, 1952, https://www.newspapers.com.
18. (USOC), *1952 US Olympic Souvenir Book: Tryouts*, 25, 38; SportsDefinitions.com, "Heats."
19. Thoreau, *1953 NCAA Track and Field Guide*; *Track and Field News*, "Men—Los Angeles—June 27-28"; AP, "Stone and Moore Set U.S. Records in Final Tryouts for Olympic Track Team: Ex-Penn State Ace Outraces Santee, Stone Wins 5,000 Meters in 14:27 and Moore Hurdles 400 Meters in 0:50.7, Whitfield Ties 800 Mark, Engel of N.Y.U Is First in Olympic Hammer Toss Trial—Bragg Takes Sprint," *NYT*, June 28, 1952, https://nyti.ms/3bjm3jp.
20. Thane competed in the original event of the ancient Greek Olympics. Even during Thane's lifetime, track meets offered this race in a straight line. Running the 200 meters around a curve was a new idea. IOC, "Run Leonidas Run."
21. Smith, interview, (see note 5 above).
22. Billings, interview, (see chap. 3, n. 4).
23. Dr. Lafene served as the doctor at KSC in 1952. In February 1951, Thane Baker pledged to the Delta Tau Delta fraternity. Lafene Health Center, https://www.k-state.edu/lafene/; *Hutchinson (KS) News*, "Barbara Hanna Wins Tri-Delt Scholarship," February 18, 1951, https://www.newspapers.com; ΔΤΔ Delta Tau Delta, https://www.delts.org/.
24. Towers, interview, (see chap. 3, n. 3).
25. Morris, "The End Is Near for 3.2 Beer."
26. Ted Smits, "'On to Helsinki' For Thane Baker: Whitfield Joins Curtis Stone as Only Trial Double Winners," AP, *Manhattan Mercury—Chronicle*, June 29, 1952.
27. The Honorable Jerry Mershon, retired and KSC track teammate of Thane Baker who knew Santee, said humility was not Santee's long suit. However, Thane Baker embodied humility according to Mershon, who has known Baker for seventy years.

AP, "Moore Best Bet to Win—Hamilton: Santee Confident," *Los Angeles Times*, July 19, 1952, https://www.newspapers.com; Kansas State Historical Society, "Wes Santee," *Kansapedia* (blog), last modified February 2020, https://www.kshs.org/kansapedia/olympic-track-shoe/10387; Mershon, interview, (see chap. 3, n. 4).
28. Smith, *Cowboy Stuntman*, 13.
29. Thane Baker marked his 1952 route from Elkhart, Kansas, to Los Angeles on a map. Rand McNally, *UTOCO: Utah Oil Refining Company Map of the US*, 48 x 32 cm, (1952 or earlier), torn from a larger map; Towers, interview, (see chap. 3, n. 3).
30. Thane received his smallpox vaccination on September 12, 1949, as a first-year college student. *Certificate of Vaccination against Smallpox*, Riley County Health Department and Student Health Services, KSC, June 4, 1952.
31. The USOC refunded a $10 passport fee to each team member. "Olympic Refund," *Daily News* (New York), July 7, 1952, https://www.newspapers.com.
32. Reverend Robert "Bob" Eugene Richards, interview with the author, September 5, 2019, and April 22, 2020. Bob Richards told the author, "Tell Thane I love him, and I'm all for him." USOC, *1952 US Olympic Souvenir Book: Tryouts*, 23; Richards, *Heart of a Champion*.
33. *Strength and Health*, "Rev. Bob Richards"; Dr. Roswell Long, "Young People Give Service to Religion: They're Responding to Churches; Offer Great Leadership," *Charlotte (NC) Observer*, July 13, 1952, https://www.newspapers.com.
34. Coach Ryun Godfrey says he believes all sprinters today do weight training to develop power. Godfrey, interview, (see chap. 3, n. 2).
35. The author interviewed Harrison "Bones" Dillard, the 1955 Sullivan Award winner, on October 1, 2019; AAU, "AAU Sullivan Award–Past Winners."
36. Franklin Wesley "Bud" Held, interview by author, April 4, 2022.
37. "New Countries Join," About the Games, Helsinki 1952, IOC, https://olympics.com/en/olympic-games/helsinki-1952.
38. When the pilot cut the power to the remaining three engines and put the airplane into a dive, the Olympians in the cabin experienced microgravity, Keplerian Trajectory, or a free-fall path. Strickland, "How Zero-gravity Flights Work," HowStuffWorks; Ramona Ritzmann, Kathrin Freyler, Anne Krause, and Albert Gollhofer, "No Neuromuscular Side-Effects of Scopolamine in Sensorimotor Control and Force-Generating Capacity Among Parabolic Fliers," *Microgravity Sci. Technol.* 28, (May 27, 2016): 477-490, https://doi.org/10.1007/s12217-016-9504-y.
39. The finish places at the national championships determined the Olympic qualifiers in the 10,000-meter run. The 10,000-meter walk participants competed in New York City, June 1, 1952; the 50,000-meter walkers met in Baltimore, Maryland. The decathlon participants competed July 1-2, 1952, in Tulare, California. A committee decided the marathon qualifiers looking at the last two years of marathon competition. Bushnell, *US 1952 Olympic Book*, 71-72; Amateur Athletic Union of the US, *64th Annual US Track and Field Championships*.
40. Many remember the plunging plane, but in the panic of the moment, where the event took place remains unknown. Thane Baker recalls it landed in Amarillo, Texas. Smith, interview; Smith, *Cowboy Stuntman*, 58; Moore and Cockerille, *Running on Purpose*, 34; Bushnell, *US 1952 Olympic Book*, 74.

Chapter 5

1. Edition, Sid Kline, "It Will Be Hot Today-Probably Not a Record," *Daily News* (New York, NY), June 30, 1952, https://www.newspapers.com; Paramount Hotel, "History," https://www.nycparamount.com/about/history; Baker, Thane, "Autograph Book of 1952 Olympians," (1952), private collection; Held, interview, (see chap. 4, n. 36).
2. Bushnell, *US 1952 Olympic Book*, 74; Bettmann, *Olympic Runners on the Track*, July 1, 1952, Getty Images, https://www.gettyimages.com/detail/news-photo/these-six-powerful-young-athletes-running-around-the-palmer-news-photo/515021068; Bettmann, *Walt Davis Practicing High Jump*, July 1, 1952, Getty Images, https://www.gettyimages.com/detail/news-photo/as-coach-clyde-littlefield-holds-the-bar-high-jumper-walt-news-photo/517760650.
3. *Dodgers Official Program and Score Card*, "Brooklyn Dodgers vs. New York Giants," (New York: Harry M. Stevens, July 3, 1952); "Brooklyn Dodgers vs. New York Giants," ticket, Brooklyn Dodgers, July 3, 1952; Baseball Reference, "New York Giants at Brooklyn Dodgers Box Score, July 3, 1952," https://www.baseball-reference.com/teams/BRO/1952-schedule-scores.shtml; AP, "U.S. Athletes Arrive in Helsinki," *Ithaca Journal*, July 9, 1952, https://www.newspapers.com.
4. Gourdine, *Untitled Memories*; Professor Traci Gourdine, MA, email messages to author, March-April 2020.
5. Dewey "Lee" Yoder, Jr. in discussion with the author, March 2020, August 2020.
6. U.S. Weather Bureau Forecast, "Daily Almanac," *Daily News* (New York City, NY), July 4, 1952, https://www.newspapers.com.
7. Kermit Jaediker, "Weather Fireworks Mark City's Fourth," *Daily News* (New York, NY), July 5, 1952, https://www.newspapers.com.
8. Asa Bushnell (Secretary, USOC), "Notice to USOC Chairmen" "Attention: All Olympic Team Members" USOC, *US Team*, 7; Daniel J. Ferris (Chairman, Pre & Post Olympic Competition Committee, AAU) to Members of the US Olympic T&F Team—Men & Women, letter, July 1, 1952, private collection; USOC, *US Olympic T&F Squad 1952*, June 1952, private collection.
9. *Mother Leone's Famous Dinner: Leone's Since 1906*, (menu, New York: n.p., July 5, 1952), private collection.
10. Richards, *Heart of a Champion*, 119, 120.
11. Arthur Mulligan, "Rush, Crush: N.Y. Starts Home," *Daily News* (New York City, NY), July 7, 1952, https://www.newspapers.com.
12. USOC, *1952 U. S. Olympic Souvenir Book: Olympic Sports Carnival*.
13. AP, "Summaries," *Spokesman–Review* (Spokane, WA), July 7, 1952, https://www.newspapers.com.
14. Hy Turkin, "Santee Sets 2 Records at Olympic Carnival," *Daily News* (New York City, NY), July 7, 1952, https://www.newspapers.com; AP, "Davis Upsets Hurdle Champ," *Fort Worth Star-Telegram* (Fort Worth, TX), July 7, 1952, https://www.newspapers.com.
15. US Weather Bureau, "Daily Almanac," *Daily News* (New York City, NY), July 6, 1952, https://www.newspapers.com.

16. "Ashbaugh Qualifies for Olympics; Red Crew Awaits Trials," *Ithaca (NY) Journal*, June 30, 1952, https://www.newspapers.com.
17. History of Branding, "History of Old Spice."
18. Bushnell, *Instructions for Members of the Olympic Teams, Trainers and Coaches*.
19. William R. Conklin, "Millions Give Record Welcome to M'Arthur; Tons of Paper Showered on 19-Mile Parade; Files Show General Expected Quick Victory–Crowds Out Early–Murphy Puts Throng at 7,500,000, Half of it from Out of Town–Fete Lasts 6 Hours–General Praises City as Force to Maintain our Way of Life," *NYT,* April 21, 1951, https://timesmachine.nytimes.com.
20. Mayor's Reception Committee, "The City of New York Reception in Honor of the 1952 Olympic Team."
21. Richards, interview, (see chap. 4, n. 32); USOC, *Information and Instruction for Members and Officials of the US Olympic Team*.
22. Kenneth L. Wilson, "Report of the Chef de Mission," in *US 1952 Olympic Book*, Bushnell, ed., 247.
23. Mayor's Reception Committee, "The City of New York Luncheon."
24. Bushnell, *Instructions for Members of the Olympic Teams, Trainers and Coaches*.
25. Pan Am, *Track, Field Stars Off for Olympics,* July 6, 1952, photograph, private collection.
26. James F. Simms, "Transportation Committee," in *US 1952 Olympic Book*, Bushnell, 77.
27. Thane sat in seat 6C. Pan Am, "Charter Ticket and Baggage Check."
28. Smith, interview (see chap. 4, n. 5).
29. Bushnell, *US 1952 Olympic Book*, 74; Smith, *Cowboy Stuntman*, 58.
30. Charles "Charlie" Hewes Moore, Jr., in discussion with the author, August 2020.
31. Charlie Dean Archives, "1952 Summer Olympic Games"; Buster Haas, "Top O' Morn," *Austin (TX) American,* July 20, 1952, https://www.newspapers.com; *Track and Field News,* "1952"; Olympedia, OlyMADMen, ed. s.v. "Jimmy Gathers," http://www.olympedia.org/athletes/78441.
32. IOC, "Andrew William Stanfield"; "US Championships (Men 1943-)," gbrathletics, http://www.gbrathletics.com/nc/usa2.htm; NJSports.com, The State of Sports! "Andy Stanfield."
33. Simms, "Transportation Committee," in *US 1952 Olympic Book*, Bushnell, 260.

Chapter 6

1. *Popular Mechanics,* "Fighting the Drouth"; The Living New Deal, "Shelterbelt Project (1934), May 6, 2018, https://livingnewdeal.org/glossary/shelterbelt-project-1934/.
2. Seutula Airport opened June 6, 1952. Kolkka, *XV Olympiad Helsinki, Finland: The Official Report,* 180-181; Arkisto *"Seutulan lentoasema* 1952."
3. Bushnell, *US 1952 Olympic Book*, 74.
4. AP, "U.S. Olympic Team Arrives in Helsinki: Fuchs Remains on Sick List," Sports, *Oakland (CA) Tribune,* July 9, 1952, https://www.newspapers.com; "Olympiakisojen aattona Helsinkiin saapui ulkomaisia edustusjoukkueita, kisaturisteja

kautta mailman-sekä 720 000 pulloa Coca-Colaa," https://yle.fi/aihe/artikkeli/2006/09/08/erik-von-frenckell-maistelee-kisacolaa-1952; "Officials Say Baker Will Run 100 in 9.3," *Manhattan (KS) Mercury*, April 24, 1952.

5. Thane Baker July 15 letter, (see chap. 4, n. 9).
6. The ride from Seutula Airport to Helsinki took about thirty minutes. Thane would have seen evergreen and birch trees. Hanna Corona, "Finland-Forests and Forestry," *Boreal Forest*, August 30, 2022, https://www.borealforest.org/finland-forests-and-forestry/.
7. British Pathé, "Helsinki Street Scenes (1952)"; Charlie Dean Archives, *"1952 Summer Olympic Games."*
8. Flemming, *Wizard of Oz*.
9. Spotting History, "Helsinki Cathedral"; Spotting History, "Senate Square: Helsinki, Finland."
10. Fodor, *Scandinavia in 1952*, 381.
11. Kolkka, *XV Olympiad Helsinki, Finland: The Official Report*, 101-102.
12. British Pathé, "Helsinki Street Scenes"; Bushnell, *US 1952 Olympic Book*, 190; Harrivirta, ed., "Muistojen kisakesä 1952" *Olympia-Filmi*; Belloni, *Finland: Land of a Thousand Lakes*, 17.
13. In total, officials flew, or athletes carried 1,152 flags during the Olympic Games. Kolkka, *XV Olympiad Helsinki, Finland: The Official Report*, 83.
14. The fifty-thousand-seat stadium dedication was on June 12, 1938, but the Finnish Olympic Organizing Committee added temporary room for twenty thousand more by the summer of 1952. Pasi Jaakkonen, "Suurten Muistojen Olympiastadion," Plus Historia, *Ilta-Sanomat Plus*, August 8, 2020, 10; Kolkka, *XV Olympiad Helsinki, Finland: The Official Report*, 44-47; Olympia Stadion, "Helsinki Olympic Stadium"; "Helsinki Olympic Stadium Reborn for Modern Age," The Stadium Business, September 9, 2020, https://www.thestadiumbusiness.com/2020/09/09/helsinki-olympic-stadium-reborn-modern-age/.
15. Much of the construction and planning for the 1952 Olympic Games took place prior to 1940. In fact, the Finnish Organizing Committee made decisions while sitting in air-raid shelters. Kolkka, *XV Olympiad Helsinki, Finland: The Official Report*, 10, 13, 22-23.
16. Wäinö Aaltonen sculpted the famous statue of a nude Paavo Nurmi running. Aaltonen, "Paavo Nurmi," Turku City Art Museum; IOC, "Paavo Nurmi Seals Record."
17. George Hirthler, *"Citius, Altius, Fortius,"* Coubertin Quote for Jan. 10, *Coubertin Speaks* (blog), https://coubertinspeaks.com/quotes/jan/10/; Bushnell, "XVth Olympic Games Biggest of All," "US Official Party in Helsinki," in *US 1952 Olympic Book*, 61, 65.
18. British Pathé, "Helsinki Street Scenes"; AP, "350 American Athletes Set for Olympics: Raise Flag over U.S. Village Today; Bob Richards Injured," *Record*, (Hackensack, NJ), July 12, 1952, https://www.newspapers.com. (Author's note: Including male and female competitors, coaches, managers, trainers, medical staff, and administrators, 498 individuals composed the American contingent at the 1952 Olympics. Bushnell, *US 1952 Olympic Book*, 63-66).
19. Bushnell, "Report of the Secretary," in *US 1952 Olympic Book*, 34-35; Metcalf,

"Administration Committee," in *US 1952 Olympic Book*, 255.
20. 1952 Helsinki Athletics Olympic participant pin, private collection.
21. Bob Busby, "U.S. in Workouts, Basketball Team has 2-Hour Drill in Helsinki After Ocean Crossing, Track Team Arrives, Santee and Baker among the Tired Athletes Who Sleep, Then Do Some Running," *Kansas City Times*, AP, July 9 or 10, 1952; "Red Olympians Get 'Friendly'–Reverse Tactics and Open 'Iron Curtain' Camp; U.S. Trackmen Workout," *Lafayette (IN) Journal and Courier*, July 10, 1952, https://www.newspapers.com.
22. At Käpylä, thirteen buildings with 545 apartments averaged 8.8 Olympians per unit. Kolkka, *XV Olympiad Helsinki, Finland: The Official Report*, 84-92; Ornstein, "Food and Housing," in *US 1952 Olympic Book,* Bushnell, ed.
23. AP, "Chinese Games Fight is Placed Before IOC," *Spokesman-Review* (Spokane, WA), July 12, 1952, https://www.newspapers.com.
24. Kolkka, *XV Olympiad Helsinki, Finland: The Official Report*, 85. The author observed a privately held photograph of the fence around the training track.
25. The Americans stayed in the same building on Koskelantie Street as the Puerto Rican delegation. Kolkka, *XV Olympiad Helsinki, Finland: The Official Report*, 86; Bushnell, *US 1952 Olympic Book*, 74; Salastie, "Olympic Village."
26. Kolkka, *XV Olympiad Helsinki, Finland: The Official Report*, 86, 95; Tassin, *Bob Mathias*, 78; Moore, interview, (see chap. 5, n. 30).
27. William Patrick O'Brien, Jr.—1959 Sullivan Award winner. Helene Elliott, "Parry O'Brien, 75; Champion Revolutionized Shotput Throw," *Los Angeles Times,* April 23, 2007, https://www.latimes.com/archives/la-xpm-2007-apr-23-me-obrien23-story.html; Frank Litsky, "Parry O'Brien, Pioneer in Shot-Putting Technique, Dies at 75," *NYT,* April 23, 2007, https://www.nytimes.com/2007/04/23/sports/othersports/23obrien.html; Marvin Stone, "American Olympic Stars Work Out at 3 a.m. in Finland's Midnight Sun," *Marysville (OH) Journal,* July 12, 1952, https://www.newspapers.com; AAU, "AAU Sullivan Award–Past Winners."
28. Germany loaned Finland the restaurant tent. "The food (in the Olympic Village) was quite good, very plentiful, and disposed of in horrendous quantity," said Robert Kane, US Team Manager. Many American companies donated food shared among all Olympians. In all, the athletes ate approximately 825,000 pounds of raw food. Bushnell, *US 1952 Olympic Book*, 264-266, 268; Kolkka, *XV Olympiad Helsinki, Finland: The Official Report*, 97; Helms Bakery District, "History," https://helmsbakerydistrict.com/about/history/.
29. "SPAM," Hormel, https://www.spam.com/; Smith, interview, (see chap. 4, n. 5).
30. KSC Coach Haylett said, "It's all right with me if he eats it (honey)–especially if he keeps on running like he has been." "Baker Claims He Gets Fuel from Eating Honey: Big Seven Dash Champ Feels He Gets Added Speed from Nature's Refinery," *Manhattan Republic,* May 30, 1951, https://www.newspapers.com.
31. Mashburn, interview, (see OM, n. 9); Bushnell, *US 1952 Olympic Book*, 75.
32. Kenneth Wilson, and Henry Matis, the US Attaché assigned to work with the Finnish Organizing Committee, both recommended that the 1956 USOC provide small charms, pins, or insignia to US athletes either by gift or purchase to allow these competitors to trade with team members from other countries. Bob Mathias reported the trading frenzy. However, Rule Nineteen of "Important Regulations"

stated, "The personnel of the Olympic Teams shall not take with them any articles for the purpose of sale or barter.... Violation of the above... shall be grounds for immediate dismissal from the team." Bushnell, *US 1952 Olympic Book*, 249; Henry Matis, "Report of Attaché," in *US 1952 Olympic Book,* Bushnell, 252; Tassin, *Bob Mathias,* 80; USOC, *Information and Instruction for Members and Officials of the US Olympic Team.*
33. Kolkka, *XV Olympiad Helsinki, Finland: The Official Report*, 91.
34. Smith, *Cowboy Stuntman*, 45-52.
35. AP, "Injured Vaulter to Miss Tuneups," *Spokane (WA) Daily Chronicle*, July 11, 1952, https://www.newspapers.com.
36. The author viewed a postcard, an Aerogram, and a letter mailed from Helsinki to the US in July 1952 along with US postcard postage during that period. Private collection; Kolkka, *XV Olympiad Helsinki, Finland: The Official Report*, 114.
37. Brylcreem, "The Look Is Back"; Gourdine, *Untitled Memories*; "Sport: The Strength of Ten," *Time*, Monday, July 21, 1952, https:// content.time.com/time/subscriber/article/0,33009,859899,00.html.
38. Richards, interview, (see chap. 4, n. 32); Stone, "Stars Work Out," see note 27 above; Kolkka, *XV Olympiad Helsinki, Finland: The Official Report*, 311; "Don Laz Pole Vault," Art of the Vault, YouTube video, 0:08, https://www.youtube.com/watch?v=zuEX_UXZcDQ.

Chapter 7

1. Mashburn, interview, (see OM, n. 9).
2. Thane July 15 letter, (see chap. 4, n. 9).
3. Bushnell, *US 1952 Olympic Book*, 75.
4. Smith, *Cowboy Stuntman*, 15, 190.
5. Gourdine, *Untitled Memories.*
6. Bushnell, *US 1952 Olympic Book*, 249-250.
7. AP, "Reds Drop Icy Attitude, OK Olympic Base Visits," *Democrat and Chronicle* (Rochester, NY), July 10, 1952.
8. AP, "Red Olympians Get 'Friendly,'" (see chap. 6, n. 21).
9. Zimmerman, "Makes Plans," (see OM, n. 9).
10. AP, "Reds' Entry Noted: U.S. Athletes Urged to Do Better Than the Best," *Ithaca (NY) Journal,* June 30, 1952, https://www.newspapers.com.
11. AP, "Moore Best," (see chap. 4, n. 27).
12. The 1952 Olympic Games instituted the Olympics as a venue for Cold War propaganda. Murray Olderman, "Brutus Hamilton, U.S. Coach, Says He'll Use 'Natural Approach' on Russ," Newspaper Enterprise Association, *La Crosse (WI) Sunday Tribune*, July 13, 1952, https://www.newspapers.com; Redihan, *Olympics and the Cold War;* Rider, *Cold War Games.*
13. UP, "U.S. Olympians Under Pressure: Past Records and Russia's Entry Cast Air of Tension about Departure," Lafayette (IN) Journal and Courier, July 8, 1952, https://www.newspapers.com.
14. AP, "Arrives," (see chap. 6, n. 4).
15. UP, "Hamilton Picks U.S. to Gain 10 Firsts in Olympic Track—Looks for Sweep

in 2 Events," *St. Louis Post-Dispatch,* July 14, 1952, https://www.newspapers.com.
16. Olderman, "Brutus Hamilton," see note 12 above.
17. *Track and Field,* "Mal Whitfield"; Kelyn Soong, "Harrison Dillard, U.S. Track Luminary Who Won Four Olympic Gold Medals, Dies at 96," *Washington Post,* November 16, 2019, https://www.washingtonpost.com/local/obituaries/harrison-dillard-us-track-luminary-who-won-four-olympic-gold-medals-dies-at-96/2019/11/16/a8d7b33e-086c-11ea-8ac0-0810ed197c7e_story.html; AAU, "AAU Sullivan Award–Past Winners."
18. One hundred days before the 1948 Olympics, Mathias had never thrown a javelin, run hurdles at Olympic height, pole vaulted, thrown a sixteen-pound shot put or competed in either the 400 or 1,500 meters. Bob Mathias said he would not compete in the 1952 Olympics if someone paid him a million dollars. Tassin, *Bob Mathias,* 24-51; "Bob Mathias Makes History by Winning the Decathlon at Just 17!"; IOC, July 29, 1948, https://olympics.com/en/news/bob-mathias-athletics; Bushnell, *Report of the US Olympic Committee 1948 Games,* 98-100; AAU, "AAU Sullivan Award–Past Winners."
19. AP, "He's Taking No Chances," St. Louis Post-Dispatch, July 14, 1952, https://www.newspapers.com.
20. UP, "Athletes' Sleeping Habits Disrupted by Midnight Sun," Spokane (WA), July 11, 1952, https://www.newspapers.com; "Helsinki, Finland–Sunrise, Sunset, and Day length, July 1952," timeanddate.com, https://www.timeanddate.com/sun/finland/helsinki?month=7&year=1952; Calendar–12, "Moon Phases July 1952"; Mashburn, interview, (see OM, n. 9).
21. The Finnish Organizing Committee printed the daily Olympic programs in four languages: Finnish, French, English, and Swedish. Kolkka, *XV Olympiad Helsinki, Finland: The Official Report,* 67, 110, 220; Programme Office of the Organising Committee for the XV Olympiad. "XV Olympia Helsinki 1952: Daily Programme, Dagsprogram, 25.7," 14.
22. Avery Brundage (President, USOA) to All Members of the US Delegation to the Games of the XV Olympiad, July 7, 1952, private collection.
23. Chandler, "Brutus Hamilton."
24. Thane Baker did not realize until he saw the developed photograph that the photographer posed Thane in front of the Coca-Cola stand.
25. Bob Busby, "U.S. in Workouts," *Kansas City (MO) Times,* July 10, 1952, https://newspapers.com.
26. By 1948, Bickle no longer lived in Elkhart. "Hit That Bell, George; Everything Set for Golden Gloves Tourney: Strongest Field in Many Years on Opening Card Monday," *Hutchinson (KS) News,* January 30, 1949, https://www.newspapers.com; Barrodale, "Boxing," in *US 1952 Olympic Book,* Bushnell, 158-160; Bear, *Official Report of the XVth Olympic Games,* 46-48.
27. The July 1951 flood in Manhattan, Kansas, brought seven feet of water inside the Wareham Hotel. Towers, interview, (see chap. 3, n. 3); "History," Harry's, https://harrysmanhattan.com/history.html; "Flood Scenes in Manhattan Kansas," Kansas Memory, Kansas Historical Society, https://www.kansasmemory.org/item/308290; *Manhattan Mercury,* "Stubblefield-Schoonover Coming Back with Plans for Expansion," August 9, 1951. https://www.newspapers.com.

28. "Thane Baker, who tied the world indoor record in the 60-yard dash and was the Big Seven outdoor champion in the 100 and 200 meters, as well as the indoor 60 and 440-yard champion, spoke on 'Sports to Me' at the Wareham Hotel." "Athletes Will Be Honored," *Manhattan Mercury-Chronicle,* April 16, 1952. https://www.newspapers.com; In a letter held in a private collection and dated April 16, 1952, Don Biggs (Outgoing President, Student Council) invited Thane Baker and other newly elected student council members to dinner at the Wareham Hotel. "Council Meets, Elects Walker," *Manhattan (KS) Mercury-Chronicle,* April 22, 1952.
29. Between July 9 and 18, 1952, Thane Baker found Bobby Bickle in the Olympic Village, and Everett Wareham came to the gate to meet Thane. The author used artistic license to place them in chapter seven.

Chapter 8

1. Bushnell stated that the athletes wore blue leather belts. However, Becky Ellis, Director of the Morton County Museum, where Thane Baker's woven belt is on loan, stated that the belt had two rows of red, a thin row of white, and two rows of blue. Swarts, "Supplies and Equipment Committee," in *US 1952 Olympic Book,* 262; History of Branding, "History of Old Spice."
2. Kolkka, *XV Olympiad Helsinki, Finland: The Official Report,* 93; Bushnell, *US 1952 Olympic Book,* 35, 248; "Flags flutter at the Olympic Village of the Helsinki Olympic Games, Photograph by UA Saarinen, Finnish Heritage Agency, https://www.finna.fi/Record/museovirasto.996BCC3E2A7303D769A58946B1095FC9; AP, "U.S. Olympic Team Raises Flag Today," *Athol (MA) Daily News,* July 12, 1952, https://www.newspapers.com; AP, "350 American Athletes, (see chap. 6, n. 17).
3. Held, interview, (see chap. 4, n. 36); International News Service, "Finland's Sun Fools American Athletes," *Minneapolis Star,* July 11, 1952, https://www.newspapers.com; Adolf Weinacker, interview by author, October 16, 2022.
4. Kolkka, *XV Olympiad Helsinki, Finland: The Official Report,* 220.
5. AP, "Hamilton Wants Wins for Present," *Spokane (WA) Daily Chronicle,* Sports, July 19, 1952, https://www.newspapers.com.
6. Bushnell, *US 1952 Olympic Book,* 72-73.
7. Charlie Dean Archives, "1952 Summer Olympic Games."
8. Kolkka, *XV Olympiad Helsinki, Finland: The Official Report,* 31, 221.
9. Norman Cudworth Armitage competed as a fencer on the US Olympic team from 1928 until 1956. "Norman Armitage, Fencing Star and Textile Executive, Dies at 65," *NYT,* March 15, 1972, https://timesmachine.nytimes.com.
10. Bushnell, *US 1952 Olympic Book,* 57, 66.
11. Kolkka, *XV Olympiad Helsinki, Finland: The Official Report,* 81.
12. Kolkka, *XV Olympiad Helsinki, Finland: The Official Report.*
13. Harrivirta, "Muistojen."
14. Marjorie Larney, another 1952 Olympian, describes the "pouring rain" along with being "chilled to the bone, my jacket, hat and skirt soaked clear through." "A Flying Javelin: Marjorie Larney," *Irish America,* August/September 2008, https://

irishamerica.com/2008/08/a-flying-javelin-marjorie-larney/; Kolkka, *XV Olympiad Helsinki, Finland: The Official Report*, 220-242.
15. Neil Ziegler, an American spectator in the stands who traveled to Helsinki on the first T&F News Tour, reported that when the small South Korean delegation entered the stadium, the crowd clapped with enthusiasm for their country beleaguered by war. Neil Ziegler, interview by author, October 7, 2022.
16. Bushnell, *US 1952 Olympic Book*, 57.
17. The Marathon gate sat on the east side of the stadium, close to the end of the southern curve near the 1,500-meter start. British Pathé, "1952 Helsinki Olympic Games: Opening Ceremony"; Arkisto, "Helsingin olympiakisojen avajaiset."
18. *Larney*, "Flying Javelin," see note 14 above; Charlie Dean Archives, "1952 Summer Olympic Games."
19. Kolkka, *XV Olympiad Helsinki, Finland: The Official Report*, 221, 236.
20. Neither the US nor the Soviets lowered their flag before the viewing stand. Kolkka, *XV Olympiad Helsinki, Finland: The Official Report*, 236; Red Smith, "Views of Sport," *Philadelphia Inquirer*, July 20, 1952. https://www.newspapers.com.
21. Harrivirta, "Muistojen."
22. Kolkka, *XV Olympiad Helsinki, Finland: The Official Report*, 238-239.
23. Aarre Merikanto wrote the music for the 1952 Olympic Fanfare. Areena Audio, "Aarre Marannon Olympic Fanfare-Helsinki Garrison Bandjoht. Martti Herantainen," https://areena.yle.fi/audio/1-61705454.
24. Two thousand five hundred birds launched. Kolkka, *Report*, (see chap. 6, n. 2), 240.
25. The Olympic torch traveled 7870 kilometers by airplane from Olympia, Greece, making it the first Olympic torch to fly. The torch relay touched down in Denmark and proceeded north through Sweden. In Tornio, Finland, this flame joined another flame kindled by the Midnight Sun at Pallastunturi, in Lapland, to symbolize unification of the northern and southern peoples. Runners, walkers, bicyclists, rowers, paddlers, and people on horseback carried the flame. One fourth of the population of Finland, whether as carriers, witnesses, or followers, involved themselves in its journey. Kolkka, *XV Olympiad Helsinki, Finland: The Official Report*, 103-105, 204-219.
26. "Paavo Nurmi Lights the Olympic Flame at the Opening Ceremony," 1952 Summer Olympics, Photographs, Urheilumuseo, https://www.urheilumuseo.fi/en/photographs/; UP, "With Torch but No Card, Nurmi Couldn't Get In," *NYT*, July 23, 1952, https://timesmachine.nytimes.com.
27. Harrivirta, "Muistojen." Charlie Dean Archives, "1952 Summer Olympic Games."
28. Hannes Kölehmainen lit the flame at the top of the tower. Smith, interview, (see chap. 4, n. 5); IOC, "Hannes Kölehmainen."
29. Barbara Rotraut-Pleyer, a German "Peace Apostle," wished to address "all nations of the world." Kluge, "The 'Peace Angel of Helsinki' Wanted to Save the World."
30. The archbishop said his prayer in Latin. The Olympic choir and spectators sang the Finnish national anthem. Kolkka, *XV Olympiad Helsinki, Finland: The Official Report*, 240.
31. *XV Olympische Sommerspiele 1952–1 Teil, Expedition Der Kölnischen Zeitung* (Cologne, Germany), August 1952, 2.

32. Smith, *Cowboy Stuntman*.
33. Clyde Littlefield had surgery in Finland and remained there to recover after the US Olympic team left Helsinki. Smith, *Cowboy Stuntman*, 65-66.
34. Harrivirta, "Muistojen."
35. Larney, *Flying Javelin*, (see note 14 above).

Chapter 9

1. Allison Danzig, "United States Takes Four T&F Tests Before 55,000 at Olympics: Remigino Wins 100 in Blanket Finish," *NYT*, July 22, 1952, https://timesmachine.nytimes.com.
2. H. D. Thoreau, "How Good Are Russian Athletes? Soviet Russia Has Been Characteristically Loud in Its Pre-Olympic Claims of What Its Athletes Can Do. Here an Olympics Expert Tells You How the Russian Athletes Really Compare to Those of the United States and Other Nations," *The Saturday Evening Post*, July 19, 1952, 26-27, 87-89.
3. Powell, *The Fastest Men on Earth*, "1952–Helsinki"; Will Grimsley, "Remigino Is Cinderella of Olympics with Sprint Win," AP, *Wisconsin Rapids Daily Tribune*, July 22, 1952, https://www.newspapers.com; Smith, *On the Line*, "Helsinki 1952–The Fastest Cowboy Stuntman"; Frank Litsky, "Lindy Remigino, Olympic Champion Runner, Is Dead at 87," Obituaries, *NYT*, July 12, 2018, https://www.nytimes.com.
4. Kolkka, *XV Olympiad Helsinki, Finland: The Official Report*, 71-73.
5. The City of Helsinki provided starting blocks for the competitors, but the Americans used their own blocks. Kolkka, *XV Olympiad Helsinki, Finland: The Official Report*, 76.
6. Kolkka, *XV Olympiad Helsinki, Finland: The Official Report*, 266.
7. "200 Metres," Kolkka, *XV Olympiad Helsinki, Finland: The Official Report*, 272; Olympedia, OlyMADMen, ed. s.v. "Levan Sanadze," https://www.olympedia.org/athletes/77623; "Camp Open to Visitors," *The State* (Columbia, SC), July 10, 1952, https://newspapers.com.
8. Bob Busby, "Thane Baker Two Steps Nearer to Winning Gold Medal in Olympics," *Kansas City Star*, July 22 or 23, 1952, private collection; Bear, *Official Report of the XVth Olympic Games*, 15.
9. International Soundphoto, "Art Bragg Wins 100 Meters Olympic Final," *Modoc County Record* (Alturas, CA), July 3, 1952, https://newspapers.com; AP, "Moore Beats Russian in 400 Hurdles to Top 40 Thrilling Minutes," *Evening Star* (Washington D.C.), July 21, 1952, https://newspapers.com; IOC, "4x100M Relay Men," Athletics, London-1948, https://olympics.com/en/olympic-games/london-1948/results/athletics/4x100m-relay-men; IOC, "Jesse Owens."
10. Smith, interview (see chap. 4 n. 5); Smith, *Cowboy Stuntman*, 61-62.
11. Kolkka, *XV Olympiad Helsinki, Finland: The Official Report*, 266; Bear, *Official Report of the XVth Olympic Games*, 22-23.
12. Richards, interview, (see chap. 4, n. 32).
13. The pole vaulters landed in a pile of sawdust. Bushnell, "Pole Vault," in *US 1952 Olympic Book*, 105; Kolkka, *XV Olympiad Helsinki, Finland: The Official Report*,

258; AP, "U.S. Wins Three Titles in Track; Kelly Ousted," *Philadelphia Inquirer,* July 23, 1952, https://newspapers.com; "Himmel," *Expedition,* (see chap. 8, n. 31), 36-37.
14. Kolkka, *XV Olympiad Helsinki, Finland: The Official Report,* 311; "Don Laz" Art of the Vault, (see chap. 6, 38); IOC, "George Frank Mattos: Biography."
15. Milestones of the Century, "1952 Olympic Games"; Richards, interview, (see chap. 4, n. 32); Kolkka, *XV Olympiad Helsinki, Finland: The Official Report,* 261.
16. Ps. 150.
17. Richards, *Heart of a Champion,* 120.
18. Isa. 40:31.
19. Richards, interview, (see chap. 4, n. 32).
20. Dillard, interview, (see chap. 4, n. 35); Kolkka, *XV Olympiad Helsinki, Finland: The Official Report,* 89."
21. A running back for the Stanford football team, Bob Mathias holds the distinction of being the only person to compete in the Rose Bowl and the Olympics in the same year. Olympedia, OlyMADMen, ed. s.v. Bob Mathias, https://www.olympedia.org/athletes/78742.
22. *Time*, "Sport: The Strength of Ten"; AP, "Whitfield Impressive in Olympic Workouts," *Corpus Christi* (TX) *Caller,* July 16, 1952, https://newspapers.com.
23. Powell, *The Fastest Men on Earth,* "1952–Helsinki."
24. Museum of the Gulf Coast, "Walter 'Buddy' Davis"; "Davis, Moore Shatter High Jump, Hurdle Records–Texan Gives U.S. First Olympic Victory," *Stars and Stripes: Unofficial Publication of the US Armed Forces in Europe,* Olympic Souvenir Edition, August 1952; British Pathé, "1952 Helsinki Olympic Games: Opening Competitions"; British Pathé, "Helsinki Olympics Various Events–Slow Motions High Jumps 1952."
25. Moore Sr. served as the alternate. AP, "Moore Best," (see chap. 4, n. 27); Moore, *Running Purpose,* (see chap. 4, n. 41), 5, 8, 47-49, 52-53; Moore, interview, (see chap. 5, n. 30); Yoder, interview, (see chap. 5, n. 5); Bushnell, "400-Meters Hurdles," in *US 1952 Olympic Book,* 95-97; Karen Rosen, "91-Year-Old Olympic Gold Medalist Charles H. Moore Jr. Is Running His Final Lap with Purpose," TeamUSA, September 15, 2020, https://www.teamusa.org/News/2020/September/15/91-Year-Old-Olympic-Gold-Medalist-Charles-H-Moore-Jr-Is-Running-His-Final-Lap-With-Purpose.
26. Harrison "Bones" Dillard said he and Jack Davis were the "two best 110-meter hurdle runners in the world at that time." Dillard, interview, (see chap. 4, n. 35); Debbie Hanson, "Harrison Dillard: Only Person to Ever Win Olympic Gold in Both Hurdles and Sprints," *Cleveland Seniors,* www.clevelandseniors.com/people/harrison-dillard.htm.
27. When a runner speaks of a quarter, they mean one lap around the track. Back when tracks were measured in yards, four laps equaled a mile. Thus, one lap is a quarter mile. Whitfield, "My Dad, Marvelous Mal"; *Track and Field,* "Mal Whitfield"; Red Smith, "Helsinki, July 22," Views of Sport, *Philadelphia Inquirer,* July 23, 1952, https://www.newspapers.com; "Whitfield, Iness and Richards Triumph but Soviet Keeps Olympic Point Lead: U.S. Sets 2 Marks, Stays in 2D Place," *NYT,* July 23, 1952, https://timesmachine.nytimes.com.

Chapter 10

1. Allison Danzig, "2 U.S. Trackmen Win, But Soviet Still Leads," *NYT,* July 24, 1952, https://timesmachine.nytimes.com.
2. Programme Office of the Organising Committee, "XV Olympia Helsinki 1952: Daily Programme, Dagsprogram, 23.7," 9; Kolkka, *XV Olympiad Helsinki, Finland: The Official Report,* 274, 294.
3. Bingisser, "The Perfect Physique for Throwing"; "Infographic: Body Shapes by Sport," Sports Medicine, Health Beat, University of Pittsburgh Medical Center, https://share.upmc.com/2015/07/infographic-body-shapes-by-sport/; Crystal Welch, "The Role of Bones, Joints & Muscles for the Javelin Throw," SportsRec, July 8, 2011, https://www.sportsrec.com/364336-the-role-of-bones-joints-muscles-for-the-javelin-throw.html; Danzig, "2 U.S. Trackmen Win, see note 1 above."
4. British Olympic Association, "BOA Honours Achievements of Sprinter Emmanuel McDonald Bailey"; Nelson, "200 Meters," *Track and Field News,* 3; IOC, "Emmanuel McDonald Bailey."
5. "Stanfield Auf Jesse Owens Spuren," *Expedition,* (see chap. 8, n. 31), 35; Olympedia, OlyMADMen, ed. s.v. "Geraldo Bönnhoff," http://www.olympedia.org/athletes/64399; Olympedia, OlyMADMen, ed. s.v. "Les Laing," www.olympedia.org/athletes/72300.
6. Olympedia, "Gathers," (see chap. 5, n. 33).
7. Way to Win, "200m World Record Evolution Leading to 18.99 Seconds"; Olympedia, OlyMADMen, ed. s.v. "Andy Stanfield," www.olympedia.org/athletes/79086.
8. The first written records of the Games appear in 776 B.C. Athletes raced about 192 meters, or one *stadion.* History.com, "The Olympic Games"; IOC, "Run Leonidas Run."
9. Bushnell, *US 1952 Olympic Book,* 96-97.
10. Programme Office of the Organising Committee, "XV Olympia Helsinki 1952: Daily Programme, Dagsprogram, 23.7," 12.
11. McAllister, "Why Do Runners Line Up Staggered?"; Boylan-Pett, "How Do Lane Assignments and Starting Spots Work in Track?".
12. *Iola (KS) Register,* "K-State Runner Avoids Tension Now and Becomes a Big Track Star," April 17, 1952, https://www.newspapers.com; "Relaxation Pays Off for K-State Whiz," *Elkhart (KS) Tri-State News,* April 18, 1952.
13. Smith, interview, (see chap. 4, n. 5); Moore, interview, (see chap. 5, n. 30); Richards, interview, (see chap. 4, n. 32).
14. Programme Office of the Organising Committee, "XV Olympia Helsinki 1952: Daily Programme, Dagsprogram, 23.7," 14.
15. Bushnell, "200-Meters Dash," in *US 1952 Olympic Book,* 81.
16. AP, "America's Three Speedsters Planned 200 Race That Way," *Elmira (NY) Advertiser,* July 24, 1952, https://newspapers.com.
17. Kolkka, *XV Olympiad Helsinki, Finland: The Official Report,* 64.
18. Kolkka, *XV Olympiad Helsinki, Finland: The Official Report,* 169. The attendance was 62,680 spectators.
19. Eight thousand Finns worked at the Olympic Games including five thousand

volunteers. "Workmen were present to smooth every mark made on the track." Bushnell, "Olympic Men's T&F Championships," in *US 1952 Olympic Book*, Bushnell, 78.

20. "The 200 metres final was run in Helsinki with a following wind along the home straight of a velocity of 1 metres/sec." Kolkka, *XV Olympiad Helsinki, Finland: The Official Report*, 250.
21. In "200 Metres," Harold Abrahams, the British 1924 100-meter Olympic champion, reports "a perfect start." At fifty meters, Stanfield had made up much of the stagger against Bailey, who was even with Gathers and Baker. Bear, *Official Report of the XVth Olympic Games*, 15; *Chariots of Fire*, directed by Hugh Hudson, (Great Britain: Allied Stars, Enigma Productions, 20th Century Fox, 1981); Bushnell, *US 1952 Olympic Book*, 81; Nelson, "200 Meters," *Track and Field News*.
22. British Pathé, "Helsinki 1952 The Olympic Games: Latest Events."
23. Thane Baker had number 984. Jim Gathers in lane six wore 985. Andy Stanfield's number was 983.
24. The 200 meters race claims from 5:41 until 6:32 of this video. Thane Baker is not visible at the beginning, but comes into view running in lane seven, closest to the stands. Charlie Dean Archives, "1952 Summer Olympic Games."
25. Thane exerted a "tremendous burst of speed to come on for second." "200-Meter, Javelin Titles Won by U.S.–Stanfield Leads to Tape; Young's Toss Takes Crown," *Stars and Stripes*, (see chap. 9, n. 24), 9; "History of the Olympic Results: 200 Meters–Men," *T&F News*, https://trackandfieldnews.com/olympic-results/history-of-olympic-results-200-meters-men/.
26. Bushnell, *US 1952 Olympic Book*, 82; *Expedition*, "Stanfield Auf Jesse Owens Spuren," (see chap. 8, n. 31), 35.
27. Programme Office of the Organising Committee, "XV Olympia Helsinki 1952: Daily Programme, Dagsprogram, 23.7," 15.
28. Kolkka, *XV Olympiad Helsinki, Finland: The Official Report*, 77, 106; Bushnell, *US 1952 Olympic Book*, 67.
29. Prior to the Rome Olympics in 1960, winners did not receive medals to wear around their necks. "All Medals," IOC, https://olympics.com/en/olympic-games/olympic-medals.
30. Charlie Dean Archives, "1952 Summer Olympic Games."
31. Tears welled in Thane Baker's eyes whenever he heard the Star-Spangled Banner for decades after his Olympic experiences. Stan Burnette, "Thane Baker Relates Olympic Experiences: Finishing Second in Dash Is a "Great Thrill" for Kansan," *Manhattan (KS) Mercury–Chronicle*, September 3, 1952, https://www.newspapers.com.
32. UP, "Token of Greatness," Here 'n' There at Games, *Salt Lake (UT) Telegram*, July 22, 1952, https://www.newspapers.com; British Pathé, "Helsinki Olympics Various Events–Men's Discus, Men's Pole Vault, Men's 100 Meters, Women's 200 Meter 1952," filmed July 20-July 25, 1952, 3:49, https://www.britishpathe.com/video/oly12-helsinki-olympics-various-events-mens-discus-mens-pole-vault-mens-100-meters-womens-200-meters/query/1952+world+record.
33. Urheilumuseo, "Thane Baker, Andrew Stanfield and Jim Gathers," Sports Photos.
34. Gourdine, *Untitled Memories*.

35. AP, "Speedsters," see note 16 above.
36. "Sprinters Happy Over 1-2-3 Finish in 200," Sports, *Deseret News* (Salt Lake City, UT), July 23, 1952, https://www.newspapers.com.
37. Oscar Fraley, "Meter Winners Say–Not Surprised at Victory," UP, *Scranton (PA) Tribune*, July 24, 1952, https://www.newspapers.com.
38. AP, "200–Meter Winners Had It Planned," *Shreveport (LA) Journal*, July 24, 1952, https://www.newspapers.com.
39. Ted Smits, "Young Brings U.S. 1st Javelin Crown in Olympics: Stanfield Leads American Slam in 200 Meters; 5 Marks Broken," AP, *Elmira (NY) Advertiser*, July 24, 1952, https://newspapers.com.
40. AP, "Speedsters," see note 16 above.
41. Fraley, "Not Surprised," see note 37 above.
42. Dick O'Malley, "Had a Lot of Confidence in Stanfield—Hamilton," *Elmira (NY) Advertiser*, July 24, 1952, https://newspapers.com.
43. The 1952 Olympics marked the third time that the US won first, second, and third in the 200 meters since the modern Olympics began. Olympedia, OlyMADMen, ed. s.v. "Athletics-200 Metres, Men," https://www.olympedia.org/event_names/41.
44. Bob Busby, "Thane Baker, Like Cunningham, Brings Honor to Elkhart, Kas.– The Fleet Kansas State Dash Man Says He Ran All Out but Was Fresh at End of Second Place Finish in the 200-Meter," *Kansas City (MO) Times*, July 24, 1952, https://www.newspapers.com; Burnette, "Baker Relates," see note 31 above.
45. "Thane Baker Second in 200-Meter Run," *Elkhart (KS) Tri-State News*, July 25, 1952.
46. British Pathé, "Helsinki Street Scenes"
47. Billings, interview, (see chap. 3, n. 4).
48. Nelson, "200 Meters," *Track and Field News*, 3.
49. USOC, *Instruction*, (see chap. 5, n. 21).
50. Bushnell, *Report of the 1948 Games*, p. 71.
51. Ward Haylett to Mr. & Mrs. W. Baker, postcard, August 12, 1952, private collection.
52. "Thane Baker Wins Firsts in Big Seven Meet," *Elkhart (KS) Tri-State News*, March 7, 1952; "Ability to Relax Big Factor in Baker's Success," *Manhattan (KS) Mercury*, April 11, 1952, https://www.newspapers.com.
53. "Cat Harriers Fun Wild, Gym Team Closes Season," *Kansas State Collegian*, March 31, 1952.
54. Nick Kominus, "Baker's Last 10 Yards Was Fastest Ever, Haylett Says," Manhattan newspaper, 1951-1953.
55. IOC, "Jesse Owens completes the Hat-Trick"; IOC, "Melvin Emery Patton."
56. Charlie Cutler, "The Second Guesser," *Council Grove (KS) Republican*, October 14, 1952, https://www.newspapers.com; "Thane Baker Breaks 220 Record–Shot Put Toss Erases Localite's (word unavailable)," *Manhattan (KS) Daily Tribune*, May 18, 1952.
57. Emeritus Professors, KSU's Centennial Year, *K-Stater*, June 1963, Socolofsky, "Haylett," (see chap. 3, n. 4).
58. University Travel Service, *Join At Masters Director of Athletics Jack Weiershauser*

Track Coach at Stanford University at the Olympic Games and Visit Europe in '52, (pamphlet, Palo Alto, CA: n.p., 1952). (Note: original name may have been marked through in 1952, based on where the author found this.)

59. "Haylett in Manhattan; Readies for Olympics," *Manhattan (KS) Mercury—Chronicle,* July 2, 1952, https://www.newspapers.com.
60. "Thane Baker Wins Second in Olympic Finals," *Elkhart (KS) Tri-State News,* July 25, 1952.
61. "Fraction off Record: Baker Second in Finals," *Manhattan (KS) Mercury,* July 23, 1952, https://www.newspapers.com; Baker Fulfills Haylett's 25-Year-Old Wish," *Mercury (KS) Chronicle,* July 1, 1952. https://www.newspapers.com.
62. Oren Campbell, "Baker Overcomes Inexperience to Lead Big Seven Sprinters," *Kansas State Collegian,* February 21, 1952.
63. As of the date of this writing, the metal from Thane Baker's 1945 injury is still under his kneecap.
64. Charlie Dean Archives, "1952 Summer Olympic Games."
65. AP, "Navy Eight Scores Over Soviet Crew: Extends U. S. Olympic Streak to Seven Straight–Rutgers Pair Defeats Belgians," July 24, 1952, https://timesmachine.nytimes.com; Danzig, "Trackmen Win," see note 1 above. Burnette, "Baker Relates," see note 32 above.
66. Philip Noel-Baker, M.P. Commandant of the British Olympic Team, "Good Feeling at the Games," (London) *Observer,* August 3, 1952, https://www.newspapers.com.
67. Loewen, "Sundown Towns," and Black Holocaust Museum, "Racial Segregation Past and Present," (see OM, n. 13).
68. "Veryl Switzer," K-State Athletics Hall of Fame, https://www.kstatesports.com/honors/k-state-athletics-hall-of-fame/veryl-switzer/13; Bill Felber, "Greatest 8 Athletes in the Spotlight Again," *Manhattan (KS) Mercury,* October 7, 1990.
69. Charlie Moore said when track team from Cornell competed in Washington, DC, the first hotel they visited refused to allow Flash Gourdine to stay in their establishment because of the color of his skin. The Cornell team left and found another that accepted all of them. Moore, interview, (see chap. 5, n. 30).
70. The KSC track team encountered racial discrimination against its Black members multiple times, but the entire team faced it together. Towers, interview, (see chap. 3, n. 3); Mershon, interview, (see chap. 3, n. 4).
71. Jjr799, "The Intersection of Athletics and Race on the 40 Acres," Diversity and Community Engagement, University of Texas at Austin, November 18, 2014, https://diversity.utexas.edu/integration/2014/11/the-intersection-of-athletics-and-race-on-the-40-acres/.
72. Held, interview, (see chap. 4, n. 36); AP, "Games Results: Track-Field, Men, Javelin Final," *San Francisco Examiner,* July 24, 1952, https://www.newspapers.com.

Chapter 11

1. Programme Office, "XV Olympia Helsinki 1952: Daily Programme, Dagsprogram, 25.7," 2.

2. Thane Baker to Mr. and Mrs. Walter F. Baker, July 25, 1952, private collection.
3. The four by one refers to the 4x100-meter relay.
4. Olympedia, OlyMADMen, ed. s.v. "Athletics-4 x 100 metres Relay, Men: Medal Winners," https://www.olympedia.org/event_names/57.
5. Bonnie Berkowitz and Artur Galocha, "Medal or Nothing: U.S. Men's Sprinters Have a Handoff Problem," *Washington Post*, August 5, 2021, https://www.washingtonpost.com/sports/olympics/2021/08/04/relay-baton-handoff-usa-olympics/.
6. Programme Office, "XV Olympia Helsinki 1952: Daily Programme, Dagsprogram, 25.7," 4-6, 8-9.
7. IOC, "Bob Mathias"; "Floyd Macon Jr. Simmons," Biography, IOC, https://olympics.com/en/athletes/floyd-macon-jr-simmons#b2p-athlete-olympic-results; IOC, "Milton Grey Campbell."
8. Bear, *Official Report of the XVth Olympic Games*, 30.
9. Queen, "US Veterans in the Olympics" *Big Picture–Your Army in Action*; Harrivirta, "Muistojen."
10. Thane Baker to Mr. and Mrs. Walter F. Baker, August 4, 1952, private collection.
11. Bushnell, *US 1952 Olympic Book*, 74.
12. Dillard, interview, (see chap. 4, n. 35).
13. Held, interview, (see chap. 4, n. 36).
14. British Pathé, "Discus."
15. IOC, Chakraborty, "Steeplechase: Rules, Regulations."
16. Moore, interview, (see chap. 5, n. 30).
17. Bear, *Official Report of the XVth Olympic Games*, 23. Kolkka, *XV Olympiad Helsinki, Finland: The Official Report*, 298-300.
18. Young, "Finnish Scholarship Fund," in *US 1952 Olympic Book*, Bushnell, 274.
19. Richards, *Heart of a Champion*, 42-43. Leased Wires, "Ashenfelter Goes Directly to Drill after Record Run," *Des Moines Tribune*, July 23, 1952.
20. Kolkka, *XV Olympiad Helsinki, Finland: The Official Report*, 266.
21. Schuster, "Distance Around a Running Track for Each Lane?" LiveStrong.com.
22. ESPN, "Horace Ashenfelter"; Bowman, "Horace Ashenfelter Dies at 94"; TF Filmarchiv, "Helsinki 1952 [Horace Ashenfelter] 3000m Steeplechase"; Robert D. McFadden, "Horace Ashenfelter, Olympic Victor of a Cold War Showdown, Dies at 94," *NYT*, January 7, 2018, https://www.nytimes.com/2018/01/07/obituaries/horace-ashenfelter-dead-olympic-steeplechase.html?_r=0; Kolkka, *XV Olympiad Helsinki, Finland: The Official Report*, 298-299; AAU, "AAU Sullivan Award–Past Winners."
23. As of the date of this publication, Horace Ashenfelter is the only American to win the Olympic 3000-meter steeplechase. James Lightbody from the US in the 1904 St. Louis Games won a 2,590-meter steeplechase. Olympedia, OlyMADMen, ed. s.v. "James 'Jim' Davies Lightbody," http://www.olympedia.org/athletes/78697.
24. New York Athletic Club, "Olympic History"; Programme Office, "XV Olympia Helsinki 1952: Daily Programme, Dagsprogram, 25.7," 4.
25. Bushnell, "5000-Meters Run," "10,000-Meters Run," *US 1952 Olympic Book*, 88-89.
26. Kolkka, *XV Olympiad Helsinki, Finland: The Official Report*, 252-255, 284-292.
27. "Dana Ingrova-Zatopkova: Biography," IOC, https://olympics.com/en/athletes/

dana-ingrova-zatopkova; Frank Litsky and William McDonald, "Dana Zatopkova, Champion Javelin Thrower, Is Dead at 97," *NYT,* March 13, 2020, updated March 15, 2020, https://www.nytimes.com/2020/03/13/sports/olympics/dana-zatopkova-dead.html.
28. "Emil Zátopek the Pioneer of Hypoventilation Training," Hypoventilation Training, YouTube video, 1:04, https://www.youtube.com/watch?v=shR8pIU7iLo.
29. Weinacker, interview, (see chap. 8, n. 4).
30. Helsingin Osakepankki, *Welcome to Helsinki*; "Stockmann"; GPSMYCITY, "Three Smiths Statue, Helsinki."
31. Visit Finland, "Suomenlinna–The Sea Fortress of Helsinki; Belloni, *Finland: Land of a Thousand Lakes*, 20-21.
32. Wikipedia, s.v. "Linnanmäki," last modified April 14, 2020, 17:19, https://en.wikipedia.org/wiki/Linnanmäki.
33. AP, "Finnish Belle Miss Universe," *Daily News* (New York, NY), June 30, 1952, https://www.newspapers.com.
34. Thane July 15 letter, (see chap. 4, n. 9).
35. History of Branding, "History of Old Spice."
36. "Baker Sets New Record," *Elkhart (KS) Tri-State News,* June 6, 1952.
37. Linnanmäki, "Welcome to the Merriest Part of Helsinki!"
38. Wikipedia, "Linnanmäki," (see note 32 above).
39. Wikipedia, s. v. *Billboard* year-end top 30 singles of 1952, last modified June 11, 2021, https://en.wikipedia.org/wiki/Billboard_year-end_top_30_singles_of_1952#.
40. Stephens, "The Bombing of Helsinki in World War II."
41. British Pathé, "Helsinki Street Scenes"; *suomalaista emmental juustoa kosken laskija* cheese label, one and a half inches per side.
42. Helsinki Kuvia.FI, "Linnanmäki."
43. Mashburn, interview, (see OM, n. 9).
44. National Weather Service, "Aurora Borealis."
45. City Guides & Bookings, Experience the Northern Lights in Helsinki," Helsinki.com, https://www.helsinki.com/blog.2017/08/17/experience-northern-lights-helsinki.

Chapter 12

1. Calendar–12, "Moon Phases August 1952."
2. Tidmarch, "Vienna 1945 or Wien Ist eine 'Perle'"; PeriscopeFilm, "Visit to War Ravaged Vienna."
3. In 1945 at the end of World War II, more than twenty percent of housing was uninhabitable, which included 87,000 apartments. In the late 1940s, Viennese citizens suffered great hardship, not only from the wartime destruction of their property, but also from starvation. City of Vienna, "The Years of the Allied Forces in Vienna"; Time Travel: Magic Vienna History Tour, "Occupied Vienna"; Lindtberg, *Four in a Jeep (Die Vier im Jeep)*.
4. History.com, "Korean War."
5. Spanish Riding School, "About Us."

6. Brownlow, "Around Vienna's Ring (Ringstrasse)," *Visiting Vienna*.

Chapter 13

1. Kolkka, *XV Olympiad Helsinki, Finland: The Official Report*, 96, 266.
2. Ferris, Members, (see chap. 5, n. 8).
3. Baker to Be Home August 15," *Elkhart (KS) Tri-State News*, August 1952; Baker to parents, August 4, 1952, (see chap. 11, n. 10).
4. Fodor, *Scandinavia in 1952*, 394.
5. Turun Urheiluliito r.y (The Turku Athletic Union) and Turku Toverit r.y. (The Turku Comrades), Invitation to Competition: Post–Olympics in Turku. July 1952, private collection; "31 Amris Tävlar på Landsorten," Swedish newspaper clipping, unknown publisher, late July 1952.
6. Åbo is the Swedish name for Turku, which is the oldest city in Finland. In 1952, Finland had two official languages, Finnish and Swedish. Wikipedia, s.v. "Turku," last updated August 28, 2020, 20:53, https://en.wikipedia.org/wiki/Turku; Fodor, *Scandinavia in 1952*, 374.
7. AP, "Finns Amazed at U.S. Cagers," Sports, *Oakland (CA) Tribune*, July 9, 1952, https://www.newspapers.com.
8. Bushnell, "Shot Put," In *US 1952 Olympic Book*, 100-101; AP, "Jim Fuchs Called 'Hard Luck Boy' of Olympic Games," *Gazette* (Montreal, Quebec), July 22, 1952, https://www.newspapers.com; Douglas Martin, "James E. Fuchs, Shot-Put Innovator, Dies at 82," *NYT*, October 17, 2010, https://www.nytimes.com/2010/10/18/sports/18fuchs.html; UP, "'Bench' Power Gave U. S. Four Medals," *Salt Lake (UT) Telegram*, July 22, 1952, https://www.newspapers.com; First Since Czars, *American–Statesman* (Austin, TX), July 20, 1952, https://www.newspapers.com; Bushnell, "Hammer Throw," in *US 1952 Olympic Book*, 101; "Martin Engel–Class of 1954–Hall of Fame–New York University," NYU Athletics, https://gonyuathletics.com/hof.aspx?hof=96&path=&kiosk=.
9. Bushnell, "400-Meters Run," "1600-Meters Relay," *US 1952 Olympic Book*, 82-84, 91-92; Frank Litsky, "Ollie Matson, an All-Purpose Football Star, Is Dead at 80," *NYT*, February 20, 2011, https://www.nytimes.com/2011/02/21/sports/football/21matson.html.
10. "Former Trojan Olympic Hurdler Davis Passes Away," T&F 200 Olympians, University of Southern California, July 23, 2012, https://usctrojans.com/news/2012/7/23/Former_Trojan_Olympic_Hurdler_Davis_Passes_Away.aspx.\
11. Bushnell, "Hop, Step, and Jump," in *US 1952 Olympic Book*, 107; Cornell University, "Walter Ashbaugh," CBS Sports Digital.
12. *Track and Field News*, "Men's World High Jump Rankings"; Bushnell, *US 1952 Olympic Book*, 105.
13. Bushnell, *US 1952 Olympic Book*, 95-96.
14. Visit Turku, "Turku Cathedral"; GPSMYCITY, "Samppalinna Park, Turku."
15. AP, "Jim Fuchs Called 'Hard Luck Boy' of Olympic Games," see note 8 above.
16. IOC, "USA's Golden Moment in the Helsinki 1952 4x100m," :30, https://olympics.com/en/video/usa-s-golden-moment-in-the-helsinki-1952-4x100m; "4 x 400 Metres Relay," Kolkka, *XV Olympiad Helsinki, Finland: The Official Report*,

301-303; Bushnell, "Olympic Women's T&F Championships," *US 1952 Olympic Book*, 114-116.
17. IOC, "Zátopek Completes Incredible Long-Distance Treble"; Grantland Rice, "Emil Zátopek Draws Praise: Fuchs Calls Czech Olympic Hero 'Remarkable Man,'" *Baltimore (MD) Sun*, August 20, 1952, https://www.newspapers.com; Yoder, interview, (see chap. 5, n. 5).
18. IOC, "Robert Mathias: Biography."
19. Turku, "Turku Castle."
20. Baker to parents, August 4, 1952, (see chap. 11, n 10).
21. Yoder, interview, (see chap. 5, n. 5).
22. Daniel J. Ferris, "Pre- & Post-Olympic Competition Committee," in *US 1952 Olympic Book*, Bushnell, 269-270.
23. K.L.M. Royal Dutch Airlines charter 9005, ticket number 0742 190937, issued to W. Thane Baker for 10 AM flight from Helsinki to London on August 2, 1952. A blue-inked circle stamped on the front and back of the ticket contained the Olympic rings and the Finnish flag. Written around the center were the words "In commemoration of your flight by KLM to the Olympic Games 1952–Helsinki," private collection.
24. Fred Smith, "15th Modern Olympiad Ends Sunday," International News Service, *Wichita (KS) Beacon*, August 3, 1952.
25. Roy Tomizawa, "The White City Stadium in London: The Birth of the Mega-Multi-Purpose Stadium," *The Olympians from 1964 to 2020* (blog), April 14, 2016, https://theolympians.co/2016/04/14/the-white-city-stadium-in-london-the-birth-of-the-mega-multi-purpose-stadium/.
26. UP, "U.S. Trackmen Top British Empire in Meet, Cut World 2-Mile Relay Mark: Americans Score in 11 of 16 Tests; U. S. Olympic Track Aces Beat British Empire as 50,000 Fans Watch at London; "Moore Ties Hurdle Mark; Quartet Timed in 7:29.2 for 2 Miles–World Records Cut in 2 Women's Events," *NYT*, August 5, 1952, https://timesmachine.nytimes.com.
27. Gourdine, *Untitled Memories*.
28. Bushnell, *US 1952 Olympic Book*, 82-84, 91-92.
29. Harold Keith, "Snub at Olympics Spurs Mashburn," *Daily Oklahoman* (Oklahoma City), September 7, 1952, https://www.newspapers.com. Mashburn, interview, (OM, n. 9).
30. Stan Burnette, "From the Sidelines," *Manhattan (KS) Mercury–Chronicle*, August 5, 1952, https://www.newspapers.com; "World Records Beaten Three Times–U.S. Defeat Empire," *Daily Telegraph & Morning Post* (London, England), August 5, 1952.

Chapter 14

1. British European Airways Passenger ticket and baggage check 0602 730639, London to *"Kärntner Ring,"* Vienna, August 5, 1952, 9:20 AM.
2. *Track and Field News*, "Men's World High Jump Rankings."
3. AP, "Moore Best," (see chap. 4, n. 27).
4. Dillard, interview, (see chap. 4, n. 35).

5. Zimmerman, "Makes Plans," (see OM, n. 9).
6. Kolkka, *XV Olympiad Helsinki, Finland: The Official Report*, 320; "Obituary, William P. Miller, Mariposa Gardens Memorial Park & Funeral Care, Dignity Memorial, October 27, 2016, https://www.dignitymemorial.com/obituaries/mesa-az/william-miller-7145312.
7. Kolkka, *XV Olympiad Helsinki, Finland: The Official Report*, 311; "Don Laz" Art of the Vault, (see chap. 6, n. 38).
8. "400-Meters Run," (see chap. 13, n. 29).
9. IOC, "Fortune Edward Gordien: Biography."
10. Larry Snyder, "My Boy Jesse," *Saturday Evening Post*, February 19, 2016, reprinted from November 7, 1936, https://www.saturdayeveningpost.com/2016/02/boy-jesse/; "Larry Snyder, USTFCCCA Special Inductees, Ohio State University," US Track & Field and Cross County Coaches Association Coaches Hall of Fame, https://www.ustfccca.org/awards/larry-snyder-ustfccca-special-inductee.
11. Museum of London, "London's Great Smog, 1952"; Klein, "The Great Smog of 1952."
12. Dillard, interview, (see chap. 4, n. 35).
13. IOC, "George Patton: Biography."
14. Zimmerman, "Makes Plans," (see OM, n. 9).
15. British Pathé, "London Traffic (1952)."
16. Baker to parents, August 4, 1952, (see chap. 11, n. 10).
17. The Hôtel Höller is now Sans Souci Wien. Sans Souci Wien, "The Philosophy & History."
18. Walter Elkins ed., "1952," Headquarters, US Forces, Austria, European Command, *US Army Germany*, (blog), http://usarmygermany.com/Sont_USFA.htm.
19. Walter Elkins ed., "European Exchange Service History," Army & Air Force Exchange Service, Europe, US Army, Europe, *US Army Germany* (blog), http://www.usarmygermany.com/Sont.htm?http&&&www.usarmygermany.com/Units/AAFES-Eur/USAREUR_AAFES.htm.
20. Dillard, interview, (see chap. 4, n. 35).
21. Jewelry Shopping Guide, "What is Marcasite Jewelry?"
22. The July and August 1952 newspapers calculated daily totals to determine which countries had the most points in the Olympic Games as of that date by assigning values to the medals issued. "United States win… the unofficial team title of the 1952 Olympics, 610 to 553 ½," Jack Ellis, "Olympic Games Finest Ever—U.S. Edges Russia in Team Standings," *Stars and Stripes* (see chap. 9, n. 24); "United States Clinches Team Title in Olympics: U. S. Triumphs in Basketball and Swimming; Boxers Set All-Time High of 5 Victories," *Post–Standard* (Syracuse, NY), August 3, 1952, https://www.newspapers.com; "Soviet Claims Games Victory– Moscow Works Out Its Own Placings," British newspaper, August 1952, in private collection; Harrison E. Salisbury, "Russians Hail Olympic 'Victory' But Fail to Substantiate Claim: Pravda Cites 'World Superiority of Soviet Athletes in Helsinki Games' without Providing Tabulation of Points," *New York Times*. August 5, 1952, https://timesmachine.nytimes.com.
23. "The IOC today unanimously passed a resolution "deploring the practice of publishing the standings of the nations in the Games . . . ." AP, "I.O.C. Deplores

Point Standings," *Calgary Herald* (Alberta, Canada), July 28, 1952, https://www.newspapers.com; Joseph Singer, "Olympic Head Fears Danger in Nationalism," International News Service, *Wichita Beacon,* August 4 or 5,1952.
24. Bushnell, *US 1952 Olympic Book*, 270.
25. Friedrich Burger, "Die Gründungsgeschichte des WAC," Wiener Athletiksport Club, 1946, https://www.wac.at/verein/geschichte/.
26. *Handbuch der Stadt Wien*.
27. *Festschrift, Internationales Leichtathletikmeeting*.
28. Ward Haylett to Thane Baker, postcard, August 11, 1952.
29. City of Vienna, "Vienna City Hall."
30. City of Vienna, Das Wiener Rathaus.
31. *Wien, Vienne, Vienna, Vieno—Ein Bilder-Album*.
32. Hoeffkes, "Wien in den 50ern"; City of Vienna, "Alte Filme–Soziales Bauen in Wien 1952."
33. Vienna Now–Forever, "In the Footsteps of Famous Musicians."
34. Vienna Now–Forever, "Sightseeing."
35. Domkirche St. Stephan, "History of the Cathedral Church"; British Pathé, "Big Bell for Vienna."
36. Hotel Sacher, "The Original Sacher–Torte."
37. *Wiener Kurier*, "Weitere Österreichische Rekorde: Prachtleistungen der USA-Athleten, Don Laz Übersprang mit der Bambusstange 4,45 m Miller Warf den Speer 73,95 m–Baker Lief die 200 m in 21 Sekunden–Hürdenkönig Harrison Dillard Ernstlich Verleizt," Sport in Aller Welt, August 8, 1952.
38. AP, "U. S. Trackmen Win 7 Tests at Vienna: Sweep Closing Program for a 14-of-15 Total in Two-Day Meet–Miller Excels," *NYT,* August 8, 1952, https://timesmachine.nytimes.com; "Baker Wins Dash in International Meet at Vienna," *Manhattan (KS) Mercury–Chronicle,* August 8, 1952, https://www.newspapers.com; *Hutchinson (KS) Herald,* "American Athletes Win in Vienna Meet," August 7, 1952.
39. *Festschrift, Leichtathletikmeeting*.
40. Karl Waldbrunner possessed the title of Central Secretary of the Socialist Party of Austria in 1952. He was also the Federal Minister for Transport and Nationalized Enterprises. Wer ist Wer, "Dipl. -Ing. Karl Waldbrunner."

Chapter 15

1. News of the World, "Post-Olympic British Games: White City Stadium Saturday 9th August 1952."
2. Biography Online, "Emil Zátopek Biography."

Chapter 16

1. News of the World, "Post-Olympic British Games," 12, 22, 24, 27-28.
2. "British Games at the White City," Athletics, *Observer* (London, England), August 10, 1952, https://www.newspapers.com.

3. Olympic medals for Herb McKenley, Mal Whitfield, and Gene Cole verified at IOC, https://www.olympics.com/.
4. Saturday Sport Round-Up, "Remigino Wins," *Evening Standard* (London), August 9, 1952, https://www.newspapers.com.
5. "Yanks Shine in British Meet," *Long Beach (CA) Press,* August 10, 1952.
6. British Pathé, "British Athletes Compete at the White City 1952."
7. AP, "Yanks Shatter 2 Track Marks in British Meet," *Chicago Tribune,* August 10, 1952, https://www.newspapers.com.
8. "Yanks Shine," Long Beach, see note 5 above.
9. "1952 British Games—200-Yards Final," Getty Images, https://www.gettyimages.com/detail/news-photo/american-athlete-andy-stanfield-american-athlete-thane-news-photo/1391394977?adppopup=true.
10. "British Games at the White City," Athletics, *Observer* (London, England), August 10, 1952, https://www.newspapers.com.
11. AP, "U. S. Sets 2 World Records to Dominate British Track." *NYT,* August 10, 1952. https://timesmachine.nytimes.com; AP, "U.S. Captures London Games," *Wichita (KS) Beacon,* probably August 10, 1952.
12. British Pathé, "Records Go in British Games (1952)."
13. Mashburn, interview, (see OM, n. 9).
14. "Mr. W. Emsley Carr, Chairman of the News of the World, requests the company of _____ at the banquet following the British Games to be held at the Dorchester Hotel on Saturday, August 9, 1952, 6.30 (for 7.15 p.m.)" Invitation printed on 4.5 x 3.5 inches poster-board material with rounded corners and gold gilt around the edge. Private collection.
15. "The Dorchester," https://www.dorchestercollection.com/en/london/the-dorchester/; "History of the Dorchester," The Dorchester, https://www.dorchestercollection.com/en/london/the-dorchester/history/.
16. News of the World, "Dinner to Athletes and Officials—Post-Olympic British Games."
17. Bear, *Official Report of the XVth Olympic Games,* 14, 23.
18. Mashburn, interview, (see OM, n. 9).
19. Smith, interview, (see chap. 4, n. 5) and Smith, *Cowboy Stuntman,* 68.
20. Gourdine, *Untitled Memories.*
21. George Raborn, "Olympics Star Visits in Waco," *Waco News-Tribune,* August 15, 1952, https://www.newspapers.com.
22. "What is the Army's World Class Athlete Program?" ArmyWCAP, https://www.armywcap.com/about.
23. Litsky, "Matson," (see chap. 13, n. 10).
24. Museum of the Gulf Coast, "Walter 'Buddy' Davis."
25. Richards, *Heart of a Champion.*
26. Redihan, *Olympics and the Cold War,* 15, 103; Erin Redihan, "The 1952 Olympic Games, the US, and the USSR," Process: a blog for American history, blog of Organization of American Historians, Journal of American History and American Historian, February 8, 2018, https://www.processhistory.org/redihan-1952-olympics/.
27. Gordien autograph in Wien, Vienne, Vienna, Vieno—Ein Bilder-Album, iv, private collection.

28. Fleming, *Gone with the Wind*; Smith, interview, (see chap. 4, n. 5); Mashburn, interview, (see OM, n. 9).
29. Imperial War Museums, "Rationing in the Second World War."
30. Dillard, interview, (see chap. 4, n. 35); Meinhardt, "Harrison Dillard: 'Wow, all for my sake!'"
31. Organising Committee for the XIV Olympiad, *Olympic Newsletter: XIVth Olympiad London 1948*.
32. Bushnell, *US 1952 Olympic Book*, 91-92, 264.
33. IOC, "Relay Quartet Make Jamaica Proud"; Wint, "Jamaican Olympic Heros"; Moore, interview, (see chap. 5, n. 30); Rosen, "Final Lap," (see chap. 9, n. 26).
34. Email, Traci Gourdine, (see chap. 5, n. 4).
35. Gourdine, *Untitled Memories*; Larry Getlen, "Brooklyn's Blight Years: From the Birth of 'the Projects' to Death of Ebbets," *New York Post*, September 30, 2019, https://nypost.com/2019/09/30/brooklyns-blight-years-from-the-birth-of-the-projects-to-death-of-ebbets/.
36. Lowe, "Friendship of the 1948 Olympians,", 4.
37. Olympedia, OlyMADMen, ed. s.v. "Levan Sanadze," http://www.olympedia.org/athletes/77623.
38. Coubertin, the founder of the modern Olympics, said, "We shall not have peace until the prejudices which now separate the different nations shall have been outlived. To attain this end, what better means than to bring the youth of all countries periodically together for amicable trials of muscular strength and agility." George Hirthler, "History's Greatest Forgotten Olympic Hero: Baron Pierre de Coubertin," *Coubertin Speaks* (blog), https://coubertinspeaks.com/the-baron/.
39. "Coubertin Quote for Jan 03," *Coubertin Speaks*(blog), https://coubertinspeaks.com/quotes/jan/03/; IOC, "What is the Olympic Creed?"

Chapter 17

1. Liberal: Crossroads of Commerce, "Mid-America Air Museum."
2. "Thane Baker arrived home Saturday evening. His parents, Mr. and Mrs. Walter Baker, went to Liberal to meet him." *Elkhart* (KS) *Tri-State News*, August 22, 1952.
3. Baker to parents, August 4, 1952, (see chap. 11, n. 10).
4. UP, "Saturday Expected to Be Cooler," *Iola (KS) Register*, August 15, 1952, https://www.newspapers.com.
5. "New Record," *Elkhart (KS) Tri-State News* (see chap. 11, n. 35).
6. "Thane Baker to Track Meet on West Coast," *Elkhart (KS) Tri-State News, June 13, 1952.*
7. Lobosco, "Telethon," (see chap. 4 n. 3).
8. Bushnell, *US 1952 Olympic Book*, 63-66.
9. Pan Am, "Passenger Ticket and Baggage Check, No. 0261-20 292454," August 10, 1952, private collection.
10. Joseph M. Sheehan, "Remigino, Moore in Group of 68 as Olympic Track Stars Return: Last Mass Homecoming of U. S. Athletes Includes Dillard and Young–

Manhattan Ace Greeted by College Officials," *NYT,* August 12, 1952, https://timesmachine.nytimes.com; Powell, *The Fastest Men on Earth,*"1952—Helsinki."
11. Raborn, "Waco," (see chap. 16, n. 21).
12. Elkhart sits in Morton County, Kansas, which contains 400,000 acres of land. Herriman, Graber, and McDowell, "Soil Survey of Morton County, Kansas."
13. Fleming, *Wizard of Oz.*
14. "Elkhart Boys in News Reel," *Elkhart (KS) Tri-State News,* July 18, 1952.
15. "Thane Baker Second," *Elkhart (KS) Tri-State News, (see chap. 10, n. 46).*
16. "Kansan Measures," *Wichita (KS) Beacon,"* July 1952.
17. IOC, "Helsinki 1952: The Medals."
18. "Baker Day to Be Celebrated August 22," *Elkhart (KS) Tri-State News,* August 15, 1952.
19. Baker to parents, July 25, 1952, (see chap. 11, n. 2). "Parton-Baker," Announcing the Marriage Of, *Hutchinson (KS) News,* February 15, 1951, http://www.newspapers.com; "Baker-Parton," Engagements, *Hutchinson (KS) News,* November 18, 1950, http://www.newspapers.com.
20. Wat1950, "1946 Ford Business Coupe."

Chapter 18

1. Rislakki, *Suomen Kuvalehti,* 1, 12-15, 18-20.
2. Bear, *Official Report of the XVth Olympic Games,* 14-32; Bushnell, *US 1952 Olympic Book,* 70-110, 211.
3. "Large Crowd Attends Baker Barbeque," *Elkhart (KS) Tri-State News,* August 29, 1952.
4. Kansas University Relays gave Bulova watches to their first-place finishers. Thane earned four of them and gave one to his father.
5. "Weather," *Salina (KS) Journal,* August 21, 1952, https://www.newspapers.com.
6. "Glenn Returns for Big Baker Party," *Elkhart (KS) Tri-State News,* August 22, 1952.
7. "Congratulations and Welcome Home Thane Baker," *Elkhart (KS) Tri-State News,* August 22, 1952.

Appendix 1

1. Baker, *Autographs,* (see chap. 5, n. 1).
2. Bear, *Official Report of the XVth Olympic Games,* 14-32; Bushnell, *US 1952 Olympic Book,* 70-110.

Appendix 2

1. Elliot Denman, "The 1952 Olympic Team Reunion, New York March 27, 2002," *Official Newsletter of the US Olympians,* Summer 2002, pg. 8-9.
2. Sally Baker, "1952 Olympians, 50th Reunion, New York City," unpublished scrapbook, 2002, private collection.

3. Lynn Lipinski, "In Memoriam: Sammy Lee, 96," *USC News* (University of Southern California), December 3, 2016, https://news.usc.edu/112049/two-time-olympic-gold-medal-diver-sammy-lee-dies-at-96/.
4. Frank Litsky, "Bob Mathias, 75, Decathlete and Politician, Dies," *NYT*," September 3, 2006, https://www.nytimes.com/2006/09/03/sports/othersports/03mathias.html.
5. "1952 Olympic 400m Hurdles Champion Moore Dies," IAAV News, WA, October 11, 2020, https://www.worldathletics.org/heritage/news/charles-moore-obituary.
6. IMDb, "Dean Smith," https://www.imdb.com/name/nm0807911/.
7. Frank Litsky, "Mal Whitfield, Olympic Gold Medalist and Tuskegee Airman, Dies at 91," *NYT,* November 19, 2015, https://www.nytimes.com/2015/11/20/sports/mal-whitfield-olympic-gold-medalist-and-tuskegee-airman-dies-at-91.html
8. Litsky, "Lindy Remigino," (see chap. 9, n. 3).

Appendix 3

1. IOC, "Melbourne 1956, Athletics 4x100M Relay Men Results."
2. IOC, "Melbourne 1956, Athletics 100M Men Results."
3. IOC, "Melbourne 1956, Athletics 200M Men Results."
4. "Baker Ties 60-Yard Dash Record," (see chap. 4, n. 17); "Baker Stars for Wildcats but Kansas Cops Dual Meet," *Manhattan (KS) Mercury,* February 8, 1953, https://www.newspapers.com.
5. "National College Outdoor Track Records: Best Undergraduate Performances," *Indianapolis (IN) News,* June 18, 1953, https://www.newspapers.com.
6. "Iness Shatters Discus Mark; Santee Does 4:03.7 Mile: 190-Foot Heave Tops World Figure; O'Brien Sets Meet Record in Shot," *Boston Globe,* June 21, 1953, https://www.newspapers.com.
7. Thane Baker also ran a wind-aided 100 yards in 9.3 seconds at the Ohio State Relays in 1956; "This Mermaid Real Shark," Sports in Short, *Vancouver Sun,* April 23, 1956, https://www.newspapers.com.
8. World Athletics, "World Record Progression of 200 Metres."
9. Thane Baker's 10.2 second 100-meter time came in the first heat of the Olympic Trials, where he placed second to Ira Murchison, who also ran 10.2. Bob Busby, "High Jump Over 7 Feet: Charles Dumas of Compton, Calif., Junior College Tops Magic Mark by 5/8 Inch in Olympic T&F Finals. Thane Baker, Bill Nieder on Team, Kansans Will Make Trip to Melbourne After Each Finishes Third—Glenn Davis Cracks World Hurdle Mark—Dave Sime Out," *Kansas City (MO) Times,* June 30, 1956, https://www.newspapers.com; AP, "Outlook Bright for Olympic Team: Coach Terms Squad Greatest Ever Assembled in U.S." *News-Pilot* (San Pedro, CA), July 2, 1956. https://www.newspapers.com; World Athletics, "World Record Progression of 100 Metres."
10. World Athletics, "World Record Progression of 4x200 Metres Relay."
11. Masters Athletics: Track and Field –World Rankings, "100 meter Dash."
12. Masters Athletics: Track and Field –World Rankings, "200 metres Dash." (The author could not independently verify the Masters records for relays and races run

in yards. However, Thane Baker holds certificates confirming the yards records.)
13. NCAA, "All-Time Honors Award Winners"; NCAA, "Silver Anniversary Award."
14. Thane and Tuija continued their friendship until her death in 2018.
15. The K-Club is a group of former Kansas State letter winners. Megan Moser, "Olympian Thane Baker an underdog success story," *The Mercury* (Manhattan, KS), October 30, 2023, https://themercury.com/opinion/from-the-editor-olympian-thane-baker-an-underdog-success-story/article_7b01602f-f468-51db-b66c-a7369b1c9285.html; D. Scott Fritchen, "K-State Was Everything to Me," *K-State Sports Extra*, October 31, 2023, https://www.kstatesports.com/news/2023/10/30/sports-extra-k-state-was-everything-to-me.
16. To hear Thane Baker's story in his own words, please see BYU Sports Nation, "The Dream: Kansas State Big Story," https://www.youtube.com/watch?v=ny3KaKWbPdA.

BIBLIOGRAPHY

AAU USA James E. Sullivan Award. "AAU Sullivan Award—Past Winners." https://image.aausports.org/images/Sullivan/AAUSullivanAwardRecipients.pdf.

Amateur Athletic Union of the United States. *64th Annual United States Track and Field Championships*. Long Beach, California: Press—Telegram, June 20–21, 1952.

America's Black Holocaust Museum. "Sundown Towns: Racial Segregation Past and Present." Bringing Our History to Light. https://abhmuseum.org/category/about-abhm/.

Bailey, Joanna. "The Lockheed Constellation—The Plane That Changed the World." Simple Flying, July 18, 2019. https://simpleflying.com/lockheed-constellation/.

Barrodale, Dr. Barry J. "Boxing." In *United States 1952 Olympic Book, Quadrennial Report United States Olympic Committee*. Edited by Asa S. Bushnell, 157-163. New York: United States Olympic Association, 1953.

Baseball Reference. "New York Giants at Brooklyn Dodgers Box Score, July 3, 1952." https://www.baseball-reference.com/teams/BRO/1952-schedule-scores.shtml.

Batens, Alain S. and Ben C. Major. "Class 9 Items: Drugs, Chemicals and Biological Stains Sulfa Drugs: Miscellaneous Medical Equipment." WW2 US Medical Research Centre. https://www.med-dept.com/medical-kits-contents/class-9-items-drugs-chemicals-and-biological-stains-sulfa-drugs/.

Bear, Cecil, ed. *Official Report of the XVth Olympic Games*. London: World Sports, British Olympic Association, August 1952.

Belloni, Stefania. *Finland: Land of a Thousand Lakes*. Translated by Prof. Brian Williams. Florence, Italy: Centro Stampa Editoriale, n.d.

Bingisser, Martin. "The Perfect Physique for Throwing." HMMR Media, November 14, 2013. https://www.hmmrmedia.com/2013/11/the-perfect-physique-for-throwing/.

Biography Online. "Emil Zátopek Biography." Last modified February 15, 2018. https://www.biographyonline.net/sport/athletics/emile-zatopek.html.

Blicker, Josh. "Ether in Surgery." Historical Medical Library of the College of Physicians of Philadelphia. December 18, 2020. http://histmed.collegeofphysicians.org/ether-in-surgery/.

Bowman, Ian, narr. "Horace Ashenfelter Dies at 94," Voxipop, YouTube video, :48, https://www.youtube.com/watch?v=0helvn_uSwk.

Boylan-Pett, Liam. "How Do Lane Assignments and Starting Spots Work in Track?" Summer Olympics, Olympic Track and Field, SBNation, August 15, 2016. https://www.sbnation.com/2016/8/15/12486250/rio-2106-track-athletics-lane-staggered-start-400-record-wayde-van-niekerk.

Bridwell, E. Nelson, ed. *Superman: From the Thirties to the Seventies.* New York: Bonanza, 1971.

British European Airways Passenger ticket and baggage check number 0602 730639 issued to W. T. Baker. London to *Kärntner Ring*, August 5, 1952, 9:20 AM.

British Olympic Association. "BOA Honour Achievements of Sprinter Emmanuel McDonald Bailey." December 9, 2013, 12:03. https://www.teamgb.com/news/boa-honour-achievements-sprinter-emmanuel-mcdonald-bailey.

British Pathé. "1952 Helsinki Olympic Games: Opening competitions (1952)." July 20, 1952. YouTube video, 1:46. https://www.youtube.com/watch?v=cQKf9VItAK8.

———. "1952 Helsinki Olympic Games: Opening Ceremony." Filmed July 1952, 3:53. https://www.youtube.com/watch?v=cxNAs7541Ro.

———. "Big Bell for Vienna." Filmed April 26, 1952. YouTube video, :42. https://www.youtube.com/watch?v=RSWSWcpu-UA.

———. "British Athletes Compete at the White City 1952." Gaumont—British News. Filmed August 9, 1952, 1:51. https://www.britishpathe.com/asset/171640/.

———. Hawkins. "Helsinki Olympics Various Events—Slow Motions High Jumps 1952." Filmed July 20, 1952. British Pathé. https://www.britishpathe.com/video/oly12-helsinki-olympics-various-events-slow-motion-high-jumps/query/1952+world+record.

———. "Helsinki 1952 The Olympic Games: Latest Events." Gaumont-British Newsreel. Filmed July 28, 1952. https://www.britishpathe.com/video/VL-VA956CUFKBZPDZZ32RCNGAFUMMA-1952-HELSINKI-OLYMPIC-GAMES-LATEST-EVENTS/query/British+Games+1952.

———. "Helsinki Opening, Track and Pool—Opening Ceremony and Torch Lighting 1952." Filmed July 19, 1952, 3:41. https://www.britishpathe.com/video/oly12-helsinki-opening-track-and-pool-opening-ceremony-and-torch-lighting/query/Games+Open+1952.

———. "Helsinki Street Scenes (1952)." Filmed in Helsinki, Finland, in summer 1952. YouTube video, 1:57. https://www.youtube.com/watch?v=dUx0A9s07co.

———. "London Traffic (1952)." YouTube video, 4:04. https://www.bing.com/videos/search?q=youtube+london+1952&docid=6079917819227708240&mid=3A69F-319B4E5B20AF0EB3A69F319B4E5B20AF0EB&view=detail&FORM=VIRE.

_____. "Records Go in British Games (1952)." Filmed August 9, 1952, 2:06. https://www.youtube.com/watch?v=4Ubgt4X_uoI.

Brooklyn Dodgers. "Brooklyn Dodgers vs. New York Giants." Ticket. July 3, 1952.

Brownlow, Mark. "Around Vienna's Ring (Ringstrasse)." *Visiting Vienna*. http://www.visitingvienna.com/ring/.

Brylcreem. "The Look Is Back." https://www.brylcreemusa.com/#get-the-look.

Bushnell, Asa ed., *Report of the United States Olympic Committee 1948 Games: XIV Olympiad, London, England, V Olympic Games, St. Moritz, Switzerland,* New York: United States Olympic Association, 1949.

_____. ed. *United States 1952 Olympic Book, Quadrennial Report United States Olympic Committee: Games of the XVth Olympiad Helsinki, Finland July 19 to August 3, 1952, VI Olympic Winter Games Oslo, Norway February 14 to 25, 1952, 1st Pan American Games Buenos Aires, Argentina February 25 to March 8, 1951.* New York: United States Olympic Association, 1953.

_____. (Secretary, United States Olympic Committee). "Attention: All Olympic Team Members, Managers, Coaches, and Other Personnel." July 4, 1952.

_____. "Instructions for Members of the Olympic Teams, Trainers and Coaches." July 2, 1952. Private collection.

_____. "Notice to United States Olympic Committee Chairmen, Managers, Coaches, and Team Members." Distributed by United States Olympic Committee. July 1952.

Calendar—12. "Moon Phases August 1952." http://www.calendar-12.com/moon_calendar/1952/august.

_____. "Moon Phases July 1952." http://www.calendar-12.com/moon_calendar/1952/july.

Case IH. "Supporting Producers Yesterday, Today, and Tomorrow." https://www.caseih.com/en-us/unitedstates/company/about-case-ih#0.

Chandler, Otis and Elizabeth, ed. "Brutus Hamilton." Quotes, Goodreads, https://www.goodreads.com/author/quotes/1537691.Brutus_Hamilton.

Charlie Dean Archives. "1952 Summer Olympic Games in Helsinki, Finland." YouTube video, 25:45. https://www.youtube.com/watch?v=YUWULnmP04Q&t=394s.

Chen, C. Peter. "Finland." World War II Database. Last modified August 2008. https://ww2db.com/country/finland.

City of Vienna. "Alte Filme—Soziales Bauen in Wien 1952." YouTube video, 12:21. https://www.youtube.com/watch?v=bqK_yP7Vcq4.

_____. *Das Wiener Rathaus*. Vienna: Press Office, 1952.

_____. "The Years of the Allied Forces in Vienna (1945 to 1955)—History of Vienna: Occupation." Culture & History. https://www.wien.gv.at/english/history/overview/reconstruction.html.

_____. "Vienna City Hall." https://www.wien.gv.at/english/cityhall/.

Cornell University Sports Hall of Fame. "Walter Ashbaugh." CBS Sports Digital. https://cornellbigred.com/hof.aspx?hof=125.

Cunningham, Glenn and George X. Sand. *Never Quit.* Lincoln, VA: Chosen Books, 1981.

Division of Diversity and Community Engagement. Jjr799. "Intersection of Athletics and Race on the 40 Acres." The History of Integration at the University of Texas at Austin. November 18, 2014. https://diversity.utexas.edu/integration/2014/11/the-intersection-of-athletics-and-race-on-the-40-acres/.

Dodgers Official Program and Score Card. "Brooklyn Dodgers vs. New York Giants." New York: Harry M. Stevens, July 3, 1952.

Domkirche St. Stephan. "History of the Cathedral Church." https://www.stephanskirche.at/?setLang=en.

Dorchester Collection. "The Dorchester." https://www.dorchestercollection.com/en/london/the-dorchester/.

———. "History of the Dorchester." https://www.dorchestercollection.com/en/london/the-dorchester/history/.

Egan, Timothy. *The Worst Hard Time: The Untold Story of Those Who Survived the Great American Dust Bowl.* Boston: Mariner Books, 2006.

Elävä Arkisto. "Helsingin olympiakisojen avajaiset: 'Rauhanenkeli' ja Nurmi olivat Helsingin Olympia-avajaisten vetonauloja." Opening Ceremony. Recorded July 19, 1952, Olympic Stadium, Helsinki, Finland. 44:15. https://yle.fi/aihe/artikkeli/2008/06/05/rauhanenkeli-ja-nurmi-olivat-helsingin-olympia-avajaisten-vetonauloja.

———. "*Seutulan lentoasema* 1952." Filmed July-August 1952. Audio, 6:59. https://yle.fi/aihe/artikkeli/2009/03/03/seutulan-lentoasema-1952.

Ensio Rislakki ed. *Suomen Kuvalehti.* Helsinki, August 2, 1952.

ESPN. "Horace Ashenfelter." Filmed July 25, 1952, in Helsinki, Finland. YouTube video, 2:21. https://www.youtube.com/watch?v=fulj2D1eYx8.

Ferris, Daniel J. (Chairman, Pre & Post Olympic Competition Committee, AAU). "Members of the United States Olympic Track and Field Team—Men & Women." July 1, 1952. Private collection.

———. "Pre- and Post-Olympic Competition Committee." In *United States 1952 Olympic Book, Quadrennial Report United States Olympic Committee.* Edited by Asa S. Bushnell, 269-270. New York: United States Olympic Association, 1953.

Festschrift, Internationales Leichtathletikmeeting, Veranstaltet vom Österr. Leichtathletick-Verband u. Österr, Olymp. Comitée, Offizielles Programm, Mittwoch 6. August u. Donnerstag 7. August 1952, Beginn 17.45 Uhr WAC-Platz, Freiexemplar. Program. Vienna, Austria: Wiener Kurier, August 1952.

Fleming, Victor, dir. *Gone with the Wind.* Written by Margaret Mitchell, featuring Clark Gable, Vivien Leigh. Culver City, CA: Selznick International Studios, 1939.

Fleming, Victor, with Mervyn LeRoy and King Vidor, dir. *Wizard of Oz*. Written by L. Frank Baum, featuring Judy Garland. Culver City, CA: Metro-Goldwyn-Mayer, 1939.

Fodor, Eugene, ed. *Scandinavia in 1952: with Finland and the Olympic Games*. Netherlands: Mouton, 1952.

Gourdine, Meredith. *Untitled Memories: Tape 1, Side B, and Tape 2, Side A*. Recorded prior to 1998. Private collection.

GPSMYCITY: Lose Yourself Without Getting Lost. "Samppalinna Park, Turku." https://www.gpsmycity.com/attractions/samppalinna-park-41247.html.

———. "Three Smiths Statue, Helsinki." https://www.gpsmycity.com/attractions/three-smiths-statue-33019.html.

Guest, Edgar Albert. *Just Glad Things*. Detroit: self-pub., 1911. https://allpoetry.com/The-Dreams-Of-Youth.

Handbuch der Stadt Wien: 67.-68 amtlich redigierter Jahrgang, Verzeichnis der Übungsstätten in Wien, Sportplätze, Spielplätze, Eislaufplätze, Tennisplätze, Bootshausanlagen, Spezialanlagen, Schwimmbäder, stand vom January 1, 1952, Vienna: Verlag für Jugend und Volk Gesellschaft M.B.H., 1952/1953. https://digital.wienbibliothek.at/periodical/pageview/1494322?query=Sportpl%C3%A4tze.

Hanson, Debbie. "Harrison Dillard: Only Person to Ever Win Olympic Gold in Both Hurdles and Sprints." *Cleveland Seniors*. http://www.clevelandseniors.com/people/harrison-dillard.htm.

Harrivirta, Holger, edit. "Muistojen kisakesä 1952: Minnenas Olympiasommar 1952." *Olympia-Filmi*. Elävä muisti video, 49:58. https://elavamuisti.fi/aikajana/muistojen-kisakesa-1952.

Harry's. "History." https://harrysmanhattan.com/history.html.

Haylett, Ward—Athletic Teams, Track and Cross Country, Vertical Files. Morse Department of Special Collections, Kansas State University Libraries, Manhattan, KS.

Health Beat. "Infographic: Body Shapes by Sport." Sports Medicine, University of Pittsburgh Medical Center. https://share.upmc.com/2015/07/infographic-body-shapes-by-sport/.

Helms Bakery District. "History." https://helmsbakerydistrict.com/about/history/.

Helsingin Osakepankki—Helsingfors Aktiebank. *Welcome to Helsinki*. Map. 1952. 1:15,000 scale. 11.69 x 16.38 inches. Private collection.

Helsinki Kuvia.FI. "Linnanmäki." Album: Rasvaletti (Image 72/196). https://www.helsinkikuvia.fi/collection/678/?rid=11250.

Herriman, Stephen C., Steven P. Graber, and James L. McDowell. "Soil Survey of Morton County, Kansas." Natural Resources Conservation Service in cooperation with Kansas Agricultural Experiment Station, United States Department of Agriculture, text regarding soil identification finalized in 2004. https://www.nrcs.usda.gov/Internet/FSE_MANUSCRIPTS/kansas/KS129/0/morton_KS.pdf.

History & Social Justice. "Information about Sundown Towns." https://justice.tougaloo.edu/sundown-towns/information/

History of Branding. "History of Old Spice." http://www.historyofbranding.com/oldspice/.

History.com. ed. "Korean War." A&E Entertainment. Last modified January 31, 2020. https://www.history.com/topics/korea/korean-war.

———. "Olympic Games." A&E Television Network. Updated August 21, 2018. https://www.history.com/topics/sports/olympic-games.

———. "Plessy v. Ferguson." Last modified January 20, 2021. https://www.history.com/topics/black-history/plessy-v-ferguson.

———. "Title IX Enacted." History. https://www.history.com/this-day-in-history/title-ix-enacted.

Hoeffkes, Karl. "Wien in den 50ern." YouTube video, 1:41. https://www.youtube.com/watch?v=n2me1v5bm8Y.

Hormel. "SPAM." https://www.spam.com/.

Hotel Sacher. "The Original Sacher—Torte: Sweet Secret." https://www.sacher.com/en/original-sacher-torte/recipe/.

Hypoventilation Training. "Emil Zátopek the Pioneer of Hypoventilation Training." YouTube video, 1:04. https://www.youtube.com/watch?v=shR8pIU7iLo.

Imperial War Museums. "What You Need to Know About Rationing in the Second World War." https://www.iwm.org.uk/history/what-you-need-to-know-about-rationing-in-the-second-world-war.

International Olympic Committee. "All Medals." https://olympics.com/en/olympic-games/olympic-medals.

———. "Andrew William Stanfield: Biography." https://www.olympic.org/andy-stanfield.

———. "Bob Mathias Makes History by Winning the Decathlon at Just 17!" July 29, 1948. https://olympics.com/en/news/bob-mathias-athletics.

———. Chakraborty, Samrat. "Steeplechase: Rules, Regulations and All You Need to Know: Avinash Sable will represent India in 3000m steeplechase at the upcoming Tokyo Olympics." May 14, 2021. https://olympics.com/en/featured-news/steeplechase-rules-regulations-and-all-you-need-to-know.

———. "Dana Ingrova-Zatopkova: Biography." https://olympics.com/en/athletes/dana-ingrova-zatopkova.

———. "Emmanuel McDonald Bailey." https://olympics.com/en/athletes/emmanuel-mcdonald-bailey#.

———. "Fortune Edward Gordien: Biography." https://olympics.com/en/athletes/fortune-edward-gordien.

———. "George Patton: Biography." https://olympics.com/en/athletes/george-patton.

_____. "Hannes Kolehmainen: Biography." https://olympics.com/en/athletes/hannes-kolehmainen.

_____. "Helsinki 1952, Athletics Results." https://olympics.com/en/olympic-games/helsinki-1952/results/athletics.

_____. "Helsinki 1952: The Medals." https://olympics.com/en/olympic-games/helsinki-1952/medal-design.

_____. "Jesse Owens Completes the Hat-Trick with 200M Win." News, August 5, 1936. https://olympics.com/en/news/jesse-owens-completes-the-hat-trick-with-200m-win.

_____. "Melvin Emery Patton." https://olympics.com/en/athletes/melvin-emery-patton.

_____. "Melbourne 1956 Athletics 100M Men Results." https://olympics.com/en/olympic-games/melbourne-1956/results/athletics/100m-men.

_____. "Melbourne 1956, Athletics 200M Men Results." https://olympics.com/en/olympic-games/melbourne-1956/results/athletics/200m-men.

_____. "Melbourne 1956, Athletics 4x100M Relay Men Results." https://olympics.com/en/olympic-games/melbourne-1956/results/athletics/4x100m-relay-men.

_____. "Milton Gray Campbell: Biography." https://olympics.com/en/athletes/milton-gray-campbell.

_____. "Paavo Nurmi Seals Record Medal Tally at Amsterdam 1928." News. July 29, 2019. https://olympics.com/en/news/paavo-nurmi-seals-record-medal-tally-at-amsterdam-1928.

_____. "Robert Mathias: Biography." https://olympics.com/en/athletes/robert-mathias.

_____. "Relay Quartet Make Jamaica Proud." News, July 27, 1952. https://olympics.com/en/news/relay-quartet-make-jamaica-proud.

_____. "'Run Leonidas Run': Meet the Starts of the Track at the Ancient Olympic Games: From Completing Three Marathons in One Day—Post Olympic Title—To Chasing Down a Live Hare, the Achievements of the Running Idols at Olympia were Remarkable." https://olympics.com/ioc/ancient-olympic-games/running.

_____. "Sports." https://olympics.com/en/sports/.

_____. "What is the Olympic Creed?" https://olympics.com/ioc/faq/olympic-symbol-and-identity/what-is-the-olympic-creed.

_____. "Xth Olympiad Los Angeles 1932." https://olympics.com/en/olympic-games/los-angeles-1932.

_____. "XIth Olympic Games Berlin 1936." https://olympics.com/en/olympic-games/berlin-1936.

_____. "Zátopek Completes Incredible Long-Distance Treble." May 30, 2014. https://olympics.com/en/news/zatopek-completes-incredible-long-distance-treble.

Jewelry Shopping Guide. "What is Marcasite Jewelry? -A Quick Guide." https://www.jewelryshoppingguide.com/what-is-marcasite-jewelry.

Kane, Robert. "Men's Track and Field, Report of the Team Manager." In *United States 1952 Olympic Book, Quadrennial Report United States Olympic Committee*. Edited by Asa S. Bushnell, 74-75. New York: United States Olympic Association, 1953.

Kansas Historical Society. "1951 Flood Scenes in Manhattan, Kansas." Kansas Memory. https://www.kansasmemory.org/item/308290.

Kansas State University. "Nichols Hall Story." http://www.k-state.edu/maps/buildings/N/.

Klein, Christopher. "The Great Smog of 1952." History.com ed. A&E Television Network. Last modified August 22, 2018. https://www.history.com/news/the-killer-fog-that-blanketed-london-60-years-ago.

K.L.M. Royal Dutch Airlines charter 9005, ticket number 0742 190937 issued to W. Thane Baker. Helsinki to London, August 2, 1952, 10:00 AM.

Kluge, Volker. "The 'Peace Angel of Helsinki' Wanted to Save the World." *Journal of Olympic History*, 25, no. 1 (2017). http://isoh.org/wp-content/uploads/2019/02/314.pdf.

Kolkka, Sulo, ed. *XV Olympiad Helsinki, Finland: The Official Report of The Organising Committee for the Games of the XV Olympiad*. Translated by Alex Matson. Pavoo, Helsinki: Werner Soderstrom, 1955. https://library.olympic.org/Default/doc/SYRACUSE/70779/the-official-report-of-the-organising-committee-for-the-games-of-the-xv-olympiad-ed-sulo-kolkka?_lg=en-GB.

K-State Athletics Hall of Fame. "Elmer Hackney." K-State: Official Site of K-State Athletics. https://www.kstatesports.com/honors/k-state-athletics-hall-of-fame/elmer-hackney/18.

———. "Veryl Switzer." https://www.kstatesports.com/honors/k-state-athletics-hall-of-fame/veryl-switzer/13.

Larney, Marjorie. "A Flying Javelin: Marjorie Larney." Irish America, August/September 2008. https://irishamerica.com/2008/08/a-flying-javelin-marjorie-larney.

Liberal: Crossroads of Commerce. "Mid-America Air Museum." City of Liberal (KS). http://www.cityofliberal.org/191/Mid-America-Air-Museum.

Lindtberg, Leopold, dir. *Four in a Jeep (Die Vier im Jeep)*. Switzerland: I. Westcsler, 1951. Re-released by VCI Entertainment, Kit Parker Films and Blair & Associates, 2010. DVD.

Linnanmäki. "Welcome to the Merriest Part of Helsinki!" https://www.linnanmaki.fi/en.

Loewen, James W. *Sundown Towns: A Hidden Dimension of American Racism*, rev. ed. New York: The New Press, 2018.

Los Angeles Coliseum. *The Story Behind the Largest and Finest Stadium in America*. Los Angeles: Citizen Print Shop, distributed 1952.

Lowe, Devin. "Friendship of the 1948 Olympians Stands the Test of Time." *The Olympian Newsletter*, Summer 2018.

Marsh, Allison. "When X-Rays Were All the Rage, a Trip to the Shoe Store Was Dangerously Illuminating: The shoe-fitting fluoroscope was unnecessary and hazardous, but kids loved it." *IEEE Spectrum.* October 30, 2020. https://spectrum.ieee.org/tech-history/heroic-failures/when-xrays-were-all-the-rage-a-trip-to-the-shoe-store-was-dangerously-illuminating.

Masters Athletics: Track and Field—World Rankings. "All Time World Rankings–100-meter Dash." http://www.mastersathletics.net/fileadmin/html/Rankings/All_Time/100metresmen.htm.

_____. "200 metres Dash." http://www.mastersathletics.net/fileadmin/html/Rankings/All_Time/200metresmen.htm.

Metcalf, T. Nelson. "Administration Committee." In *United States 1952 Olympic Book, Quadrennial Report United States Olympic Committee.* Edited by Asa S. Bushnell, 253-255. New York: United States Olympic Association, 1953.

Matis, Henry A. "Report of the Attaché." In *United States 1952 Olympic Book, Quadrennial Report United States Olympic Committee.* Edited by Asa S. Bushnell, 251-252. New York: United States Olympic Association, 1953.

Mayor's Reception Committee. "The City of New York Luncheon in Honor of the 1952 U. S. Olympic Team." Menu, New York: Waldorf- Astoria, July 7, 1952, private collection.

_____. "The City of New York Reception in Honor of the 1952 Olympic Team." Program, New York: New York City Hall, July 7, 1952, private collection.

McAllister, Joseph. "Why Do Runners Line Up Staggered?" SportsRec, November 16, 2018. https://www.sportsrec.com/8586499/why-do-runners-line-up-staggered.

McLaughlin, Thad G. *Geology and Ground-Water Resources of Morton County, Kansas.* Bulletin 40, State Geological Survey of Kansas. Lawrence, KS: University of Kansas Publications, 1942. http://www.kgs.ku.edu/General/Geology/Morton/04_geog.html.

Meinhardt, Gunnar. "Harrison Dillard: 'Wow, all for my sake!'" *Journal of Olympic Historians,* 26, no. 3 (2018): http://isoh.org/wp-content/uploads/2019/02/370.pdf.

Milestones of the Century. "1952 Olympic Games." Pathé News, filmed July 1952, released 1960. YouTube video, 3:12. https://www.youtube.com/watch?v=dYH1V-f5YZoI.

Miller, Darci. "Three-Time Olympic Track Champion Mal Whitfield Dies at 91." *Team USA News,* November 19, 2015. https://www.teamusa.org/News/2015/November/19/Three-Time-Olympic-Track-Champion-Mal-Whitfield-Dies-At-91.

Mintz, Steven. "Statistics: Education in America, 1860-1950." New York: Gilder Lehrman Institute of American History, n.d. https://www.gilderlehrman.org/history-resources/teaching-resource/statistics-education-america-1860-1950.

Moore, Charles H. Jr. and James Cockerille. *Running on Purpose: Winning Olympic Gold, Advancing Corporate Leadership, and Creating Sustainable Value.* Self-published, Edgemoor Ink, 2017.

Morris, Frank. "The End is Near for 3.2 Beer." Morning Edition, National Public Radio, April 5, 2019. https://www.npr.org/2019/04/05/709515770/the-end-is-near-for-3-2-beer.

Mother Leone's Famous Dinner: Leone's Since 1906. (menu), New York: n.p., July 5, 1952.

Museum of London. "London's Great Smog, 1952." YouTube video, 1:47. https://www.youtube.com/watch?v=k6Ww0ONdhg4.

Museum of the Gulf Coast. "Walter 'Buddy' Davis, Born: January 5, 1931, in Beaumont, Texas." https://www.museumofthegulfcoast.org/buddy-davis.

National Weather Service—National Oceanic and Atmospheric Administration. "Aurora Borealis (Northern Lights)." https://www.weather.gov/fsd/aurora.

NCAA. *31st Annual National Collegiate Athletic Association Track and Field Championships*. Berkeley, CA: Lederer, Street & Zeus, June 13-14, 1952.

———. "All-Time Honors Award Winners." http://www.ncaa.org/about/resources/events/awards/all-time-honors-award-winners.

———. "Silver Anniversary Award: Honors Celebration." http://www.ncaa.org/about/resources/events/awards/silver-anniversary-award.

Nelson, Cordner. "200 Meters." Edited by H. D. Thoreau. Special Olympic Edition, *Track and Field News*. August 1952.

News of the World. "Dinner to Athletes and Officials—Post-Olympic British Games: W. Emsley Carr in the Chair." The Dorchester, Park Lane, W.1. Saturday, 9th August 1952. Invitation and Program. Private collection.

———. "Post-Olympic British Games: White City Stadium Saturday 9th August 1952." Program. Private Collection.

New York Athletic Club. "Olympic History." https://www.nyac.org/olympic-history.

Next Big Idea Club. "David Goldblatt on the Impact of Olympics on the World Stage." https://nextbigideaclub.com/magazine/conversation-beyond-the-gold-a-conversation-with-david-goldblatt-on-the-effect-of-the-olympics-on-the-world-stage/10633/.

NJSports.com. The State of Sports! "Andy Stanfield." Track and Field. http://njsportsheroes.com/andystanfieldtf.html.

Oil-Dri Corporation of America. "History." https://www.oildri.com/about/history/.

Olympia Stadion. "Helsinki Olympic Stadium: History of the Stadium." https://www.stadion.fi/helsinki-olympic-stadium.

Ornstein, Charles L., Committee Chairman. "Food and Housing." In *United States 1952 Olympic Book, Quadrennial Report United States Olympic Committee*. Edited by Asa S. Bushnell, 264-268. New York: United States Olympic Association, 1953.

Organising Committee for the XIV Olympiad, ed. *Olympic Newsletter: XIVth Olympiad London 1948*. London: Press Dept of the Organising Committee, 1947. https://library.olympic.org/Default/doc/SYRACUSE/25827/olympic-newsletter-xivth-olympiad-london-1948-issued-by-the-press-department-of-the-organising-commi?_lg=en-GB.

Pan American World Airways System. "Charter Ticket and Baggage Check, No. 0261-20 214522." Olympic Charter 060. July 7, 1952, private collection.

_____. "Passenger Ticket and Baggage Check, No. 0261-20 292454." August 10, 1952, private collection.

Paramount Hotel. "History." https://www.nycparamount.com/about/history/.

PeriscopeFilm. "Visit to War Ravaged Vienna Post-WWII—Home Movies Feldkirch 60284." YouTube video, 12:10. https://www.youtube.com/watch?v=2B9k454Xbhw#action=share.

Popular Mechanics. "Fighting the Drouth." October 1934. https://books.google.com/books?id=xd8DAAAAMBAJ&pg=PA483#v=onepage&q&f=false.

Powell, Robert, narr. *The Fastest Men on Earth*. Episode 12 of 20, "1952—Helsinki." Thames Television, 1988. YouTube video, 6:53. https://www.youtube.com/watch?v=dmgTQJBokr4.

Programme Office of the Organizing Committee for the XV Olympiad. "XV Olympia Helsinki 1952: *Yleisurheilu—Athletisme—Athletics—Fri-Idrott, Olympiastadion, Helsinki—Helsingfors, Keskiviiko, Mercredi, Wednesday, Onsag, Päväohjelma, Programme Journalier, Daily Programme, Dagsprogram, 23.7.*" *XV Olympia Helsinki 1952,* Helsinki: Programme Office, 1952.

_____. "XV Olympia Helsinki 1952: *Yleisurheilu, Athletisme,* Athletics, *Fri-Idrott; Olympiastadion* Helsinki, *Helsingfors; Perjantai, Ventredi,* Friday, *Fredag; Päiväohjelma, Programme Journalier,* Daily Programme, *Dagsprogram.* 25.7." Helsinki: Programme Office, 1952.

Public Broadcasting Network. "Surviving the Dust Bowl-Timeline: The Dust Bowl." American Experience. http://www.pbs.org/wgbh/americanexperience/features/dust-bowl-surviving-dust-bowl/.

Queen, Master Sergeant Stewart, United States Army, host. "US Veterans in the Olympics—1952 Helsinki Finland Summer Olympic Games." *Big Picture—Your Army in Action*. Produced by Signal Corps Pictorial Center, presented by United States Army, 1952. YouTube video, 28:33. https://www.youtube.com/watch?v=cX6xffQat24&t=347s.

Rand McNally. "*UTOCO: Utah Oil Refining Company Map of the United States.*" 48 x 32 cm, (1952 or earlier), torn from a larger map.

Rare Historical Photos. "The Amazing Story of Finland in World War II, 1939-1945." August 16, 2017. https://rarehistoricalphotos.com/finland-world-war-ii/.

Redihan, Erin Elizabeth. *Olympics and the Cold War, 1948-1968: Sport as Battleground in the U.S.—Soviet Rivalry*. Jefferson, NC: McFarland, 2017.

Richards, Rev. Bob. *Heart of a Champion: Inspiring True Stories of Challenge and Triumph*. Grand Rapids, MI: Revell, 2009, Kindle.

Rider, Tobey C. *Cold War Games: Propaganda, The Olympics, and U.S. Foreign Policy*. Sport and Society Series Urbana: University of Illinois Press, 2016. Kindle.

Riley County Health Department and Student Health Services, Kansas State College. *Certificate of Vaccination against Smallpox.* June 4, 1952.

Rise of Automobiles After World War II. "During WWII: Automobile Growth Halted." http://theriseofautomobilesafterwwii.weebly.com/wars-of-the-time-period.html.

Salastie, Ritta. "Olympic Village." Finnish Architecture Navigator. https://finnisharchitecture.fi/olympic-village/.

Sans Souci Wien. "The Philosophy & History of the Sans Souci Wien." https://www.sanssouci-wien.com/en/hotel/philosophy-and-history/.

Santavirta, Torsten, Nina Santavirta, and Stephen E. Gilman. "Association of the World War II Finnish Evacuation of Children with Psychiatric Hospitalization in the Next Generation." JAMA Psychiatry. 2018 Jan 1;75(1):21-27. https://jamanetwork.com/journals/jamapsychiatry/fullarticle/2664260.

Schuster, Kurt. "What is the Distance Around a Running Track for Each Lane?" LiveStrong.com. https://www.livestrong.com/article/168904-what-is-the-distance-around-a-running-track-for-each-lane/.

Simms, James F. "Transportation Committee." In *United States 1952 Olympic Book, Quadrennial Report United States Olympic Committee.* Edited by Asa S. Bushnell, 259-260. New York: United States Olympic Association, 1953.

Smith, Dean. *Cowboy Stuntman: From Olympic Gold to the Silver Screen.* With Mike Cox and foreword by James Garner. Lubbock: Texas Tech University Press, 2013.

_____. narr. *On the Line.* Season 1, Episode 4, "Helsinki 1952—The Fastest Cowboy Stuntman to Ever Compete in the Olympics." Olympic Channel video, 7:54. https://www.olympicchannel.com/en/original-series/detail/on-the-line/on-the-line-season-season-1/episodes/helsinki-1952-the-fastest-cowboy-stuntman-to-ever-compete-in-the-olympics/.

Smithsonian National Museum of American History Behring Center. "Separate Is Not Equal: Brown v. Board of Education: White Only: Jim Crow in America." https://americanhistory.si.edu/brown/history/1-segregated/white-only-1.html.

_____. "Beef, Iron & Wine." https://americanhistory.si.edu/collections/search/object/nmah_213916.

Socolofsky, Homer. "Ward Haylett Chronology." October 28, 1993. Vertical Files Collection. Athletic Teams. Track and Cross Country-Haylett, Ward. Morse Department of Special Collections. Kansas State University Libraries.

Spanish Riding School, "About Us." https://www.srs.at/en/about-us/the-spanish-riding-school/.

SportsDefinitions.com: All You Need to Know about Every Sport on the Planet. "Heats." www.sportsdefinitions.com/track-events-general-terms/heats._3/.

Spotting History. "Helsinki Cathedral." https://www.spottinghistory.com/view/131/helsinki-cathedral/.

_____. "Senate Square: Helsinki, Finland." https://www.spottinghistory.com/view/138/senate-square/.

Stavropoulos, Vasileios. "The Evolution of Women Participation in Sports Events." Statathon, February 9, 2018. https://statathlon.com/the-evolution-of-women-participation-sports-events/.

Stephens, Brian. "The Bombing of Helsinki in World War II." 20th Century Battles. January 28, 2021. https://20thcenturybattles.com/the-bombing-of-helsinki-in-world-war-ii/.

"Stockmann." https://www.stockmann.com.

Strength and Health. "Rev. Bob Richards: Sullivan Award Winner; Training Schedule of the World's Best Pole Vaulter and Decathlon Champion." July 1952. https://www.tias.com/strength--health-magazine-july-1952-rev-bob-richards-617344.html/.

Strickland, Jonathan. "How Zero-gravity Flights Work." HowStuffWorks. August 8, 2007. https://science.howstuffworks.com/zero-g.htm.

Swarts, H. Jamison. "Supplies and Equipment Committee." In *United States 1952 Olympic Book, Quadrennial Report United States Olympic Committee.* Edited by Asa S. Bushnell, 261-262. New York: United States Olympic Association, 1953.

Tassin, Myron. *Bob Mathias: The Life of the Olympic Champion.* New York: St. Martin's Press, 1983.

TF Filmarchiv. Helsinki 1952 [Horace Ashenfelter] 3000m Steeplechase AMATEUR FOOTAGE, filmed July 25, 1952, in Helsinki Finland. YouTube video, 1:27. https://www.youtube.com/watch?v=4GIqVrWzKK4.

Thoreau, H. D., ed. *1953 Official NCAA Track and Field Guide: The Official Rules Book and Record Book of College Track & Field.* New York: National Collegiate Athletic Bureau, 1953.

———. "How Good Are Russian Athletes?" *Saturday Evening Post.* July 19, 1952.

Tidmarch, Bobby. "Vienna 1945." YouTube video, 3:50. https://www.youtube.com/watch?v=fhBn9cWtdxs.

Time Travel: Magic Vienna History Tour. "Occupied Vienna." https://www.timetravel-vienna.at/en/highlights-history-vienna/highlightsoccupied-vienna/.

Track and Field. "Mal Whitfield." Team USA. https://www.teamusa.com/hall-of-fame/hall-of-fame-members/mal-whitfield.

Track and Field News. "1952: Men—Los Angeles, June 27-28." https://trackandfieldnews.com/wp-content/uploads/2019/10/1952.pdf.

———. "History of the Olympic Results: 200 Meters—Men." https://trackandfieldnews.com/olympic-results/history-of-olympic-results-200-meters-men/.

———. "Men's World High Jump Rankings by Athlete, 1947-2019." https://trackandfieldnews.com/mens-world-rankings-by-athlete-2/mens-world-high-jump-rankings-by-athlete/.

Trans World Airlines. *Skyline New York.* Dudley Pictures, 1952. YouTube video, 26:51. https://www.youtube.com/watch?v=dkvznbIJyNA.

Trees of Texas. "Osage-Orange." Texas A&M Forest Service. http://texastreeid.tamu.edu/content/TreeDetails/?id=61.

Turku. "Turku Castle." https://www.turku.fi/en/turku-castle/visiting.

Turun Urheiluliito r.y The Turku Athletic Union and *Turun Toverit r.y.* The Turku Comrades, *Invitation to Competition: Post—Olympics in Turku.* July 1952, private collection.

United States Food and Drug Administration. "Fluoroscopy." https://www.fda.gov/radiation-emitting-products/medical-x-ray-imaging/fluoroscopy.

United States Olympic Committee. *1952 U.S. Olympic Souvenir Book: Olympic Sports Carnival.* Lynn, MA: H. O. Zimman, July 6, 1952.

_____. *1952 United States Olympic Souvenir Book: Track and Field Tryouts for Men.* Los Angeles: United States Olympic Committee, June 27-28, 1952.

_____. *Information and Instruction for Members and Officials of the United States Olympic Team: XV Olympiad—Helsinki, July 19-August 3, 1952. VI Olympic Winter Games—Oslo, February 14-25, 1952.*

_____. *Instructions to Athletes: U.S. Olympic Track and Field Try-Outs.* Handout. Los Angeles Memorial Coliseum. June 27-28, 1952.

_____. *United States Team for 1952 Olympic Games.* Brooklyn Eagle Press, July 1952.

University Travel Service. *Join ~~Al Masters Director of Athletics~~ Jack Weiershauser Track Coach at Stanford University at the Olympic Games and Visit Europe in '52.* Palo Alto, California, 1952.

Urheilumuseo. "Paavo Nurmi Lights the Olympic Flame at the Opening Ceremony." 1952 Summer Olympics. https://www.urheilumuseo.fi/en/photographs/.

_____. "Thane Baker, Andrew Stanfield and Jim Gathers at the Summer Olympics in Helsinki 1952." Sports Photos, Summer Olympics, 1952 Helsinki. https://verkkokauppa.tahto.com/en/tuote/thane-baker-andrew-stanfield-and-jim-gathers-at-summer-olympics-in-helsinki-1952/.

USATF. "U.S. Olympic Team Trials–Track & Field." https://www.usatf.org/events/2021/2020-u-s-olympic-team-trials-track-field.

Vienna Now—Forever. "In the Footsteps of Famous Musicians," Vienna Now-Forever. https://www.wien.info/en/recommendations/in-the-footsteps-of-famous-musicians

_____. "Sightseeing." https://www.wien.info/en/sightseeing.

Visit Finland. "Suomenlinna—The Sea Fortress of Helsinki." https://www.visitfinland.com/article/fortress-by-the-water/.

Visit Turku. "Turku Cathedral." http://www.visitturku.fi/en/turku-cathedral_en.

WAC Wiener Athleticksport Club. "Home." https://www.wac.at/.

Wäinö Aaltonen. *Paavo Nurmi. Turku City Art Museum.* https://www.turku.fi/en/culture-and-sports/museum/collections/outdoor-sculptures/waino-aaltonen-paavo-nurmi.

Wat1950, "1946 Ford Business Coupe." YouTube video, :42. https://www.youtube.com/watch?v=NSXu6LOq8KQ&t=3s.

Way to Win. "200m World Record Evolution Leading to 18.99 Seconds." YouTube video, 10.19. https://www.youtube.com/watch?v=2OI8-XyeddI&t=316s.

Welch, Crystal. "The Role of Bones, Joints & Muscles for the Javelin Throw." SportsRec, July 8, 2011. https://www.sportsrec.com/364336-the-role-of-bones-joints-muscles-for-the-javelin-throw.html.

Wer ist Wer, *Republik Österreich Parlament*. "Dipl. -Ing. Karl Waldbrunner." Last modified February 11, 2019, 10:45. https://www.parlament.gv.at/WWER/PAD_01408/index.shtml.

Wessels Living History Farm. "J. I. Case Tractors." Farming in the 1950s & 60s. https://livinghistoryfarm.org/farminginthe50s/machines_07.html.

Whitfield, Fredricka. "My Dad, Marvelous Mal." November 22, 2015, CNN video, 6:17. https://www.cnn.com/2015/11/22/opinions/whitfield-marvelous-mal/index.html.

Wien, Vienne, Vienna, Vieno–Ein Bilder-Album mit einem Geleitwort des Bürgermeisters der Stadt Wien Franz Jonas. Vienna, Austria: Gerlach & Wiedling, 1952.

Wilkinson, Stephan. "Call Her Connie: The Legendary Lockheed Constellation." Originally in *Aviation History*, July 2009. https://www.historynet.com/the-legendary-lockheed-constellation.htm.

Wilson, Kenneth L. "Report of the Chef de Mission." In *United States 1952 Olympic Book, Quadrennial Report United States Olympic Committee*. Edited by Asa S. Bushnell, 245-250. New York: United States Olympic Association, 1953.

———. "Men's Track and Field: Report of the Committee Chairman." In *Report of the United States Olympic Committee 1948 Games: XIV Olympiad, London, England, V Olympic Games, St. Moritz, Switzerland*, edited by Asa Bushnell, 71-76. New York: United States Olympic Association, 1949.

Wint, Andrew. "Jamaican Olympic Heros Wint, Rhoden, McKenley, and Macdonald." YouTube video, 2:20, https://www.youtube.com/watch?v=rfxrMy9pQcc&t=26s.

World Athletics. "World Record Progression of 100 Metres: Male-Senior-Outdoor." https://www.worldathletics.org/records/by-progression/16647?type=1.

———. "World Record Progression of 200 Metres: Male-Senior-Outdoor." https://www.worldathletics.org/records/by-progression/13243?type=1.

———. "World Record Progression of 4x200 Metres Relay: Male-Senior-Outdoor." https://www.worldathletics.org/records/by-progression/339?type=1.

Young, Ralph H. "Finnish Scholarship Fund." In *United States 1952 Olympic Book, Quadrennial Report United States Olympic Committee*. Edited by Asa S. Bushnell, 274. New York: United States Olympic Association, 1953.

Zirin, Dave, and Jules Boykoff. "Racist IOC President Avery Brundage Loses His Place of Honor: The decision to remove his bust from the San Francisco Asian Art Museum was long overdue." *Nation*, June 25, 2020, https://www.thenation.com/article/society/avery-brundage/.

INDEX

Åbo, 219, **334**, 363n6
Air Force, 52, 82, 320, 327
Airport: Idlewild, New York, 78, 84; Inglewood, California, 43; La Guardia, New York, 275; Liberal, Kansas, 273; Seutula, Finland, 85, 348n2, 349n6
Amateur Athletic Union (AAU): 220 yards, 322; 1952 All-College Track and Field Team, 322; Exhibition Meets, 74, 221, 217, 222, 231-32, 236, 275; National Track and Field Championships, 45, 74, 83, 268, 270, 320; organization, 2
Amateur Code, 2, 74, 265
Ashbaugh, Walter, 194, 221, 304
Ashenfelter, Horace "Nip": 50th reunion, 312; autographs, 203-4, 300; scholarship, 195, 361n18, steeplechase, 122, 160, 194-99, 300, 361n22-23
Ashenfelter, William, 122, 160, 195, 301
Backus, Bob, 81, 122, 306
Bailey, McDonald "Mac": 100 meters, 144,159, 257; 200 meters, 159, 164-65, 168, 170-71, 173, 284
Baker, Ruthene: Child 9, 11, 13, 15-17, 39; Adult, 281-82
Baker, Sally vii, xv, 311-18, 320, 322, 324-27, 329
Baker, Susie (Mother): at seven, 7, 9, 11, 13-16; at fourteen, 18-19, 26-28, 30; at eighteen, 36, 54; at Olympics, 101, 162, 175, 215, 236; after Olympics, 273-79, 281-84, 286-87, 289-90, 293; as Susie, 17, 288-89, 329

Baker, Walter Franklin (Father): at seven, 7-9, 11, 13-16; at fourteen, 18-20, 22-24, 26-28; at eighteen, 37; at Olympics, 54, 101, 152-53, 162, 175; after Olympics, 273-75, 277-79, 281-84, 286-89, 293; as mechanic, 153, 281; as Walter or Walt, 17, 37, 288-90, 343n12
Barnard, Art, 122, 299
Barnes, John, 122, 296
BEA (British European Airways), 255-56
Betton, Arnold: autographs, 240, 302; photographs, 122, 235, 238, 249, 256; in Turku, 221-22; in Vienna, 231,249, 256
Berliner, Harold, 122, 309
Bickle, Bobby, 112-13, 352n26, 353n29
Biffle, Jerome, 122, 303
Big Seven, 32, 148, 270, 296, 353n28
Biltmore Hotel, 74
Blackman, Roland, 122, 231-32, 244, 246, 300
Bönnhoff, Geraldo, 159, 164, 171
Bragg, Arthur, 122, 143, 295
British European Airways (BEA), 233, 255-56
British Empire Games, 226-30
British Games, News of the World, 255, 258, 262
Brooklyn Dodgers, 69-71
Brown, George, 122, 304
Brundage, Avery, 3-4, 109,117, 119, 127, 352n22
Campbell, Milt, 150, 192, 199, 201, 308
Capozzoli, Charles, 122, 297
Carnival, Olympic, 76, 180

387

Citius, Altius, Fortius, 90, 126, **335**
Coca-Cola, 67, 111, 208-9, 352n24
Cold War, 3, 107, 351n12
Cole, Gene: autographs by, 240, 296; in London, 255, 260; photographs, 122, 238, 249, 256; relays with Thane Baker, 227-28, 231, 246
Colorado Relays, 47-48
Corbitt, Ted, 122, 299
Creed, Olympic, v, 132
Crosby, Bing, 275
Cunningham, Glenn: Parade, 7-8, 10, 12-14, 16, 129; Thane Baker Day, 287-88, 290; Thane's hero, 27, 39, 172, 175, 326
Davis, Jack, 121-22, 221, 284, 299, 356n26
Davis, Walter "Buddy," autograph, 302; basketball, 151, 265; high jump, 69; photograph, 118, 122, tall, 116
Delta Tau Delta, 52, 345n23
Deni, John, 122, 302
Depression, 9, 20, 85, 266, 291
Dillard, Harrison "Bones": autographs, 154, 240, 299, 311; Davis, Jack, 370n26; expectations for, 108; London, 262; meeting, 59-61; Olympic results of, 158, 193, 221; photographs of, 60, 122, 238, 249, 256; Vienna, 231, 238-40, 245, 253, 284
Dillon, Jim, 122, 306
discrimination, racial, 3, 82, 183-85, 222, 360nn70-71
Dorchester, The, 262-63, 291
Dreams of Youth, The (Guest), viii
Druetzler, Warren, 122, 297
Dust Bowl, 1, 266
Dyrgall, Vic, 122, 299
Eläintarha, 123, 335
Elkhart: 1939 Parade, 129; Bickle, Bobby, Olympian, lived in, 112-13, 352n26, 353n29; childhood, 7-17; high school in, 27, 32, 215; Muncy & Sons, 21, 218-19 (*see* Ford garage); prohibition in, 22; Thane Baker Day, 283-293; Thane's hometown, 19, 23, 31, 37; Thane's memories of, 68, 112, 243, 253; Thane's return to, 273-282
Engel, Martin, 221, 306
Father, of Thane: at seven, 7-9, 11, 13-16; at fourteen, 18-20, 22-24, 26-28; at eighteen, 37; at Olympics, 54, 101, 152-53, 162, 175; after Olympics, 273-75, 277-79, 281-84, 286-89, 293; as mechanic, 153, 281; as Walter or Walt, 17, 37, 288-90, 343n12

Felton, Sam, 121-22, 306
fire on the plane, xi, 63-64, 346n40
flag ceremony, 118
fluoroscope, 23
Ford
  Baker cars: 1936, 24; 1942, 24; 1946, 24, 281-82
  Garage: adult Thane work in, 218-19, 265, 279, 286; child labor in, 19, 21-22, 24; father in, 153, 281 (*see also* Muncy & Sons)
Fuchs, Jim, 61, 122, 219, 222-24, 305
Gathers, Jim: autographs, 186, 295; finals, 163-64, 167, 170-72, 174, 358n21, 358n23; London, 229, 259; photographs of, 82, 121-22, 168, 171; prelims, 139, 142; semifinals, 159; travel with, 82-83
Gerhardt, Jim, 122, 304
Gordien, Fortune, 1948, 61; autographs, 238, 240, 265, 306; photographs, 72, 122, 249, 256; Vienna, 231
Gourdine, Meredith: autographs, 102, 303; daughter, 329; Fort Green Projects, 269; Helsinki, 102, 121-22; London, 227-28, 260, 262, 264, 268; Moore, Charlie, friend of, 228, 360n69; New York, 69; photograph, 72, 121-22; Stanfield, Andy, friend of, 228
Guest, Edgar Albert: *Dreams of Youth, The,* viii
Hamilton, Brutus: autographs, 185, 308; birthday, 119; comments by, 136, 142, 146, 172, 174-75; Cunningham and Baker's coach, 288; instructions from, 104, 106-9, 118, 173; Mashburn, 261-62
Haylett, Ward: coaching, 343n4, 344n8, 345n12, 350n30; Hamilton, Brutus, 104, 185; Helsinki, 176-77, 179-81; integration, 184-85; Kansas State, 47, 51-53; Mathias, Bob, 33, 108; photographs, 34, 56, 182; pistol for, 234; Thane speaks of, xii, 55-56, 175, 268, 275, 286, 289; Thane recalls, 108-9, 114, 160, 172, 186, 239
Hays, Kansas, hospital, 18-19, 23-30, 110
Hill, Ike, 122, 310
Held, Bud: autograph, 307; London, 260; pool player, 68; and Richards, Bob, 61-62, 119, 185-86, 193-94
Helsinki, Finland: AAU exhibition meets after, 219, 226, 228, 231, 245; assistance from residents of, 332; comparisons to, 58, 232, 260, 267-68, 291; introduction, 1-4; journey to, 43, 54, 74, 78, 84; memories

of 218, 277, 283, 288; Olympians, older, from, 311, 315-17, 327; Thane's Olympics in, 85-210; winning country in, 236
Helsinki Stadium: construction of, 89-90, 349n14; maintenance of, 142, 161; map of, 139, 149; Opening Ceremony, 123-33; photographs, 90, 127-28, 130-32, 140-42, 171, 198; warm-up area, 137-38, 159-63
Hitler, Adolf, 8-9, 208
Hooper, Darrow, 122, 305, 312
Hope, Bob telethon, 43, 275, 344n3
Hotel Höller, 234, 247, 251, **336**, 365n17
Houston, Larry, 122, 309
Howard, Ken, 122, 310
IOC, 3, 335, 344n7, 366n23
Iness, Sim, 305
Integrated teams: Kansas State, 184-85; US Olympians, 3, 81-82, 96, 183-84, 222
International Olympic Committee, 3, 344n7, 366n23
Jones, Tom, 122, 299
Kane, Bob, 122, 309
Kansas State College: architecture at, 68, 224 (*see* Nichols Gym); athletic directors, Mullins, Moon, 278, Taylor, Gene, 326; borrowed shoes, 146, 157, 170, 176; Haylett, Ward, 108, 182, 289; integration at, 184-85; Santee, Wes and, 54; telegrams from, 188-89; Thane attended, 1, 97, 219, 270, 315; Thane, competed for, 47, 51, 166, 191, 319; Thane, honored by, 326-27; Thane volunteered for, 322. *See* K-State and Kansas State University.
Kansas State Collegian, 31
Kansas State University, xii, 322, 326. *See* K-State and Kansas State College.
Kansas Relays, 45, 49, 87, 135
Käpylä Olympic Village: buses, 90, 124; details, 92-94, 114, 201, **336,** 350n22; map, 149; photographs, 93-95
King, Price, 122, 301
KLM Royal Dutch Airlines, 226, 364n23
Korean War: Cold War, 3, 62, 107, 215; Olympic athletes and, 265, 312, Opening Ceremony, 354n15
K-State: borrowed shoes, 106, 170, 176, 275; Haylett, Ward, 51-52, 55-56, 179; photographs, 32, 182; rivalry University of Kansas (K.U.), 260, 298; Santee, Wes, 54; Switzer, Veryl,184; Thane, walk on at, 50;

Wareham, Everett, 114. *See* Kansas State College and Kansas State University.
Laing, Les, 159, 164, 170, 259, 261
Laskau, Henry, 122, 301
Laz, Don: autographs, 240, 303; handstand race, 102-3; Olympics, 147; photographs, 81, 122, 238, 249, 256; Vienna 231, 245
Lee, Sammy, 310
Linnanmäki Amusement Park or *Lintsi,* 202-3, 207,217, **337**
Littlefield, Clyde: autograph, 308; illness of, 134, 355n33; photographs of, 81, 122; and Smith, Dean, 69, 104, 106, 133-4
London: 1948 Olympics, 58, 62, 108, 199, 257; British Empire Games, 226-230; memories of, 243, 275, 277, 291; News of the World British Games visit, 255-270; Vienna, 247, 253
Los Angeles: 8; 68, 101,182, 278
Manhattan, Kansas, 31-39, 113, 115, 180, 189, 343n1, 352n27
markka, 99, 101, 203, 207, **337**
Mashburn, J. W.: 4x400-meter relay, 98, 228; 4x440-yard relay, 227-29, 259-62; 440 yards, 257; autograph, 296, 311; fifty-year reunion, 315; photographs, 97, 120-22, 316; post-Olympic contact, 326
Mathias, Bob: 1948 decathlon, 33, 108, 180, 352n18; 1952 decathlon, 192, 199, 201, 224, 284; autographs, 307, 311; fiftieth reunion, 312; Rose Bowl 356n21; Thane, 150
Matson, Ollie, 122, 190, 221-22, 265, 295
Mattos, George, 122, 147, 303
McCormick, Pat, 310
McKenley, Herb: London, 229, 255, 261; Olympics, 144, 150, 267
McMillen, Bob, 122, 297
Miller, Bill: autographs, 240, 307; photographs of 121, 238, 249, 256; Olympics, 231; Vienna, 244, 246
Montez, Javier, 122, 297
Moore, Charlie: advice, 154,162; autograph, 300; father, 356n25; Gourdine, 228, 360n69; London, 228-29, 259, 262, 267-68; after Olympics, 315, 326; photographs of, 122, 316; Randall's Island, 76; spectator, 194-95, 198; Olympics, 151-53
Mother, of Thane: at seven, 7, 9, 11, 13-16; at fourteen, 18-19, 26-28, 30; at eighteen,

36, 54; at Olympics, 101, 162, 175, 215, 236; after Olympics, 273-79, 281-84, 286-87, 289-90, 293; as Susie, 17, 288-89, 329
Mullins, Moon, K-State AD, 279
Muncy and Sons, 19, 21, 218-19
Nazis, 2, 135, 208, 214, 270
National Collegiate Athletic Association or NCAA: collegiate championships, xiv, 2, 36, 268, 270; Silver Anniversary Award, 324; Thane 1952, 45, 47, 74, 159; Thane 1953, 319-20; track meet starter, 321
News of the World British Games, 255, 262, 264
New York Athletic Club or NYAC, 195, 198, 311-14, 318
New York City: airport, 78, 84, 275; compared to, 215, 287, 291; to Finland, 89, 114; Hall, 77, 313; Los Angeles to, 43-44, 66; visiting, 67-84
Nichols Gym or Hall, 31-32, 39, 224
Nurmi, Paavo: Olympic Torch 129-31; statue, 90, 129, 349n16
O'Brien, Parry, 95, 145, 151, 305
Olympia, 158, **337**
Olympiad, 40, 43, 85, 89, 108, **337**
Olympic: Carnival, 76, 180; Creed, v, 132; Torch 129-31; Tryouts in Los Angeles, 4, 43-44, 74, 83; Olympic Spirit, 148-49, 270
Olympic Stadium
-Helsinki: construction of, 89-90, 359n14; maintenance of, 142, 161; map of 139, 149; Opening Ceremony, 122-33; photographs of, 90, 127-28, 130-32, 140-42, 171, 198; warm-up area, 137-38, 158-63
-London, 267
-Los Angeles, 45
Olympic Village: Eastern Bloc (*Otaniemi*), 149, **337**; West, the, (*Käpylä*): 90-95, 98-99, 102, 112, 114, **336**; women, western, 92
Opening Ceremony, 122-33
Otaniemi, 149, **337**
Owens, Jesse, 60, 159, 170, 174, 179, 295
Pan American World Airlines or Pan Am, 78, 80-81, 86, 232, 276
Parade: Elkhart, 7, 9, 11; New York City, 67, 76-77; Opening Ceremony, 124, 126, 133, 135
Paramount Hotel, 68, 74, 215, 276
Patton, Jr. General George, 232
Pearman, Reggie, 122, 229, 261, 296, 326-27

Price, Tom, 310
prohibition, Elkhart, 22
racial discrimination, 3, 82, 183-85, 222, 360nn70-71
Remigino, Lindy: autographs, 152, 294, 311; fiftieth reunion 312-13, 315, 317; London, 255, 257; Olympics, 136, 150-51, 315; photographs, 122, 144, 284; Randall's Island race, 76
restaurant tent: compared to, 291, Germany and, 361n28; photograph, 93, meals in, 95-96, 117, 133-34, 142, 181, 203
Rhoden, George, 229, 257, 261
Richards, Bob: on airplane, 57-59, 61-63; autographs, 185, 187, 303; Held, Bud, 61-62, 119, 186, 193-94; Laz, Don, 102-3, 147-48, 231; Mathias, 150;in New York, 78, 81; Olympic Village, 95-103; pastor, 76, 147-48, 162, 265; pole vault gold, 147, 284; Soviet athletes, 62, 148-49; spectator, 188-89, 192-96, 198; years later, 326, 346n32
Riddell, 36, 170
Ross, Browning, 122, 301
Saint Anthony Hospital, 23, 25-26
Sanadze, Levan, 138, 141, 148, 270
Santee, Wes: autographs, 240, 298; boastful, 54, 148, 345n27; fiftieth reunion, 315-16; Olympics, 104-5, 146, 156; London, 260; photographs, 55, 105, 120-22, 235, 238, 249, 256; Vienna 231, 245
Simmons, Floyd, 33, 122, 150, 192, 201, 308
Sisters of Saint Agnes, 24-25
Shaw, George, 122, 304
Schick electric razor, 98, 100
Sjogren, Leo, 122, 302
Smith, Dean: 100-meter, 136 142-45, 159; 4x100 meter, 144, 189, 222, 284; airplane, 44-50, 52-62, 64-65; autographs, 143-44, 146, 294; Dorchester, The, 262-69; encouragement from, 147, 162; extraverted, 150; fiftieth reunion, 312-13, 315-17; Helsinki, 89; 350n5; later years, 322, 324, 326; Littlefield, Clyde, 69, 104, 106, 133-34; London, 226, 257, 260, 262-69; New York, 67-69, 75-76, 78, 80; Opening Ceremony, 124, 133-35; photographs, 50, 122, 143-44, 313, 316; Restaurant tent, 95-98, 142-47; spectator, 188-90, 192-96, 199, 201-3; Village, 92, 100-1, 103-4, 106; Yoder, 154

Snyder, Larry, 122, 231, 239, 249, 256, 308
Sober, Pincus, 122, 309
Soviet Union or USSR: athletes, 136, 139, 143-44, 265, (see Ashenfelter, Horace and Sanadze, Levan); Austria, 214, 235-37, 252-53; and Finland 1-3, 135; Hamilton, Brutus, 107-8; *Otaniemi,* 149, 337; Porkkala, 219; Richards, Bob, 62, 148-49, Thane start meets, 321
Stadium
-Helsinki: construction of, 89, 359n14; Opening Ceremony, 123-33; maintenance of, 142, 161; map of 139, 149; photographs of, 90, 128, 140-42, 171, 198; warm-up in, 137-38
-Triborough, 76, 180
-White City, 226, 255, 257, 267
Stanfield, Andy: 200-meter, 159-60, 163-65, 167, 170, 284, 373n22, 373n24-25; awards ceremony, 172; autograph, 185, 295; Thane Baker, 219, 319-20; Gourdine, Meredith, 102, 228; Opening ceremony,124, 135; photographs of, 83, 122, 167-68, 171; and press, 173-74; White City Stadium, 259-60
Stockmann Department Store, 201
Stone, Curtis, 122, 298
Suojärvi, Tuija Timonen; dancing with, 205-9, life-long friends, 325-26, 371n14; talking about, 283, 286; thoughts of, 217, 219, 233
Suomi, 85, **338**
Switzer, Veryl, 184
Texas Relays, 14, 45, 48, 82, 321
ticker-tape parade, 77
Times Square, 67-68
The Dorchester, 262-63, 291
Towers, Dick, 32, 37, 53-54, 172, 331
Track and Field Tryouts. *See* Olympic Tryouts.
Trans World Airlines, 43, 44
Trials, Olympic. *See* Olympic Tryouts.
Triborough Stadium, 76, 180
Tuija Timonen Suojärvi: dancing with, 205-9, life-long friends, 325-26, 371n14; talking about, 283, 286; thoughts of, 217, 219, 233

Turku or Turun, Finland, 219-225, 231, 241, 277, **338**
Union of the Soviet Socialist Republics. *See* the Soviet Union.
United States Olympic Committee: Brundage, Avery, 3, 117, 119; expenses, 57, 75, 99, 277; flag, 123; fundraising, 2, 76; London, 267; processing,56, 74; rules, 177; travel, 80; uniforms, 124, 275; work for, 65, 312, 315
USSR. *See* the Soviet Union.
Vienna, Austria: competition in, 231-250; hiding in, 213-216, 251-254; memories of, 266, 277, 284, 287, 291
Waldbrunner, Karl, 247-49
Waldorf-Astoria, 78-79, 114, 291, 315-16
Wareham: Everett, 113-14; Hotel, 113-15, 352n27
Weinacker, Adolph, 119, 201, 301
Werner, Chic, 122, 308
White City Stadium, 226, 255, 257, 267
"Whites only," 3, 82, 184-85, 222, 360nn70-71
Whitfield, Mal: accomplishments, 315; autograph, 296; expectations, 108; London, 229, 255, 257, 261; meeting, 61; Olympics, 154-55, 190; photographs of, 156, 317
Wiesner, Ken, 121-22, 302
Wilt, Fred, 298
Wint, Arthur, 257, 260
Wojecki, Eddie, 122, 310
World War II: 1940 Games cancelled, 89; Austria after, 214, 362-3n3; Dorchester, The, 262; Finland, 1; rationing, 28, 266; recovery, 4, 183
XV Olympiad, 3, 43, 85, 128
Yhdysvallat, 123, 125, **339**
Yoder, Lee: autograph, 300; Dodgers game, 69, 72-73; Helsinki, 122, 153-54; Turku, 222, 224
Young, Cy, 81, 122, 307
Zátopek, Emil, 199-200, 223-24, 252, 284
Zatopkova, Dana, 199
Ziegler, Neil, 330, 366n15

ABOUT THE AUTHOR

CATHERINE BAKER NICHOLSON had her own athletic career and even won a collegiate national championship in the 800-meter run. She gave up the practice of law to raise and homeschool her four children, one of whom later died of brain cancer. Today, she lives in the Omaha, Nebraska, area with her husband and near her father, Thane Baker. Beginning each day with prayer, she studies, writes, volunteers, and adores her children and grandchildren.

Printed in the USA
CPSIA information can be obtained
at www.ICGtesting.com
CBHW020304030824
12651CB00004B/382